# Jabal al-Akhḍar, Cyrenaica:

## An Historical Geography of Settlement and Livelihood

Douglas L. Johnson
*Clark University*

THE UNIVERSITY OF CHICAGO
DEPARTMENT OF GEOGRAPHY
RESEARCH PAPER NO. 148

1973

*Library of Congress Catalog Card Number: 73-79883*

*Research Papers* are available from:
The University of Chicago
Department of Geography
5828 S. University Avenue
Chicago, Illinois 60637
Price: $5.00 list; $4.00 series subscription

# PREFACE

The present study has two foci. One investigates the contemporary pastoral ecology of the eastern Jabal al-Akhḍar both in its traditional context and as it has experienced change in this century. The second thrust of the study uses these ecological insights to illuminate the settlement history of the area and the historical interrelationships of agrarian and pastoral livelihood modes in eastern Cyrenaica. The understandings thus gained support three general observations.

First, the bedouin livelihood patterns of eastern Cyrenaica are a sophisticated adjustment, at a given technological level, to subtle variations in the ecology of the Jabal al-Akhḍar. Variations in the vegetative resources available to support animals, combined with the differential ability of various animals to exploit these resources, leads to complex herding patterns in which different bedouin groups specialize in herding the animals best suited to the ecology of their tribal homeland. Contrary to the common view that bedouin have an antiagricultural bias, the nomads of Cyrenaica also actively engage in agricultural pursuits. Both speculative cropping of barley in marginal areas as well as the raising of barley and wheat in the better-watered upper elevations of the jabal are practised. Thus, complex patterns of movement must be followed to accommodate both agricultural and pastoral activities and to deal with the climatic instability characteristic of the region.

In theory, each nomadic family strives for the maximum degree of self-sufficiency and to a remarkable degree is able to attain independent economic status. Until the development of a rural periodic market system in the last twenty years in response to rapid changes in transportation technology, the bedouin economy had only limited contacts with a sedentary agricultural population. The basic mechanism making this level of independence possible is the division of al-Jabal al-Akhḍar into tribal strips running from the coast to the fringes of the Sahara and comprising a full range of the environmental variations present in the region. Lower level segments of the tribal genealogy are associated with discrete portions of the tribal territory and each segment tends to specialize in the production of the animals and grains best suited to its area.

iii

Marriage and kin ties both within one tribal strip and between two strips link the system together in patterns of mutually obligatory aid and reciprocal gift-giving. In this way deficits in one area are exchanged against the surpluses of another zone and access to a neighbor's pasture in times of drought carries with it the obligation to return such aid at the first likely opportunity. Thus, each tribe or subtribe represents a relatively closed, self-sufficient economy with little need for contact with the outside world except for a limited range of luxury goods.

Historically, the fluctuating frontiers of settled agriculture and the periodically hostile interactions of nomadic and sedentary folk can be explained by the ecology of Cyrenaica. Although pastoral activities can be undertaken throughout the jabal, there are certain areas of high agricultural potential that pastoralists must control if their economy is to function smoothly. These same areas are the only ones in which sedentary agriculturalists can operate productively, so competition between the two livelihood modes is inevitable. Yet the historical record of violent conflict between nomad and farmer is a sporadic one and indicates both periods of relative stability in the allocation of resources between the two modes as well as the long-term military superiority of the settled population. Only under special conditions, when the agricultural population expanded into areas vital to the nomad, when ethnic and kin ties between the two groups were absent or broken so that exchange patterns were interrupted, when nomadic mobility was increased (particularly after the introduction of the camel), when the organization and authority of the sedentary government collapsed into chaos and anarchy, and when nomadic coalitions formed around the personality of charismatic leaders, did violent and sustained levels of hostility occur.

Finally, although the nomadic life style gradually replaced settled farming as the dominant livelihood after the twelfth century A.D., continuity between the two settlement patterns was maintained. Just as the first Greek settlers used the same springs and fields as did the Berber nomads before them, so too did the Arab bedouin incorporate many elements of the classical settlement pattern into their own system. These elements were reshaped and reordered to meet the needs and express the aspirations of a different culture. Agricultural fields, though reduced in extent, classical roads, now maintained as footpaths, cemeteries and corrals, reusing the stone of ruined farmhouses, and Roman wells, springs, and cisterns continued in use and formed the fixed points in a now nomadic way of life. Even though the nomadic population, pressured by changes introduced first by Italian colonists and subsequently as part of the modern oil-boom economy, is beginning to abandon nomadic pursuits and become

iv

sedentary, many of the same points in the classical settlement pattern loom as constants in today's emerging landscape.

In transliterating place names every effort is made to retain fidelity to the Arabic spelling while preserving the advantages of standardization. To this end the transliteration system of the International Journal of Middle East Studies is followed except in instances where documentary sources are too vague to permit determination of the original form. Arabic words frequently used, such as jabal (mountain), wadi (seasonal stream), suq (market), funduq (market place/ hotel), and sabkha (salt marsh), are underscored in their initial appearance but not subsequently. In addition, the reader's attention is called to the following list of journal titles which have been shortened for use in both footnote and bibliographic entries.

| AJA | American Journal of Archaeology |
|-----|---------------------------------|
| AAAG | Annals of the Association of American Geographers |
| AESC | Annales, Economies, Sociétés, Civilisations |
| ABSA | Annual of the British School of Athens |
| BRSGI | Bollettino della Reale Società Geografica Italiana |
| BAAPG | Bulletin of the American Association of Petroleum Geologists |
| BFA | Bulletin of the Faculty of Arts, University of Libya |
| BSGE | Bulletin de la Société de Géographie d'Egypte |
| JJS | Journal of Jewish Studies |
| JRS | Journal of Roman Studies |
| JRAI | Journal of the Royal Anthropological Institute |
| LA | Libya Antiqua |
| PBSR | Papers of the British School at Rome |
| QAL | Quaderni di archeologia della Libia |
| TESG | Tijdschrift voor Economische en Sociale Geografie |
| TIRS | Traveau de l'Institut de Recherches Sahariennes |

Debts incurred during research are too numerous for a brief expression of thanks to suffice, yet, although omissions are inevitable, my gratitude to all who either aided or encouraged me is profound. The Foreign Area Fellowship Program provided financial support both for field work and data analysis and its staff was a constant source of enthusiasm and encouragement. While in the field, the American and British communities in Banghāzī and Darna, and in particular the American consul, Hon. George M. Lane and family, were an invaluable source of comfort and support. A host of Libyans, especially Shoeib Yunis al-Mansury, Muftah Burzeiza, Suleman Luhaishi, Ashur Burashid, Idris El-Hareir, Mohamed Heneish, Suleiman El-Ollaigy, and Shobaki Ali, as well as Drs. Muktar Buru, Hadi Bulugma, and Mansour Kikkia of the University of Libya, contributed in manifold ways to the project and without their selfless interest it could not have succeeded. Illustrations are the product of the diligent and competent care of Dr. Daniel Irwin and staff of the Cartographic Laboratory, Southern Illinois

University. My appreciation is extended to Professors Berry, Butzer, Harris, and Mikesell of the University of Chicago who read all or part of the manuscript and contributed numerous provocative and helpful suggestions. While the final conclusions remain my own responsibility, the result has been materially improved by their care and insight. Special acknowledgement must be made of my debt to Marvin W. Mikesell, my academic advisor, whose unflagging support and encouragement has been responsible in large part for the successful completion of this project. Finally, to my wife, who shared the experience with me, my gratitude and thanks.

TABLE OF CONTENTS

Chapter

# LIST OF TABLES

# LIST OF ILLUSTRATIONS

# CHAPTER I

## ORIENTATION TO THE PHYSICAL ENVIRONMENT

Cyrenaica is in many respects an island and an outpost of Europe on the shores of North Africa. Jutting northward into the Mediterranean, Cyrenaica is only 300 kilometers south of Crete and historically has maintained close ties with the Greek mainland (Figure 1). To the south, the arid Sahara approaches within a few kilometers of the Mediterranean coast in the Gulf of Sirt and, save for a narrow coastal strip between Darna and Alexandria, barren desert effectively isolates Cyrenaica from the remainder of the African continent. The flora of the northern coastal regions, the product of increased precipitation in the moderate elevations of a coastal upland, is composed of large numbers of northern and circum-Mediterranean species not typical of nearby coastal districts. Relatively lush flora, moderate rainfall, locally rich pockets of soil, and limestone relief combine to make Cyrenaica a familiar setting conducive to settlement by a succession of European colonizers. The relative richness of the Cyrenaican environment for both agricultural and pastoral pursuits is even more striking when considered in the context of the marginality of areas east, west, and south of the Cyrenaican plateau. With Cyrenaica's resource potential appearing greater to both farmer and nomad by comparison with surrounding territories, the plateau has formed a focus for competing livelihood and settlement forms as Berber and Greek, Roman and Arab, Sanūsī bedouin and Italian peasant have struggled for possession of its resources.

## Landforms

al-Jabal al-Akhḍar, the Green Mountain of Cyrenaica, is a structural cuestaform plateau of generally moderate relief which has experienced successive phases of uplift, erosion, and dissection to produce the present hill-to-low-mountain country.[1] The basic configuration is a step-like arrangement of alter-

---

[1] Considerable controversy exists as to the origin of this cuestaform configuration. Ardito Desio, "Brève synthèse de l'évolution morphologique du territoire de la Libya," BSGE, XXV (1953), 18-19, and other Italian investigators

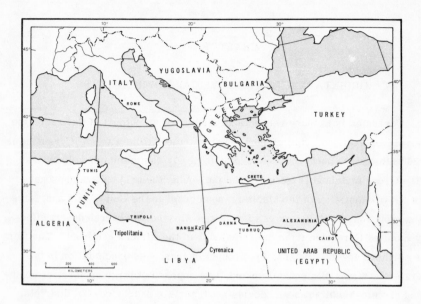

Fig. 1.--The central and eastern Mediterranean

nating platforms or "terraces" and escarpments rising 800 meters above the
Mediterranean (Figure 2). Two main escarpments, further apart in western
Cyrenaica but drawing gradually closer together as they are followed eastward,

---

believed that the scarps were the result of faulting and major block movements.
Recent geological studies undertaken in support of petroleum exploration have
identified the existence of fault lines coincident with the major scarp-faces.
This position is summarized by Eberhard Klitzsch, "Die Structurgeschichte der
Zentralsahara: Neue Erkenntnisse zum Bau and zur Paläographie eines Tafellandes," Geologische Rundschau, LIX (1969), 508-10, and Louis C. Conant and
Gus H. Goudarzi, "Stratigraphic and Tectonic Framework of Libya," BAAPG,
LI (1967), 726-29. An alternative viewpoint contends that the scarps and terrace
platforms represent wave-cut features generated between intermittent periods of
block uplift. In this way each pause in uplift was accompanied by the planation of
the uplifted surface and the construction of a marine beach scarp and terrace on
the seaward face. The main exposition of this view is found in C. B. M. McBurney and R. W. Hey, Prehistory and Pleistocene Geology in Cyrenaican Libya
(Cambridge: University Press, 1955). A briefer statement is contained in R. W.
Hey, "The Pleistocene Shorelines of Cyrenaica," Quaternaria, III (1956), 139-44.
In contrast, Roger Coque, "Morphogenèse quarternaire du piémont méditerranéen du djebel Akhdar (Cyrénaïque)," Annales de Géographie, No. 433 (1970),
375-85, suggests that karst erosion processes may have played a crucial role in
the ultimate shape of the Cyrenaican upland. Gus H. Goudarzi, Geology and
Mineral Resources of Libya - A Reconnaissance (Washington: U.S. Government
Printing Office, 1970), p. 53, maintains an intermediate position by ascribing the
scarps to faulting and the terrace platforms to erosional processes.

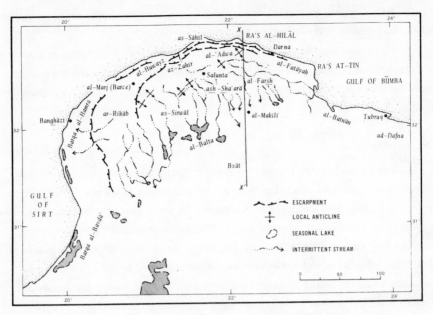

Fig. 2.--Morphology of Cyrenaica

swing in broad arcs roughly parallel to the coast. There are also very limited remnants of a third scarp and terrace in the highest areas of the jabal between Salunṭa and Marawa. Although the lower scarp-faces often rise abruptly from the coastal plain, the second scarp is a less dramatic break from the lower terrace surface and the boundary between the upper terrace surface and the high scarp and terrace remnants is almost imperceptible. Both the coastal plain and the lower terrace follow a similar pattern; they are broader in the Barqa al-Hamra and al-Marj Plain on the west but become constricted further east.

All of these features lie close to the Mediterranean coast and the drainage divide is seldom more than 40 kilometers inland. South of the jabal crest is a long, gradual dip-slope, broken into a series of low, parallel north-south ridges by the seasonal wadis that drain the area. No marked break in elevation occurs along the dip-slope. Instead, the seasonal streams gradually descend into a series of playa lakes in the Balṭa zone. Beyond al-Makīlī and the Balṭa[1]

---

[1]Literally, a large depression, usually with limited vegetation, that becomes muddy during the autumn and winter rains. The surface experiences severe cracking when it dries out in summer. For the local Arabic usage of physiographic terms, see E. E. Evans-Pritchard, "Topographic Terms in Common Use among the Bedouin of Cyrenaica," JRAI, LXXVI (1946), 177-88.

stretch flat, featureless, arid plains which in the extreme south merge with the dunes of al-Ghard, the Kalanshīyyu sand sea.

The structural features left by alternating periods of orogeny and erosion are depicted in Figure 3. This figure is a north-south cross-section extending from the coast at Ra's al-Hilāl into the desert south of al-Makīlī along the line X-X' on Figure 2.

## The Coastal Plain

The coastal plain, as-Sāḥil, between Marsā Susa and Darna is narrow, seldom more than one kilometer in width, and at times fades out completely as the scarp approaches the present shoreline. In many places it is veneered with a variety of continental gravels which attain considerable thickness where streams descend onto the plain. In addition to these alluvial deposits numerous small marine scarps and correlated beach deposits are located in the coastal plain and along the lower slopes of the first escarpment (below 200 meters). [1] Also notable features of as-Sāḥil are small off-shore islands, the fossilized remnants of coastal sand dunes left by lower sea levels, [2] which give precarious shelter to coastal fishing craft.

The lower scarp-slope rises spectacularly from the coastal plain with the minor terraces noted by McBurney and Hey[3] being scarcely apparent to the observer in the Ra's al-Hilāl area, although some of these assume greater prominence further east at Darna. The scarp-face, however, is not the barrier that it might appear to be in Figure 2. The local anticline which runs from al-Aṭrūn to beyond Qayqab and dominates the local drainage pattern[4] is located

---

[1] At least one of these abrasional terraces, that standing 15 meters above sea level, might also have correlations with similar marine terraces at the same elevation in Marmarica, Syrtica, and southern Tunisia. See Anta Montel, "Les terrasses marines de la côte nord de Cyrénaïque," Compte-rendu sommaire des séances de la Société géologique de France, Nos. 13-14 (November 7, 1955), pp. 256-58.

[2] As Amilcare Fantoli, "Le isole della Tripolitania e dello Cirenaica," L'Universo, XXXVII (1957), 923-30, points out, these islands were also utilized as breakwaters in Greco-Roman ports.

[3] McBurney and Hey, Prehistory and Pleistocene Geology in Cyrenaican Libya, pp. 33-34.

[4] R. W. Hey, "The Geomorphology and Tectonics of the Gebel Akhdar (Cyrenaica)," Geological Magazine, XCIII (1956), 10-11, was the first to recognize the local importance of this anticline. It also is apparently responsible for the surface exposure of Upper Cretaceous rocks in the Ra's al-Hilāl area, one of

5

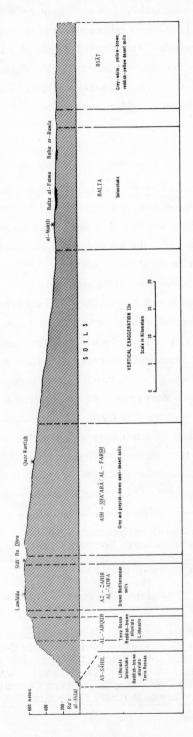

Fig. 3.--Cross-section Ra's al-Hilāl to al-Makīlī.  Source:  U.S. Army Map Service, Beda Littoria (1:250,000).

close to the coast. The combination of an elevation of 650 meters and proximity to the coast has resulted in the deep entrenchment of the northward-draining wadis into the lower terrace (al-'Arqūb) and a spectacular notching of the lower scarp as well. Thus, the lower scarp-face is not a continuous, impenetrable wall, but rather a series of vertical segments broken by wadis whose beds serve as natural highways for the movement of men and animals between the coastal plain and the interior.

The Lower Terrace

The lower terrace, al-'Arqūb, is also known by a number of local names referring to the platform's regional characteristics. al-Huwayz, for example, in the northern portion of the al-Marj plain near Baṭṭa conveys the meaning of enclosed space[1] at a point where the lower terrace begins to be constricted between the upper and lower scarp slopes. All of al-'Arqub, however, has one thing in common, for karst erosion, while present in other parts of the jabal, is particularly well developed here. The al-Marj Plain is structurally a giant sink-hole (polje), saucer-shaped and without drainage to the sea, in the center of which a seasonal lake develops during the winter rains. Smaller sinkholes in the narrower eastern al-'Arqub serve to break up surface regularity. Karst erosion plus the deep incision of wadis into the lower terrace give it much greater local relief than in the al-Marj Plain. Accessibility from one segment of the lower terrace to the next is thereby reduced, although the moderate slope of the upper scarp and the presence of small alluvial fans at the foot of scarp-face make access to the upper terrace much easier.

Of the various limestone formations outcropping along the cross-section only the Oligocene deposits of the Cyrene and Faidia formations[2] have any impor-

---

the few places such rocks appear in Cyrenaica. See F. T. Barr, "Upper Cretaceous Stratigraphy of Jabal al Akhdar, Northern Cyrenaica," in F. T. Barr (ed.), Geology and Archaeology of Northern Cyrenaica, Libya (Tripoli: Petroleum Exploration Society of Libya, 1968), pp. 138-41.

[1] Evans-Pritchard, "Topographical Terms in Common Use among the Bedouin of Cyrenaica," p. 181.

[2] The basic characteristics of these two formations are discussed by W. F. J. Kleinsmeide and N. J. van den Berg, "Surface Geology of the Jabal al Akhdar, Northern Cyrenaica, Libya," in F. T. Barr (ed.), Geology and Archaeology of Northern Cyrenaica, Libya, pp. 119-21, and Constans R. Pietersz, "Proposed Nomenclature for Rock Units in Northern Cyrenaica," in F. T. Barr (ed.), Geology and Archaeology of Northern Cyrenaica, Libya, pp. 128-29.

tant implications for human settlement. Each of these formations has an impervious marl member along its lower-most horizon that acts as a trap for groundwater percolating down from above. Once encountering this layer the subsurface water is forced to move laterally until it appears in the form of springs. The marl member of the Cyrene Formation outcrops to the west of the cross-section near the crest of the upper escarpment at Shaḥḥat (ancient Cyrene) where it gives rise to the famous Greek fountain of Apollo. At decreasing elevations further east it results in a number of copious springs which occur near the base of the upper scarp or along the course of wadis near Ra's al-Hilāl. The marl member of the Faidia Formation reaches the surface in a very important series of springs running in an east-west direction south of Lamlūda. These springs serve as a focus of the nomadic population during the summer months since they represent a relatively dependable supply of water for their herds throughout the driest months of the year.

The Upper Terrace and Southern Slope

The relief of the upper terrace, az-Zahir, is gentle and without any evidence of major tectonic disturbance. The moderate relief is a product of the initial emergence of the land from the sea in the Upper Miocene which did not produce a land mass of any great elevation. Instead, a long, low island of monotonous relief was shaped by subaerial erosion at a time when the level of the sea stood considerably higher than at present.[1] The transition from the upper terrace to the interior is imperceptible for, in contrast to the steep slopes found along the northern cuesta escarpments, the dip-slope is gentle and descends gradually into the interior. Subparallel hills with moderate slopes separate the southward-draining wadis and give the area its Arabic name, as-Sirwāl.[2] In eastern Cyrenaica this same topography is variously called ash-Sha'arā (the region of juniper) and al-Farsh (the carpet) because of the pure stands of juniper, often existing in densely matted thickets, found in the area between Qayqab and Khūlān. Shallow alluvium-filled depressions that on occasion are valuable for agriculture, and the broad potentially productive wadi beds emptying into them, are conspicuous features of this region.

---

[1] R. W. Hey, "The Geomorphology of the Jabal al-Akhdar and Adjoining Areas," in F. T. Barr (ed.), Geology and Archaeology of Northern Cyrenaica, Libya, pp. 168-69.

[2] The analogy in Arabic is between the shapelessness of the traditional Arab-style baggy trousers and the formless arrangement of the hills.

At the base of the southern dip-slope is the Balta zone, a region of playa
lakes which collects most of the drainage of the jabal and serves as a focus of
the summer migration movements of the nomadic population. Only in a few
instances, such as the Wādī an-Naqa and the Wādī Darna, do streams originating on the south slope of the jabal break through the mountain barrier and reach
the northern coast. A few stream valleys drain directly eastward and empty
into the Gulf of Būmba on the rare occasion when they carry water. The further south one goes the more poorly defined is the drainage system. South of
al-Makīlī it is difficult to discern any clear pattern in the streams for, like the
Wādī al-Mra, they are characterized by braided and intermittent channels.
Relief is very slight in the Bsāt and most of the wadis are in reality poorly connected chains of depression that wander across a featureless pediment. They
take on significance only when the winter rains bring water to the area and the
surface run-off collects in them as temporary pools.

Soils

Although little study has been devoted to the soils of Cyrenaica, the general outline of their distribution is known (Figure 3). In as-Sāḥil, the coastal
plain from Ṭulmaytha to Darna, lithosols of extreme stoniness predominate.
Saline solonchak soils are common immediately behind the coastal dunes wherever these formations have not been eroded by an encroaching sea. Unlike the
Barqa al-Hamra in western Cyrenaica, where deep terra rossa alluvials and
reddish-brown calcareous soils are common and where stony lithosols are restricted to pediments at the foot of the lower scarp, [1] extensive alluvial gravels,
lithosols, and isolated patches of terra rossa are characteristic of the Sāḥil. In
part this reflects the narrowness of the littoral plain. Seldom exceeding one
kilometer in width, little space exists between the foot of the scarp-face and the
coast in which deep alluvial soils of silt clay to loam texture can develop. Only
in isolated pockets of karst eorsion, in limited areas where Graeco-Roman
check-dams survive to retard soil erosion, or where major wadis debouch upon
the Sāḥil and form alluvial fans do reddish-brown alluvials of any depth develop.

The lower terrace contains the same soil types as does the coastal plain,
but here the relative proportions are markedly altered. Although lithosols and
bare limestone outcrops do occur frequently, the incidence of terra rossa and

---

[1]R. W. Price, Report on the Soil Survey of the Proposed Bu Traba Settlement Area (Banghāzī, n.d.), p. 2.

alluvial soils is much greater.  This is particularly true in western Cyrenaica
where the al-Marj (Barce) Plain is composed of terra rossa soils formed both in
situ and by alluvial processes,[1] while calcareous reddish-brown alluvial soils
are common on the fringes of the plain.[2]  Further east, al-'Arqūb becomes
more broken by deeply incised wadis; terra rossa soils are more restricted in
occurrence and are found in isolated pockets or as a thin soil mantle over hard
limestone parent material.[3]  Of much greater importance are the often widespread alluvial soils formed on alluvial fans at the foot of the upper scarp faces.
Composed of soil, silt, and other material washed down from the upper scarp
and terrace, they have often been preserved by Roman terraces and check-dams.

Brown Mediterranean soils, varying in hue from greyish-brown to near
black, are frequently encountered in the upper terrace.  In the more hilly region
between Salunṭa and al-Bayḍā', where slopes are often as steep as 20 per cent,
these brown soils are confined to hilltops,[4] but further east from Ṣafṣaf to al-
Qubba, where local relief is less pronounced, they become more extensive.
Here dark soils, presumably vertisols and subject to severe cracking under
summer drought conditions, predominate and are interspersed with occasional
rock outcrops and karst depressions.  Elsewhere in the upper terrace denuded
hillslopes and deep, reddish-brown alluvial valley soils are characteristic.

South of the jabal watershed soils gradually decrease in humus content as
they grade through several transitions to the regosols of the interior desert.
Grey to greyish-brown sierozems are found throughout the semi-desert zones
of the jabal dip-slope.  In the Balṭa areas at the foot of the dip-slope, extensive
playa lakes develop during the winter rains and solonchak soils of high saline
content are widespread.  Beyond the Balṭa calcareous desert soils of sandy tex-

---

[1]Mukhtar Buru, "Soil Analysis and its Relation to Land Use in el-Marj
Plain, Cyrenaica," BFA, II (1968), 41-70.  The processes operating in terra
rossa formation in Libya and the eastern Mediterranean are discussed by Kenneth Atkinson, "The Dynamics of Terra Rossa Soils," BFA, III (1969), 15-35.

[2]P. Hubert, Report on the Soil Conditions of the Ente Farm Settlement
Area of Farzūghah (Benghazi:  FAO, Libya Mission, 1964), pp. 2-3.

[3]R. W. Price, The Soils and Agricultural Potential of the El Useta Area
for Tribal Land Settlement (Benghazi:  Development of the Tribal Lands and Settlements Project, FAO, Libya Mission, 1966), p. 3.

[4]R. W. Price, General Appraisal of the Omar Mukhtar Area as a Possible Center for Tribal Lands Settlement (Tripoli:  Project for the Development of
Tribal Lands and Settlements, 1966), pp. 2-3.

ture and yellowish-brown, reddish-yellow, and grey-white color stretch in a
broad arc from the Gulf of Sirt to the Gulf of Bumba. Finally, in the extreme
south are the inhospitable mobile dunes of the Kalanshīyyu sand sea.

Many of Cyrenaica's soils are of limited agricultural value. Sterile
lithosols and rock outcrops are found throughout the jabal and the alluvial gravels of much of the Sāḥil have limited productive capacity. The grey and grey-
brown semi-desert soils of the dip-slope are often of poor quality while within
and south of the Balṭa salty solonchaks and sandy regosols are generally worth-
less. Soils of Barqa al-Baydā' and Barqa al-Hamra are often fertile, but patchy
distribution limits their usefulness.

The soils of the lower and upper terrace have the most potential. Although in pockets they are extremely fertile and in some areas, particularly al-
Marj plain in the west and al-Fatāyaḥ plain on the lower terrace above Darna,
cover extensive areas, throughout most of the jabal they are confined to relatively limited areas and are often subjected to severe soil erosion. In the upper
terrace the best of these Mediterranean soil areas is al-'Adwa north of al-
Fā'idīyya from al-Baydā' to Lamlūda, but even here soil erosion is extensive.
In almost every case it is the hilltops and the steeper upper slopes that have suf-
fered the most damage. The better soils are concentrated in the upper reaches
of the wadi beds, on miniature alluvial fans where seasonal streams spill out
onto the lower terrace, in karst hollows and pockets of internal drainage on the
upper terrace, on the few areas of extensive alluvial deposition on as-Sāḥil
between Ṭulmaytha and Darna, and in the broad reaches of the seasonal streams
draining down the gentle gradients of the southern dip-slope.

## Climate

If landforms have only a relatively subtle impact on livelihood activities
in eastern Cyrenaica, the same cannot be said for climate. All activities are
intimately dependent upon the climatic regime and relatively minor departures
from "normal" conditions can have severe consequences for the farmers and
nomads of the area. Three aspects of the climatic regime, its seasonality, its
relationship to the landforms outlined above, and its extreme variability, are of
crucial importance in understanding the potentialities of the eastern jabal and
the uses to which it is put by its inhabitants.

Seasonality and Rainfall Distribution

First, the regime is extremely seasonal. A glance at the rainfall graphs for selected stations in Figure 4 indicates the basic Mediterranean pattern of winter rain and summer drought. During the summer months of June, July, and August scarcely a drop of rain falls. Even when thunderstorms do occur, they are so sporadic in distribution, fall at such distances from the summer well zones, and evaporate so rapidly that they are of no significance to the bedouin and are without effect on the farmer's crops. Despite a concentration of rainfall in the remaining nine months of the year, the totals are unevenly distributed and most of the precipitation occurs in the period from December to February, with a January maximum. This precipitation is a product of cyclonic storms that are generated either in the Atlantic or in the western Mediterranean basin and then move eastward, or of local disturbances originating in the Tyrrhenian and Adriatic Seas which then travel directly south. Most of the Atlantic disturbances follow a northerly track, but those that do proceed by a more southerly course pass over the Cyrenaican bulge. Sometime in September or early October the rains commence, generally falling in light showers but occasionally being deposited in violent downpours that result in rapid run-off and serious flooding in the seasonal stream beds. These rains form the sole known source of water for the jabal[1] and upon the effectiveness of its storage in surface cisterns or wells or its collection at springs depends the life of herders and animals during the summer.

Rainfall distribution is closely associated with relief in al-Jabal al-Akhḍar. The combination of a coastline jutting out into the Mediterranean, a position on the southern fringes of the west-to-east storm track, and a modest,

[1] Although a considerable debate exists regarding the origin of the water supplies supporting the oases of Egypt and Libya, A. Torayah Sharaf, "The Hydrological Divisions of the Northern Belt of Libya," in Reiner Keller (ed.), Flussregime und Wasserhaushalt (Freiburger Geographische Hefte, Hefte 6; Freiburg, 1968), p. 33, points out that it is highly unlikely that any water source other than rainfall is important for northern Libya. Other alternative viewpoints, more applicable to the water supply of the southern oases, assign subsurface water origin to: (1) northward migration from intake beds in Chad (Bo Hellstrom, "The Subterranean Water in the Libyan Desert," Geografiska Annaler, XXII [1940], 206-39); (2) "fossil" survival from the Pleistocene (G. W. Murray, "The Artesian Water beneath the Libyan Desert," BSGE, XXV [1953], 81-92); or (3) leakage from the Nile into exposed Nubian sandstone strata (A. Shata, "Geologic Problems Related to the Ground Water Supply of Some Desert Area of Egypt," BSGE, XXXII [1959], 249-62).

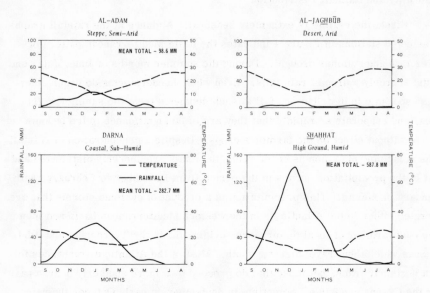

Fig. 4.--Average temperature and rainfall conditions observed at major stations in eastern Cyrenaica. Source: Kingdom of Libya, Meteorological Service, Climatological Summary, No. 147 (August, 1966).

but crucially important, rise in elevation close to the coast, produces a relatively abundant rainfall. These totals are greatest closest to the most elevated areas and the precipitation high point occurs on the upper terrace from Shahhat to west of al-Baydā' (Figure 5). From this zone of maximum concentration, rainfall totals decrease rapidly in all directions, with the maximum amounts closely following the crest line of the upper scarp. This reflects the markedly orographic nature of the precipitation. The subsidence of the upper scarp eastward and the more gentle elevation decrease southward along the dip-slope are reflected in similar configurations in the isohyets.

It is important to point out that Figure 4 represents only a crude approximation of the rainfall distribution. Gathering of climatic data, while first undertaken by the Italians,[1] was interrupted by the Second World War, recommenced

---

[1] The definitive summary of the Italian period is Amilcare Fantoli, Le pioggie della Libia: con particolare riguardo alle zone di avvaloramenta (Rome: Ministero Africa Italiana, 1952) which is especially valuable because it publishes rainfall data for the Italian meteorological stations. Unfortunately, many of these stations were able to collect material for only a few years, so that coverage for much of the country is very sporadic both in time and in space. The Kingdom of Libya resumed publishing climatic statistics (first as the Bollettino Meteorologico and subsequently in expanded publications successively entitled

13

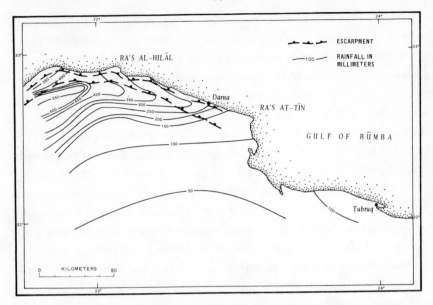

Fig. 5.--Precipitation distribution in eastern Cyrenaica. Sources: Amilcare Fantoli, Le pioggie della Libia (Rome, 1952); Kingdom of Libya, Meteorological Service, Weather Bulletin, Nos. 1-73; and idem, Climatological Summary, Nos. 74-147.

by the British during their military occupation, and then continued with gradually increasing effectiveness after independence. Unfortunately, stations are widely scattered and far too few to give more than a general indication of the pattern.

While it is doubtful that it is possible to be as precise as the recent climatic classification published by UNESCO might suggest,[1] four major climatic subtypes can be delimited (Figure 5). Similar temperature patterns are found at nearly all stations regardless of their geographical location, although mean temperatures obscure the extremes of diurnal maximum and minimum temperatures. The major distinction between each of the zones is the amount of rainfall which is directly related to the elevation of the station and inversely related to distance

the Weather Bulletin and the Climatological Summary) in 1954. The number of gathering stations has been gradually increased, but even today only four stations in the eastern half of Cyrenaica collect complete temperature and rainfall data. A combination of pre-1940 Italian statistics and post-1954 figures was used to construct the isohyets of Figure 5, but, since many of the Italian and post-independence stations have collected information for only a few years, the results of the map must be regarded as indicative rather than definitive.

[1]UNESCO-FAO, Carte bioclimatique de la zone méditerranéenne: notice explicative ("Recherches sur la zone aride, Vol. XXI"; Paris: UNESCO-FAO, 1963).

from the coast.  The coastal zone, benefitting from its position at the base of
the lower scarp, receives a moderate amount of rainfall unevenly distributed
throughout the year.  Darna is the best available representative of this type,
being reasonably analogous to stations further west.  The high rainfall totals of
Shaḥḥat, a humid station, show an uneven distribution and a dry season of nearly
six months, during three months of which almost no rain falls.  Shaḥḥat and
Darna exhibit similar basic patterns which vary only with respect to the differential impact of elevation on the overall precipitation totals.  Because rain falls in
the coolest months of the year, precipitation is doubly effective.  The rapid
decline of rainfall totals south of the upper terrace are reflected by al-Adam station which exhibits a pattern similar to that of Khūlān and al-Makīlī in the study
area cross-section.  al-Jaghbūb, a desert oasis in the south of Marmarica some
225 kilometers from the coast, is typical of conditions in the extreme south.
Here rainfall is extremely low and variable, summer temperatures are high
while winter temperatures are relatively low, and the same pattern of winter
rain and summer drought is repeated as in the areas further to the north.

Variability and Drought

The climatic regime outlined above is not as simple as it might appear.
While it is true that some climatic zones receive appreciable rainfall, and thus
possess considerable agricultural potential, precipitation remains unreliable.
Rainfall in one year is seldom similar to that of another.  Drought, with all its
implications for crop failure and herd decimation, is an ever present threat in
Cyrenaica.

A climatic factor of great importance in northern Cyrenaica is the qiblī.[1]
Most common in spring and autumn when temperature contrasts are greatest,
the qiblī is a strong, hot wind from the Sahara that is invariably accompanied by
large quantities of air-borne sand and dust.  Sandstorms are unpredictable in
occurrence and, if they persist for more than one or two days, can have an
adverse effect on exposed herds and humans as well as on agricultural crops.
Although the humid uplands usually receive enough precipitation and are well-
enough protected by altitude from sandstorms to ensure at least a meager harvest, departures from expected conditions in other areas can have serious consequences.

---

[1]The meteorology of eastern Mediterranean sandstorms is discussed by
E. A. Lunson, Sandstorms on the Northern Coasts of Libya and Egypt (London:
His Majesty's Stationery Office, 1950).

Figure 6 suggests the variability inherent in the rainfall regime. This figure depicts the wettest and driest years recorded since 1954 at the four main stations in eastern Cyrenaica. Whereas Figure 4 evens out extreme variations from month to month, Figure 6 indicates the marked and unpredictable departures from "normal" that can take place monthly in any one year. Although January usually appears as the peak month, subsidiary peaks as late as May also occur, while shifts in the timing of peak months are common from year to year. This is especially serious for the dry-farm cereal cultivation practiced in Cyrenaica, for rainfall in winter is essential if seeds are to germinate while the absence of rain in spring means that the grain will fail to mature.

Not only does rainfall vary from year to year in quantity and monthly timing, but also it differs widely from place to place in the same year. Sites only a few kilometers apart may experience the opposite extremes of drought and surplus. It is this type of variability between neighboring territories that favors the development of marriage links and other ties between the groups occupying different areas in order to overcome the short-term unpredictability of the micro-climate by activating reciprocal patterns of assistance in times of need. In the subhumid and humid jabal zones appreciable rain falls even in bad years, but the environmental hazards become much more severe in the semi-arid areas south of the jabal.

In the precarious semi-arid environments even a minor alteration can create serious difficulties, for the margin of security within which individuals must operate is much less. Superabundant rainfall as recorded for al-Adam in 1956-1957[1] is a blessing but it remains a random and fortuitous occurrence. More common is the near absence of effective rainfall recorded in a dry year for this represents a relatively smaller departure from normal conditions; indeed, only one or two fewer major storms are required to institute adverse conditions and initiate widespread dislocations in the nomadic economy.

This variability in rainfall occurrence and distribution causes rapid increases and decreases in the size of nomadic herds. During good years herds expand since more animals can be supported by the vegetation. In contrast, a succession of arid years results in dramatic reductions in the size of nomadic flocks. In one family of the Ait ʿAlalqa (located in the semi-arid steppe south of Lamlūda) a herd of fifty sheep and forty-five goats, a total reached after a series of better than average years, was reduced in 1952 to only two goats when dry

---

[1]United Kingdom of Libya, Ministry of Communications, Meteorological Service, Weather Bulletin/Bollettino Meteorologico, No. 39 (August, 1957).

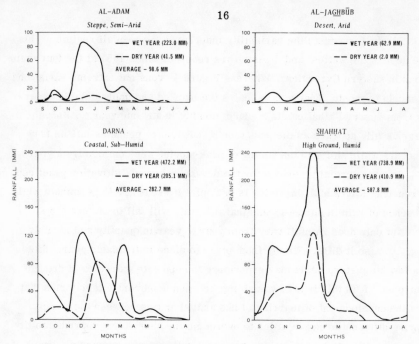

Fig. 6.--Wet and dry years at selected Cyrenaican stations. Source: Kingdom of Libya, Meteorological Service, Climatological Summary, Nos. 74-147.

years followed. The more arid the area, the more variable the monthly and yearly rainfall totals and the greater the fluctuations in animal numbers associated with them. Only on the rare occasion when storms pass far south of their normal eastward course does appreciable precipitation fall in the extreme south. Entire years without rain have been recorded at Jaghbūb, and the vagaries of the arid and semi-arid zones impose a greatly circumscribed range of options on the nomadic dwellers of the desert fringes of Cyrenaica.

Vegetation

Taking into consideration both climate and relief, two major generalized types of vegetation, maquis and steppe, can be delineated in eastern Cyrenaica. The subhumid and humid zones of the northern coast and the upper terrace, possessing an impressive local relief and receiving relatively large quantities of precipitation, support a maquis vegetation. The interior areas of the dip-slope and the eastern coastal districts with little relief, and thus with correspondingly lower rainfall totals, are dominated by a steppe vegetation of variable composition. A number of different communities can be recognized within both the maquis and the steppe divisions and the distribution of these is shown in Figure 7.

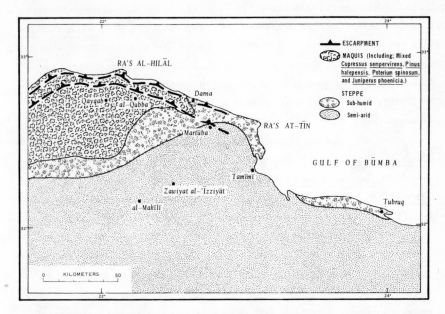

Fig. 7.--Vegetation of eastern Cyrenaica. Sources: Amilcare Fantoli, Le pioggie della Libia, pp. 16-21; UNESCO-FAO, Vegetation Map of the Mediterranean Zone; and field observation.

Maquis Communities

The maquis vegetation begins at the coast and extends across the upper terrace. A large number of the maquis species are found at all elevations, but in certain areas, in response to particular edaphic factors, certain elements of the flora achieve a local dominance. Coastal beaches and dunes, where they exist, support a vegetation dominated by Ammophila arenaria and Juncus auctus. Ridam (Salicornia fruticosa), Suaeda fruticosa, and Limonium pruniosum are usually found concentrated in and around the salt marshes (sebkha) located immediately behind the coastal dunes, while Zygophyllum album is commonly restricted to sites within the range of maritime influence.[1] Temperature constraints restrict Nerium oleander to a lowland location, while its high water

---

[1]This is not an absolute condition since the presence of Zygophyllum album in the interior oases has been noted by C. H. Gimingham, "A Note on Water-table, Sand Movement and Plant Distribution in a North African Oasis," Journal of Ecology, XLIII (1955), 22-25. In this instance its role is that of a dune former on the edges of the oasis where ground water is available. It is likely that its rather prominent occurrence near the coast is related to the presence of substantial supplies of water close to the surface immediately behind the dunes.

requirements localize it in wadi beds, particularly on the northern coast where nearly perennial stream flow is assured. In many locations along the northern coast the escarpment approaches so near the ocean that maritime erosion is taking place immediately at the foot of the scarp. In these situations there is no opportunity for dune or sebkha formation and in the absence of these physiographic features there is an immediate transition from the wave-cut rock to maquis vegetation.

A substantial number of maquis species are found throughout the jabal. Klīl (Rosmarinus officinalis), Baṭūm (Pistacia lentiscus), Zahayra (Phlomis floccosa), Shaʿāra (Juniperus phoenicea), Shibriq (Poterium spinosum), ʿAnsīl (Urginia maritima), Balūt (Quercus coccifera), Shmārī (Arbutus pavari), Quercus ilex, Drās (Thapsia garganica), Anabasis articulata, Jadhārī (Rhus oxycantha), Sakhab (Phillyrea media), Kharūb (Ceratonia siliqua), and Sidr (Zizyphus lotus) are found at all elevations from the coastal plain to the borders of the interior steppes. However, the particular distribution of these species and their relative dominance varies. South facing wadi slopes, for example, suffer from more desiccating conditions than their northward oriented counterparts; as a result more drought resistant species such as Artemisia herba-alba, Rosmarinus officinalis, and Phlomis floccosa, as well as extremely stunted representatives of the less well adapted species, dominate in these demanding conditions.[1] Other intrusives such as the wiry Poterium spinosum and the thorny Zizyphus lotus appear as prominent components of the more humid Mediterranean communuties whenever local conditions of micro-climate or human and animal pressure have created unfavorable habitats for other species. The northern face of the lower scarp between Karsa and Susa, especially where marl composes a prominent part of the substratum,[2] shows a high concentration of Qilʿiz (Pinus halepensis). Appearing first as small and often stunted individuals in the wadi bottoms and along the lower slopes of the wadis some four miles west of Karsa, Pinus halepensis gradually becomes increasingly common until on the scarp slopes behind Raʾs al-Hilāl it forms a definite tree layer. Pinus halepensis, like all the arboreous Cyrenaican species, fails to exercise shade dominance

---

[1] C. H. Gimingham and K. Walton, "Environment and the Structure of Scrub Communities on the Limestone Plateau of Northern Cyrenaica," Journal of Ecology, XLII (1954), 514.

[2] H. N. Le Houérou, Report to the Government of Libya on Natural Pastures and Fodder Resources of Libya and Problems of their Improvement (FAO Report No. 1979; Rome: FAO, 1965), p. 25.

and in many places Juniperus phoenicea is found in association, while Phlomis floccosa, Urginia maritima, Poterium spinosum are common as shrubby ground cover. Nevertheless, the Pinus halepensis stands surviving in coastal Cyrenaica probably represent remnants of the potential climax vegetation for the littoral zone if human and animal pressure is discounted,[1] a rather unrealistic assumption.

Although a few specimen of Nakhl (Cupressus sempervirens var. horizontalis)[2] are encountered in the wadi beds of the coastal plain, they are otherwise never found in a natural setting below the upper scarp. Study of the natural distribution of Cupressus sempervirens is complicated by planting under the Italian forestry program of a number of stands of Cupressus in various locations in the jabal. Thus, it is not uncommon to find specimens of Cupressus sempervirens var. stricta (Pyramidalis) near farm sites and along roads or in separate small plantations. Nevertheless, the sheer size of most of the individual specimens indicates that they were present in al-Jabal al-Akhdar long before the first effective Italian demographic settlement began after 1930. Although restricted today to a few of the more inaccessible sites near the crest of the upper scarp,[3] Cupressus sempervirens at one time occupied much larger portions of the better-watered upper terrace.

Juniperus phoenicea also occurs in isolated stands, on occasion in association with substantial numbers of olives (Olea europaea var. oleaster) as in the stretch of lower terrace between 'Ayn Marra and Wādī an-Naga, the most notable instance being on the dip-slope between Qayqab and Khūlān. In part this

---

[1] UNESCO-FAO, Vegetation Map of the Mediterranean Zone: Explanatory Notes (Paris: UNESCO-FAO, 1969), p. 64.

[2] Nakhl is the word used by northern Cyrenaican Arabs for the cypress; this is the source of some confusion since it is also the word used in the oases, and in literary Arabic, for the date palm. The origin of the colloquial usage is obscure, but it is the only term utilized by the uneducated farmers and nomads of the jabal. 'Abd al-'Azīz Turayyah Sharaf, Jughrāfīyyah Libiyā (Alexandria: Matbi'a al-Masrā, n.d.), p. 270, refers to Cupressus sempervirens as al-Arz ("the cedar"), which adds an additional element of confusion.

[3] Le Houérou, Report to the Government of Libya on Natural Pastures, p. 25, indicates that Cupressus sempervirens is only found in areas where the rainfall is greater than 550 mm. However, individual specimen and small isolated clusters of fully grown, healthy trees can be seen up to fifteen kilometers from the crest line of the upper scarp and well outside the highest precipitation areas. It appears that Cupressus sempervirens can survive in regions with as little as 300-350 mm. of yearly rainfall, given an absence of human and animal interference with growth and regeneration.

reflects the juniper's ability to survive, albeit in stunted aspect, in areas receiving less than 150 mm. of rain. Undoubtedly it also indicates the elimination due to animal and human action of some species normally associated with juniper. In other, flatter pockets with deep soils on both the upper and lower terraces, generally toward the more arid margins of the humid upland, Pistacia lentiscus, a species highly favored for grazing by goats, forms an open cover, interspersed with an occasional Ceratonia siliqua[1] and with frequent occurrence of Poterium spinosum and associates in the open areas between the shrubs.

However, the major maquis community remains a mixed one, characterized by a complex jumbling of numerous species. Arbutus pavari is conspicuous by its presence,[2] as are Juniperus phoenicea, Olea europaea var. oleaster, Quercus coccifera, Q. ilex, Rhus oxycantha, Ceratonia siliqua, Phillyrea media, the vine Smilax aspera, and a lower layer of Pistacia lentiscus, Poterium spinosum, Phlomis floccosa, and Cistus salviifolia. Darna marks the eastern limit of this mixed maquis community, although a few isolated specimen of juniper do occur along the edge of the upper scarp near Umm ar-Razam. In general this dividing line coincided with the 300 mm. isohyet although the presence of juniper as far south as Khūlān, beyond the 150 mm. isohyet, has been noted.

The transition from maquis to steppe vegetation is not an abrupt one, but rather is characterized by an unevenly distributed, extremely degraded community largely composed of Mediterranean species.[3] Poterium spinosum is clearly the dominant member of this association and with it are grouped a number of familiar species such as Phlomis floccosa, Urginia maritima, Thapsis garganica, Thymus capitatus, and a large number of annual grasses. A large band of this Poterium-dominated community runs from al-Qubba through the Italian colonization areas between the two major east-west highways and it occupies all land not directly devoted to agricultural pursuits. Its presence in this location separates

---

[1]The presence of both Ceratonia siliqua and Pistacia lentiscus in loose association, has led Gimingham and Walton, "Environment and the Structure of Scrub Communities," p. 515, to suggest that this community is analogous to a similar grouping of these same species noted by others in Palestine.

[2]In those areas where terra rossa soils are deficient in CA $CO_3$, Arbutus pavari, mixed with Cistus salviifolius, tends to form pure stands. Le Houérou, Report to the Government of Libya on Natural Pastures, p. 25.

[3]This formation is referred to as bartha by Gimingham and Walton, "Environment and the Structure of Scrub Communities," p. 515. For the use of this Biblical term see Michael Zohary, Plant Life of Palestine: Israel and Jordan (New York: Ronald Press Co., 1962), pp. 110-24.

the juniper dominated maquis south of Qayqab from the main maquis areas of
the upper terrace. Its position in the heart of the eastern Jabal al-Akhḍar
reflects the extreme pressure, both human and animal, that has removed other
elements of the natural flora and created an altered set of micro-climatic conditions (featuring increased sunlight, reduced ground cover, and augmented solar
insolation) that are more conducive to xerophytic species.

Steppe Communities

As rainfall totals diminish, a transition to a less aboreous, more open,
steppe environment is made. Like the maquis vegetation, the steppe is also
composed of a number of separate communities,[1] but in contrast to the maquis,
which is partially grouped areally in response to various human pressures as
well as edaphic factors, the steppe flora reflects more broad-scale macro-
climatic influences. Boundaries between each type of steppe community are
vague and they tend to blend imperceptibly one into the other. The first band of
steppe encountered as one proceeds southward down the dip-slope is composed
of Mediterranean biota. Characterized by such species as (Zizyphus lotus),
which becomes increasingly localized to wadi beds and shallow depressions further south, Asphodelus microcarpus, Urginia maritima, and Artemisia cam-
pestris, there are also numerous palatable annual grasses that attract large con-
centrations of grazing animals in season.

This community grades into a semi-arid steppe. Found in areas with
lighter-colored greyish soils, the semi-arid flora is dominated by Shīḥ (Artemisia herba-alba) and its associates Matnān (Thymelaea hirsuta) and Ḥalfā
(Stipa tenacissima). Large numbers of annuals are found here, the most numerous being Reaumuria mucronata, Hordeum murinum, Stipa capensis, S. retorta,
Bromus rubens, Avena alba, and Carex divisa.[2] Overuse, particularly in the
steppes around Martūba and Tamīmī, has resulted in a degradation of the community and a reduction in its carrying capacity.[3] Further south vegetation

---

[1]Hans W. Ahlman, "La Libye septentrionale," Geografiska Annaler, X
(1928), 43-46.

[2]For a fine study of the palatable species found in northern Libya and
their potential for grazing consult Le Houérou, Report to the Government of
Libya on Natural Pastures, particularly pp. 26-27.

[3]Ibid., p. 26.

becomes increasingly restricted to wadi beds and basins of internal drainage at
the foot of the dip-slope.  In more saline areas this arid steppe zone shows con-
centrations of Anabasis articulata, Salsola vermiculata, Atriplex coricea, Choe-
nolea halimus, and Atriplex halimus, while the better soils support Sabit (Aristida pugens), Rimth (Haloxylon articulatum), Safsafa (Medicago sp. ), Zilla
biparmata, and Anvillea australis.[1]

South of the balta zone, the arid steppe becomes increasingly discontinuous and localized to those areas, such as the Wādī al-Mra, where seasonal
water supplies occur.  On those occasions when rain showers reach this southern fringe of the desert, ephemeral vegetation, dominated by Retama raetam
and Aristida pugens, springs to life on the loose sandy soils or dune areas.
Sporadic and irregular in occurrence, it offers meagre pastures for the nomad
and can only be successfully exploited by the hardy camel.

Utilization of the Natural Vegetation

Four major processes have been operating through time to change the
structure and composition of the flora of Cyrenaica.  Gathering and collecting of
useful plants, burning, cutting of trees and large shrubs for firewood and charcoal or for the fabrication of domestic implements, and grazing and browsing
are the main pressures that have had an impact on the flora.  However, the
effect of these processes has been unequal in importance and some, particularly
cutting and grazing, have played the principal roles in altering the distribution
and the physical aspect of the vegetation.

An essential requirement for a community trying to extract a living from
a marginal environment under conditions of climatic variability is to utilize
every available resource to the maximum possible extent.  This requires a great
deal of expert knowledge of the potential of the natural vegetation as a source of
supplemental food and as a pharmacy containing herbal remedies for common ill-
nesses.  The traditional bedouin economy operated with only limited contacts
with an urban population largely because many required items could be produced
locally.  In achieving a considerable degree of independence from the settled
population, the collecting of useful plants and the manufacturing of the limited
number of domestic implements needed by the bedouin household played an important role.

Bedouin lore recognizes that numerous plants are valuable either for food

[1]Ibid., p. 27, and Ahlman, "La Libye septentrionale, " p. 46.

or for their medicinal properties. Foremost among these is Shih (Artemisia herba-alba). Although found throughout the jabal, Shih is most commonly encountered in the semi-arid steppe, where it is a major component of the flora. Extensively collected, it is regarded as a sovereign specific for stomach worms and it is frequently brewed with tea with this end in view. Shih's aromatic properties make it valuable as bedding; it is often used as such for young goats that are tethered in the tent during the warmest months of the year.[1] However, it is the medicinal properties of Artemisia that are renowned in local lore and many believed that those steppe zones dominated by Shih are free from disease. The 1918 cholera epidemic is cited by bedouin elders as an example of this, for it is claimed that wherever Artemisia was common the epidemic was averted, while those regions closer to the coast bore the full brunt of the disease. Whatever the merits of the claims, it is most likely that distance from the coastal cities, where inadequate sanitation facilitated the spread of cholera, was more importnat than the medicinal qualities of Shih, however high they might be.

Ja'farāz (Asparagus stipulans), sporadically encountered throughout the maquis, is also reputed to be a successful treatment for stomach complaints of various kinds, while Tafā (Salvia triloba) is thought to cure the common cold. Most of these species are consumed with tea and double as a kind of spice or flavoring. Other plants used primarily for flavoring, but which also have medicinal properties usually associated with stomach problems, are Klīl (Rosmarinus officinalis), Tafā (Salvia triloba), and Za'tar (Thymus capitatus). Shmārī (Arbutus pavari) produces a berry in season that looks something like a strawberry[2] and this is consumed with relish by the badawi.

Three other elements of the flora have a more commercial function, although their use is largely confined to the rural population. Marsīn (Myrtus communis), a somewhat rare plant, produces a small seed that is processed and used as a perfume; Birbish (Cistus salviifolius) and Balūt (Quercus coccifera) are important in skin-tanning. One of the more heavily utilized food plants is Zahayra (Phlomis floccosa). Its flowers are sucked for their sweet taste and its seed pods are crushed and mixed as a flavoring in rural cuisine. After boiling for twenty-four hours, its leaves produce a black residue (rūb) which, when mixed with samin (butter), is used as a sugar and honey substitute. The seeds

---

[1] Emrys L. Peters, "The Sociology of the Bedouin of Cyrenaica" (unpublished Ph. D. thesis, Lincoln College, Oxford University, July, 1951), p. 22.

[2] Lutfī Būlis, "az-Zuhūr al-Barrīya fī Lībiyā," al-Hisād, August, 1968, p. 9, refers to Shmārī as the "strawberry tree" for this reason.

of Qilʻiz (Pinus halepensis) are gathered, dried in the sun, and then eaten; the bedouin likened them both in taste and smell to cocoa.

These gathering activities have only a limited effect on the flora because they always are conducted on a small-scale, domestic level. Only during the summer months, when the nomads are concentrated near the springs and cisterns of the jabal, do bedouin women appear in the weekly markets selling small quantities of Zaʻtar. Similarly, stands of Qilʻiz are too limited to make commercial exploitation of its seeds profitable and it is only rarely that they appear in the Darna suq. With these exceptions, plants collected are consumed in small quantities by the people who gather them. Although exploitation of seeds obviously interferes with regeneration, there is no indication that such utilization is driving any plant to the verge of extinction.

Degradation of the Natural Vegetation

Burning of the flora takes place to a limited degree. However, there is no evidence to suggest that the nomadic population deliberately burns the steppe to improve the pasture or that such activities in the past were an important element in its origin. Although the degraded nature of much of the Artemisia steppe is all too clear, the cause can best be sought in overgrazing rather than in climatic change or uncontrolled burning. The major perennial steppe species are all adjusted to summer-drought conditions and the spacing of individual clumps is so great that fires would have no chance of catching and spreading.

There is also no evidence to suggest that any of the communities existing in the jabal today represent adjustments to repeated burning. Whatever burning is taking place at present, aside from an occasional accidental fire in the maquis, is associated with the clearing of new areas for agriculture. In these instances the method employed is to maintain a small fire at the base of a tree or shrub until either the tree falls or its bark is burned through and it is killed. The impact of this procedure is local and the more recent practice, prompted by the oil boom, has been to employ tractors and bulldozers to clear tracts of land. Occasionally fires of accidental origin, either from domestic sources or agricultural clearing operations that get out of hand, occur in the jabal, but the existence of numerous deep wadis tends to isolate the fire and prevent it from spreading widely.

A few of the most common jabal trees are fabricated into tools and household implements. Before the advent of the oil economy, both the cutting and the shaping of these implements was done by the bedouin and this activity represents one facet of their traditionally limited dependence on urban craftsmen and merchants for products in common use. The 'Asa (a walking stick that also doubled as a shepherd's crook) and the temporary brush shelters (Khūs) erected at harvest time or by individual shepherds were usually made from olive wood.[1] Juniper, oak, and the occasional cypress and arbutus furnished the material for such essential bedouin household items as the mabram (spindle), minshaz (beater; used in weaving to beat the weft firmly into the warp), qas'ah (serving bowl), muhqan (funnel), and maghraf (spoon), not to mention such crucial necessities as tent poles and pegs. Bedouin need for domestic furnishings was limited to those items that could be easily transported and this served to keep the demand small. Yet, although the household items manufactured from wood were relatively few, they did necessitate the cutting of the major arboreal species in the jabal.

These same species also were exploited by the limited urban population which, before the Italian conquest, essentially was confined to Darna and Banghāzī. Because the urban population was small, its demand for wood was limited. Yet such items as roof beams, plows, agricultural tools, doors, and domestic furniture could only be supplied by cutting the domestic vegetation, although recently the importation of lumber from foreign sources has served to reduce dependence on local supplies. Nevertheless, exploitation of local timber resources for manufacturing purposes is a relatively minor pressure on the domestic flora.

Similarly, the need for local timber as a construction material has always been small. Greco-Roman settlers seem to have built largely in stone. Local stone was relatively soft and easily worked and, although it needed considerable attention to prevent degeneration, it represented a better long term investment than wooden houses. Subsequently, those elements of the nomadic population that were nearly or completely stationary often occupied Greco-Roman tomb chambers and so required little timber for building purposes; others made use of these same facilities for storing grain or other valuables. Most houses built in the jabal today also require little timber from local sources, since the use of locally-quarried limestone blocks[2] or domestically-manufactured cement blocks is the most popular construction material. Even the tin barak favored by

---

[1]Peters, "Sociology of the Bedouin of Cyrenaica," p. 18.

[2]Robert Holz, "Sandstone as a Building Material in Libya," Pennsylvania Geographer, VIII (September, 1970), 1-10.

the sedentarizing nomadic population are built on a frame of imported lumber.

Undoubtedly fuel requirements have caused the most severe pressures on the vegetation. Juniper, pistacia, and arbutus are the most commonly utilized species today and the activities of charcoal burners are everywhere apparent. Concentration of the charcoal industry on its present set of most favored species reflects the difficulty of finding hardwoods that can be most efficiently converted into charcoal. Balūt (Quercus coccifera)[1] is increasingly restricted to the most inaccessible parts of the jabal by the pressures being put upon it. The charcoal-license authority and forest guards of the Department of Agriculture now make it very difficult to cut cypress and olive trees for charcoal or for the manufacture of wooden implements. This has forced charcoal producers to concentrate on more marginal species in terms of the efficiency of their yield of finished product.

Nevertheless, in recent years the demand for charcoal has accelerated. Not only is charcoal favored by the bedouin because of its transportation efficiency, but also its smokeless and flameless qualities make it attractive to the urban population. Although modern appliances are common in Libya and bottled gas is increasing in popularity, charcoal fires remain the main fuel source for cooking and for brewing the tea and coffee that form such an important part of Arab daily life and hospitality. The accelerated rural to urban migration of the last ten years has increased and concentrated the demand for charcoal, because many individuals who formerly gathered their own firewood now must rely on charcoal purchases in local markets. Moreover, as more nomads become sedentarized their impact on the fuel resources of their immediate neighborhood grows. Completely aside from the production of charcoal, a common sight throughout the jabal is clusters of women (whose responsibility it is to provide their family fire with fuel) trudging along the roadside burdened with gigantic bundles of faggots destined for the domestic hearth. In addition, shepherds pause several times each day to brew a pot of tea and it is the branches of immediately accessible shrubs that form their fuel supply.

Thus, both urban and rural fuel demands provide the necessary incentive for continued charcoal production. Burning pits are scattered throughout the

---

[1]It should be pointed out that the bedouin do not distinguish between the three main oak species (Q. coccifera, Q. ilex, and Q. calliprinos) present in Cyrenaica. To the bedouin an oak is an oak and serves as a source for tannic acid and for charcoal regardless of its speciation. In this sense, if in no other, the distinctions of the taxonomist have only limited significance.

jabal in close proximity to each other, and this suggests how widespread and serious is the practice. In combination with other uses of the shrubby flora for fuel, charcoal production has a dramatic impact on the morphology of the maquis vegetation. Indeed, since oak, juniper, arbutus, and pistacia tend to reproduce by sprouting, consistent cutting for charcoal production and fuel favors the development of a lateral growth form. Species that once possessed an upright aspect have developed the stunted appearance characteristic of maquis vegetation as a consequence of centuries of human use.

The long-term effect of this unremitting assault of the vegetation is difficult to assess. At present only a few stands of Cupressus sempervirens and Pinus halepensis exist to give meagre clues about the potential structure of the flora. No protected sacred groves associated with tombs of saints exist in the rural areas around Darna. Thus, it is difficult to speculate on the potential vegetation if cutting were removed as a source of interference.[1] Nevertheless, the existence of fully grown individuals of most maquis species, particularly on remote and inaccessible sites, indicates that the present shrubby and stunted aspect is not natural but rather is man-induced. The maquis flora of northern Cyrenaica represents a degraded forest community whose recumbent aspect is the result of unchecked cutting and resulting lateral sprouting.

Grazing and browsing also are important contributors to the degraded nature of the Cyrenaican flora. The goat is the prime culprit in this regard, largely because so many are kept by both the nomadic and the sedentary population. The location of the goat is directly related to the distribution of vegetation communities, for goats are excellent converters of the leafy shrubs of the northern coastal regions and it would be impossible to maintain herds of any size in these areas without them. The ability of the goat to consume the most unpalatable plants, together with its tremendous agility, make it an ideal animal for the rugged upland platforms and scarps. Pistacia lentiscus, Arbutus pavari, and Juniperus phoenicia, the three most common arboreal species in the jabal, are eaten with great gusto, and it is not unusual to see the goat ensconced in the branches of an olive tree vigorously consuming everything within reach. Artemisia herba-alba is another favorite goat fodder; its partiality for this plant enables the goat to operate effectively in the semi-arid steppe as well. The goat's consumptive habits are seasonal. It favors annual grasses during the

---

[1]For the uses to which such relic protected stands can be put in reconstructing the potential vegetation of an area, see Marvin W. Mikesell, "Deforestation in Northern Morocco," Science, CXXXII (August 19, 1960), 441-48.

winter and spring and thus relieves the pressure on the trees and shrubs for at least part of the year. But in the summer months, when the annual vegetation becomes desiccated, the goat thrives on the herbaceous shrubs.

The goat's omniverous eating habits are not responsible in isolation for the degraded nature of the maquis. Indeed, were this so it is probable that the maquis flora would have disappeared long ago as some ecologists fear it is in danger of doing at present.[1] Uncontrolled, and perhaps uncontrollable, cutting both for firewood and charcoal represents the most severe pressure on the flora. Continued cutting for fuel has undoubtedly eliminated the shrub layer from the understory of the few surviving stands of Cupressus sempervirens and replaced it with Poterium spinosum. Isolated stands of Juniperus phoenicea with only Poterium as an understory reflect the same process. Continued cutting, where it has failed to eliminate such species as Arbutus pavari and Pistacia lentiscus, has favored the development of lateral sprouting and a lower, more bushy profile. Cutting combined with grazing creates a more open environment that permits increased penetration of light to take place. Increased insolation, in turn, changes micro-climatic conditions sufficiently to allow arid intrusives such as Zizyphus lotus to invade areas capable of supporting far more luxuriant herbage.

Measured by this standard the degree of disturbance present in al-Jabal al-Akhḍar is considerable. The goat operates in conjunction with cutting by preventing the cut-over species from attaining unhindered their previous upright aspect; indeed, grazing on previously cut-over specimens facilitates additional lateral sprouting. In those areas where the undergrowth has been completely removed, the goat prevents regeneration both of groundcover species and of tree-layer seedlings. In both instances the goat maintains and extends a condition that has already been brought into existence by the activities of the human population.

---

[1] Le Houérou, Report to the Government of Libya on Natural Pastures, p. 25; Gimingham and Walton, "Environment and the Structure of Scrub Communities," p. 517.

# CHAPTER II

## TRIBAL DISTRIBUTIONS AND

## HERDING LIFE STYLES

The Cyrenaican Arab tribes represent not the initial wave of conquest led by 'Amr ibn al-'Āṣ in A. D. 643 but rather a subsequent invasion of the Banī Hilāl and Banī Sulaym tribes after A. D. 1050. This second Arab influx differed from the earlier strictly military conquest in that it involved the mass migration of entire clans complete with their families and flocks. While most of the Hilalian tribes pushed across Libya into North Africa, a number of sections of the Banī Sulaym remained in Cyrenaica and became the effective owners of its land and water resources by right of conquest.

### The Distribution of Cyrenaican Tribes

The tribes presently occupying al-Jabal al-Akhḍar can be grouped into two major subdivisions. On the one hand are the noble lineages, descendants of a common legendary ancestress, Sa'ādah, who claim exclusive access to the resources of the jabal on the basis of their conquest of Cyrenaica during the Hilalian invasion. In contrast to the noble tribes are the marābṭīn tribes, who are geneaolgically inferior in status but are generally associated as clients with particular segments of the noble lineages. The marābṭīn are themselves divided into two major classes: (1) the Marābṭīn bi-'l-Barakah, marābṭīn of blessing or goodness, who are the descendants of holy men and possess a certain saintly status both by virtue of their piety and of their role as mediators in tribal disputes, and (2) the Marābṭīn as-Sidqān, "true" or fee-paying marābṭīn, who theoretically obtain access to resources only at the sufferance of the noble clans with which they are affiliated. [1] Although their status is inferior to that of the

---

[1] The implications of this variation in status are developed by Emrys L. Peters, "The Tied and the Free: An Account of a Type of Patron-Client Relationship among the Bedouin Pastoralists of Cyrenaica," in J. -G. Peristiany (ed.), Contributions to Mediterranean Sociology (Paris and The Hague: Mouton & Co., 1968), pp. 167-88.

Sa'ādī tribes, the marābtīn are nearly as numerous as their noble patrons and in practical terms the power and prestige of the Sa'ādī clans is directly related to the support they can muster among the marābtīn.

## The Noble Tribes of Cyrenaica

Today nine noble Sa'ādī tribes (Figure 8) divide al-Jabal al-Akhḍar among them, the descendants of Jibarna occupying the western jabal and the Harabī the eastern. That this particular division of Cyrenaica is relatively recent is certain.[1] Before 1800 the Jirbana and Harabī occupied only a small portion of the central coastal districts of Cyrenaica (Figure 9). Then, as today, the object of each major genealogical segment was to occupy a full range of ecological zones. Given the east-west orientation of the Jabal al-Akhḍar and the resulting development of ecological zones parallel to the coast, each tribe had to control a north-south strip of territory beginning at the coast and extending indefinitely into the interior. Only in this way could an adequate resource base be developed that would assure access by denizens of the marginal areas to more favorable niches should environmental disasters such as drought or crop failure ensue. The Jibarna tribes of 'Abīd, 'Arafa, 'Awaqir, and Magharba, together with the Harabī tribes, crowded into the central coastal districts and the dissected plateau areas immediately to the south, were cut off from direct access to the southern regions suitable for sheep and camel herding by their Jawazī, Fawayid, and Awlad 'Alī cousins. Although some of the plateau areas occupied by the Jibarna and Harabī receive substantial rainfall totals, the rugged nature of the relief restricts agricultural possibilities. Denied access to the more productive upper plateau and dwelling in a zone of maquis vegetation suitable only for goats, there appear to have been built-in ecological inadequacies in the original Jibarna and Harabī tribal territories.

Whether environmental considerations, population pressure, or the well-established quarrelsomeness and raiding proclivities of the bedouin[2] were to

---

[1] E. E. Evans-Pritchard, The Sanusi of Cyrenaica, pp. 49-50.

[2] Louise B. Sweet, "Camel Raiding among the Bedouins of North Arabia: A Mechanism of Ecological Adaption," American Anthropologist, LXVII (October, 1965), 1132-50, points out the importance of raiding activities in the nomadic ethos. But, since what is gained in one raid might well be lost to marauding neighbors in a subsequent retaliatory raid, it is unclear what overall benefits accrue from raiding, unless, as is the case in Arabia, substantial settled communities or major caravan routes are at the mercy of the bedouin.

31

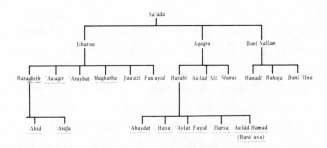

Fig. 8.--The relationship of the Saʿādī tribes of Cyrenaica (after Evans-Pritchard and de Agostini). Only underlined tribes are present in Cyrenaica.

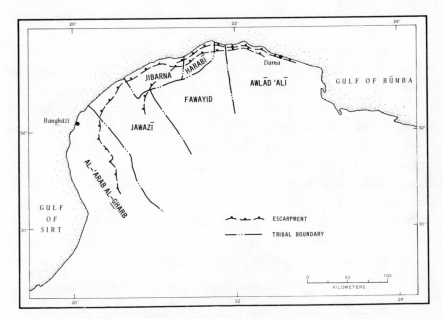

Fig. 9.--Tribal distribution in Cyrenaica before 1800

32

blame is not mentioned in existing oral traditions. However, regardless of the
initial cause, large-scale fighting broke out after 1800 between the Jibarna and
Harabī and the tribes surrounding them to the south. Aided by the Karamanlī
dynasty in Tripoli, [1] the Jibarna and Harabī were eventually successful in driving their rivals into Egypt. An additional series of wars ending about 1832
resulted in the expulsion of al-ʿArab al-Gharb (the Western Arabs) from the
coastal plain between Banghāzī and Ajadābiyah and produced the tribal distribution of today (Figure 10).

This is not to suggest that intratribal and intertribal feuding ended with
the expulsion of al-ʿArab al-Gharb. On numerous occasions internal feuding
caused the expulsion of tertiary sections from their homelands, so that a constant dribble of tribal fragments into Egypt took place. Nor were the tribes in
the central portions of Cyrenaica content to remain in their rather restricted
areas. The ʿAbaydat, successful occupiers themselves of former Awlad ʿAlī
territory, experienced pressure from their western neighbors. On at least one
occasion in the mid-nineteenth century the Barāʿasa formed an alliance with the
Darsa and Hasa and launched a series of attacks on the ʿAbaydat. Initially on
the verge of total defeat, the ʿAbaydat were able to turn back their rivals in part
as the result of the assistance of mercenary soldiers recruited in Tripolitania.
The proportion of Tripolitanians from Tajūra, Zlitan, and Misratah in the city
population of contemporary Darna is directly related to these nineteenth century
tribal conflicts. [2]

These conflicts explain the presence of components of most of the ʿAbaydat primary segments in the al-Qubbah area. Elements of Ghayth, Mansūr (of
Bū Yamāmah), Bū Dawī, ʿAbd al-Karīm (of Thana Sulayman), Mariam, Bū
Jaziyyah (of Bū Yamāmah), ʿAbayd, and Rfad of the ʿAbaydat and elements of the
Awwama and Misamir marābtīn can be found either in al-Qubbah itself or in its
immediate environs. According to tribal traditions the presence of these primary segments and the absence of others reflects division of the spoils of victory
among those subtribes that took an active part in the fighting with the Barāʿasa.
Despite conflicts of this type, however, tribal areas remained relatively constant from about 1850 until the Italian colonial period.

---

[1] Evans-Pritchard, Sanusi of Cyrenaica, p. 50.

[2] In 1922, out of a total Darnese Muslim population of 9,420, better than
one third came from Tajūra alone while more than an additional third was represented by Misratī and Zlitanī. Only 6 per cent of the population was composed
of ʿAbaydat and their associated marābtīn. See the census figures of Enrico de
Agostini, Le populazione della Cirenaica (Bengasi: Governo della Cirenaica,
1922-1923), p. 433.

33

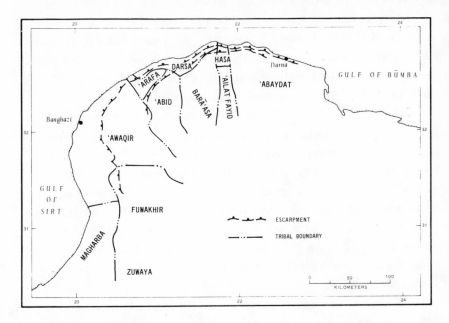

Fig. 10. --Tribal distribution in Cyrenaica since 1850 (after Evans-Pritchard).

The Abaydat Tribe

The largest Sa'ādī tribe of Cyrenaica, both in terms of numbers[1] and of territory, is the 'Abaydat, who occupy the eastern third of al-Jabal al-Akhḍar and all of Marmarica. The 'Abaydat in turn are subdivided into four major units, 'Uwār, al-'Awakla, Shīyyāhīn, and Muhammid Bū Sharī'a, the last of which now resides in Egypt. Each of the first three segments occupies a discrete portion of the jabal but the actual territories involved are unequal. This illustrates one of the major difficulties in using the genealogy as an expression of territorial organization, for the particular level of a tribal unit in the genealogy in no way

---

[1] de Agostini, Le popolazione della Cirenaica, p. 444, gives the following figures for the noble tribes and their associated marabtīn:

| Harabī: | 'Abaydat | 30,450 | Jarbani: | 'Abīd | 6,850 |
| | Hasa | 6,510 | | 'Arafa | 9,300 |
| | 'Ailat Fayid | 100 | | 'Awaqir | 27,500 |
| | Darsa | 18,850 | | Magharb | 13,000 |
| | Barā'asa | 20,000 | | | |

Although neither the census of 1954 nor that of 1964 enumerates tribal affiliation, recent population growth is unlikely to have altered the relative proportions at the tribal level.

corresponds to its physical size and extent on the ground. This is best illustrated by reference to the descendants of 'Uwār (Figure 11) to which group the
greater part of the 'Abaydat belong. Even within the 'Uwār lineage territorial
balance is skewed, for the various families of Ait Ghayth and Bū Yamāmah control the major portion of the eastern jabal while a small lineage such as Bū
Ḍawī or 'Abayd, although the genealogical equals of Ghayth, possess a propor-
tionately smaller waṭan (homeland). As a result, position in the genealogy fails
to reflect the size and prestige of a particular segment.

Moreover in response to demographic and other pressures some elements in the tribal lineage expand at the tertiary level[1] while others decline.
As this process of unequally distributed fission takes place, it is accompanied
by corresponding shifts both in the territorial arrangements of the tertiary segments and in the genealogical structure that explains the relationship of one
group to another. In this sense the genealogy is really a fictionalized expression of descent designed to comprehend the practical realities of ownership of
land and water resources.

Ideally each tribe attempts to command a full range of the resource
possibilities offered by al-Jabal al-Akhḍar. This is done by controlling a north-
south oriented strip that extends from the coast across the agricultural areas of
the high plateau and into the steppe and semi-desert grazing areas on the Saharan fringes. Because this strip is too large for each of the lowest order lineage segments to control, they are forced to occupy smaller pieces of the total
tribal whole or to fragment themselves in such a way that they are located in a
variety of ecological conditions. The presence of portions of the Thana Sulayman, a subdivision of the Bū Yamāmah, on the first plateau, on the second plateau around al-Qubbah, in the steppe south of al-Fatāyaḥ, and in the small
oasis of Umm ar-Razam is typical of attempts to control resources in all zones.
This process of lineage split on the basis of geographical position can extend to
the tertiary level; Ait 'Ali of 'Abd al-Karīm of Thana Sulayman, for example, is
located in the coastal steppe near Umm ar-Razam, while Ait 'Umar occupies a
small block of territory in the fertile upper terrace near al-Qubbah. Thus, it is

---

[1]"Tertiary" is Peters' descriptive term for a segment, numbering from
200 to 700 people, which comprises the lowest lineage level capable of functioning as a unit in the ownership of land, the payment of blood money, and the exac-
tion of vengeance. Secondary and primary are used to distinguish correspondingly more populous ascending levels in the genealogy below tribal status whose
relationships are characterized by feuding and raiding respectively. See Emrys
L. Peters, "Some Structural Aspects of the Feud among the Camel-Herding
Bedouin of Cyrenaica," Africa, XXXVII (1967), particularly pp. 262 and 269.

35

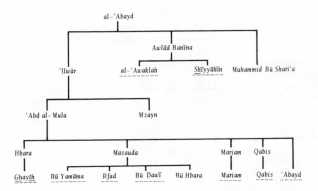

Fig. 11.--Genealogy of the 'Abaydat Tribe (after de Agostini). Underlined tribal sections are present in al-Jabal al-Akhdar.

not so much segmentary opposition that explains the proliferation of segments in
the bedouin lineage structure as it is the need to organize and control access to
particular ecological niches.[1]

A comparison of the genealogy (Figure 12) and the tribal territory (Figure 13) of Ait Ghayth points out this relationship between genealogy and area.
The widest range of environmental zones is held by the Bū Mghaytha. Although
Ait Faḍīla is concentrated in the coastal district around Ra's al-Hilāl, the
remaining two secondary sections are stretched in alternating leap-frog fashion
as they divide the remainder of the tribal strip. Similar patterns occur at the
tertiary level where, for example, Ait Ibrāhīm of Ait al-Farkh occupies the high
plateau while Ait Ḥusayn and Ait Buṣayṣ divide the western and eastern portions
of the inland steppe.[2] The same is true in Ait al-Khādim where Ait Bū Taḥīyya
occupies the northern portion of the tribal area and Ait 'Āmir the southern. Similarly, among al-Afrād, Ait aṣ-Ṣughayyir is localized on the first plateau while
Ait Jābir and Ait Bū Nḍārah are found in the eastern and western portions respectively of their high plateau zone near Zāwiyat Tīrt.

---

[1] Emrys L. Peters, "The Proliferation of Segments in the Lineage of the
Bedouin of Cyrenaica," Journal of the Royal Anthropological Institute, XC (1960),
30 ff., 39-40.

[2] de Agostini, Le populazione della Cirenaica, pp. 120-22.

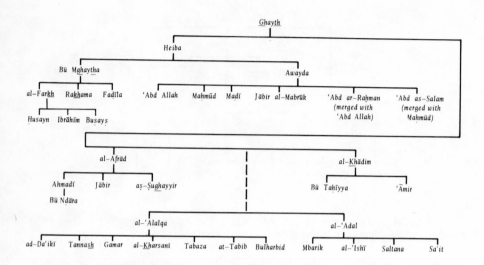

Fig. 12.--Genealogy of the Ait G̲h̲ayth (after de Agostini)

As a result of these ownership patterns, all tribesmen are fully aware of the boundaries of the various segment levels. Moreover, although land at the level of the tertiary segment is held in common and individuals gain access to ploughing land on the basis of their membership in this corporation, tradition plays a large role in determining where each lineage member will cultivate. Thus, there are well understood repetitive patterns of personal as well as of segmental land use. These traditional land-ownership patterns underlie the redistribution of former Italian colonial properties and the settlement system which emerges when pastoralists abandon their tents in favor of permanent housing in proximity to tribal wells or traditional grain fields. Tribal segments whose territory lies on the southern slopes of al-Jabal al-Ak̲h̲ḍar claim exclusive ownership only of the areas that are conducive to agriculture. Once farming possibilities become excessively marginal, generally at about the latitude of K̲h̲ūlān, all of the Ait G̲h̲ayth whose herd composition makes seasonal movements southward a necessity are free to share in the general tribal territory.

Finally, reference must be made to the marābtīn mentioned above. Although in theory all marābtīn are ineligible to own land, in practice many client

37

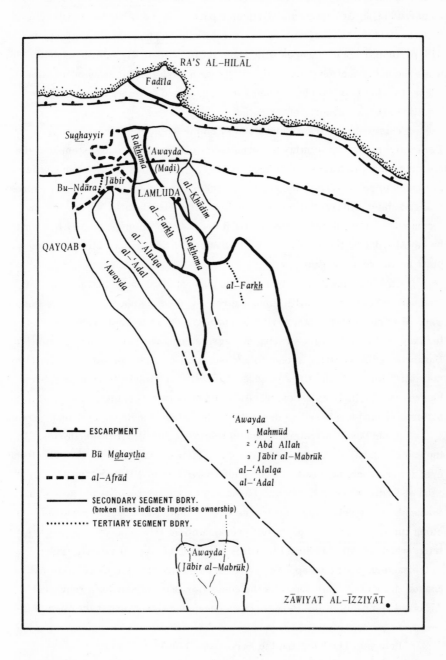

Fig. 13.--Tribal territory of the Ait Ghayth (after de Agostini)

tribes do have recognized tribal territories. The Marābtīn bi-'l-Baraka are not
numerous enough to claim any particular portion of the 'Abaydat territory for
their own. Like the majority of the Marābtīn as-Sadqān, they are associated
with particular noble lineages with whom they are mutually interdependent. For
while the noble section gains political strength from the numbers of its client
adherents, the marābtīn gain access to the land and water resources that by
tradition are the property of the Sa'ādī.

This point is stressed by Peters[1] on the basis of his work with the
Barā'asa. Somewhat similar patterns operate in the 'Abaydat system, but the
contemporary practice is undergoing change. Informants from Sa'ādī lineages
are quick to point out that there are no such distinctions and that visible expres-
sions of status differentiation are confined to the Barā'asa. "We are all one" is
a common statement among the 'Abaydat and they claim emphatically that anyone,
be he 'Abaydat or Hasa, 'Awaqir or Fawakhir, Sa'ādī or marābtīn can graze or
plant in 'Abaydat territory.

Closer inspection of these claims suggests that the actual patterns of
land use and the lineage affiliations expressing them do not work in quite this
way. It is possible for other tribal subsections or even other tribes to use a
tertiary section's land for grazing and agriculture, but permission is required.
Unsanctioned activities can lead to serious conflict. This applies especially to
marābtīn, for while the lines of separation between client and noble are being
blurred increasingly as sedentarization and modernization progress, traditional
patterns of land use based on descent still have tremendous significance.

A number of marābtīn tribes do have recognized tribal territories. In
the eastern Jabal al-Akhdar few 'Abaydat sections occupy the lower terrace and
even fewer reach the coast (the Ait Fadīla near Ras al-Hilāl and the Mansūr
'Abd al-Qādir between Karsa and Darna are exceptions). Instead, zones characterized by their relatively limited resource potential are in the possession of
client lineages. In other parts of Cyrenaica client tribes occupy distinct districts which usually are found in buffer positions between the Sa'ādī tribes,[2] but
in the eastern jabal they appear to have been pushed into the more marginal
coastal districts. This supports the contention that the marābtīn represent
Arabized remnants of the Berber tribes occupying Cyrenaica at the time of the

---

[1] Peters, "The Tied and the Free," pp. 170-72.

[2] Ibid., p. 169.

Hilalian invasion.[1]  Origin aside, such tribes as the Ḥuta and Tarākī, despite
ties to certain noble lineages, function for all intents and purposes as independent tribes.  This is particularly true for the Qat'an and Minifa marābṭīn of
Marmarica,[2] for there the number of Sa'ādī tribesmen is comparatively small
and the opportunities for a functionally independent status correspondingly
greater.  Nevertheless, for most of the client tribesmen, including those with
their own tribal territory, a combination of relatively limited resource potential
and population pressure encourages them to maintain at least some of the traditional links to the noble lineages.

Herding Life Styles in Eastern Cyrenaica

Were it not for the relatively high relief of al-Jabal al-Akhḍar and the
greater quantities of rainfall that are a consequence of it, Cyrenaica would support little more than a semi-arid steppe flora.  Under these conditions of relative environmental poverty, only limited numbers of animals and people could
be supported and the genre de vie would be much more precarious.[3]  But this is
not the case, and the peculiarities of rainfall and relief make Cyrenaica a relatively secure and reliable place in which to live.  This environmental richness
is relative, however, for the elevation of al-Jabal al-Akhḍar is not great enough
to bring forth a large number of sharply differentiated ecological zones.  Unlike
other areas of North Africa, where mountain ranges attain great height and
favor the development of isolated ecological niches suited to the production of
specialized products, Cyrenaican pastoral life exhibits a sameness in its general lifestyle that simultaneously complicates and simplifies the situation.
There is no absolute separation between the man who herds and the man who

---

[1]The ethnic origin of tribal elements in Cyrenaica is open to question,
since literary sources for the post-conquest period are almost entirely nonex-
estent. de Agostini, Le populazione della Cirenaica, p. 444, believes that the
Berber element in the 'Abaydat tribe and associated marābṭīn is very high and
he assigns an arabo-berber origin to 13,680 tribesmen out of a total population
of 30,450.  This total would ascribe Berber blood to a considerable proportion
of noble 'Abaydat, but it should be pointed out that definitive proof is lacking.

[2]Evans-Pritchard, Sanusi of Cyrenaica, p. 53.

[3]Under such hypothetical conditions the environmental regime for all of
Cyrenaica would be analogous to that of the Syrtic Gulf area and the nomadic
life style would be as marginal and as oriented to dependence on the support of
agricultural oases as that described by André Cauneille, "Le nomadisme des
Megarha (Fezzân)," TIRS, XII (1954), 41-67.

farms. With few exceptions all nomads practice agriculture and all sedentary farmers maintain at least a small herd of livestock. Combinations of herding animals and cultivating practices blend imperceptibly into one another and differences are of degree and not of kind. Although farmers do possess certain products that nomads, because of their mobile genre de vie, are unable to produce, only a limited amount of economic exchange takes place between the two groups, a consequence that is examined in detail in the following chapter.

Until the last thirty years nearly all Cyrenaicans were nomads. That is to say, they derived most of their livelihood from animals, shifted their animals about in response to seasonal variations in the location of pasture and water, and participated in a shared value system, mythos, and tribal social structure. Whether living on the coast or in the highest elevations of the jabal, in the interior steppes or in exile in Egypt, they shared a unity and common outlook that set them off from the alien population of the towns. Those differences of degree that do exist within the nomadic community are related to the types of animals being herded.

Domesticated Animals

A variety of domestic animals are herded in the eastern Jabal al-Akhḍar. Cows, goats, sheep, camels, horses, and donkeys are all owned by different tribal segments and grouped in various combinations to support the economic activities of individual tertiary sections. Each of the animals herded has its own particular characteristics, its own set of advantages and problems. However, all animals share one primary attribute: they mediate between the nomad and his environment. It is the physiological characteristics and differential abilities of the available animal species to utilize the varied vegetative resources of the jabal which determines the life style and success of the pastoral adjustment.

Goats

Goats are agile creature, tough of fibre and hardy in constitution. Their ability to browse on shrubby vegetation, combined with their sure-footedness, makes them ideal herding animals in the northern part of the jabal. Able to operate in rugged country, unselective in their eating habits, relatively undemanding in their water requirements, goats form the largest component of the herds in the upper terrace and coastal districts of al-Jabal al-Akhḍar. Some

95, 570 goats, almost entirely of the Nubian type, [1] are reported for the Darna muhafadhat. In both the al-Aṭrūn and Karsa districts no sheep are reported (Table 1) and this is an accurate reflection of available fodder resources. Only in a few coastal areas such as Ra's al-Hilāl, where grazing on wheat and barley stubble is possible, are sheep present in any numbers. Most of the northern scarps and terraces support a maquis vegetation and such species as juniper, olive, arbutus, oak, and artemisia are recognized as being the most suitable fodder sources for goats.

The goat's value to the rural population is consistently overlooked by ecologists. Most would be delighted to see it disappear entirely or drastically reduced in numbers and range. [2] This attitude is incomprehensible to the nomad. To the bedouin the goat is the indispensable element in successful utilization of the shrub vegetation of the jabal and his way of life would be impossible without it. To be sure, there are some plants that also play an important role in supplementing the food supply of other animals. The small black seeds of Sakhab (Phillyrea media) are collected in periods of drought and fed to sheep, while Halab (Periploca laevigata) is recognized as an important source of sheep fodder. The berries of Baṭūm (Pistacia lentiscus) are an additional favorite of sheep in the spring when the plant is in fruit. Finally, the Kharūb (Ceratonia siliqua) is valuable because its pods can be fed to cattle. But these exceptions aside, the maquis is the preëminent domain of the goat.

Sheep

In many respects goats and sheep possess contrasting characteristics. Libya's sheep are of the fat-tailed Barbary variety and they are often the most valuable animal which a nomad can own. While the goat represents the major subsistence animal, valued for its meat, milk, and hair, the sheep represents the productive capital of the nomadic economy. Money earned by the sale of grain, animals, or craft products, or by employment in the sedentary sector of the economy, is frequently reinvested in sheep. The prices commanded by sheep, the symbolic significance of lamb as the quintessential meat in feasting,

---

[1] D. E. Faulkner, Report to the Government of Libya on the Improvement of Cattle (Rome: FAO, 1965), p. 13.

[2] For example, N. M. H. Arnott, Report to the Government of Libya on the Improvement of the Sheep Industry (Rome: FAO, 1959), pp. 17-18, who recommended reducing the number of goats by 30 per cent while eliminating them from most of the areas of maquis vegetation where they are so prominent today.

TABLE 1

ANIMAL INVENTORY OF DARNA MUHAFADHAT

| Mudariya | Horse | Goat | Sheep | Camel | Cow | Donkey |
|---|---|---|---|---|---|---|
| Al-Aṭrūn | | 3,800 | | | 110 | |
| Ayn Marra | 200 | 12,150 | 2,450 | 300 | 350 | 800 |
| Bayt Thamir | 200 | 600 | 400 | 100 | 150 | 400 |
| Sīdī Khalid | 5 | 6,000 | | 100 | 200 | 400 |
| Umm al-Gdayh | 50 | 300 | 100 | 40 | 200 | 300 |
| Karsa | 5 | 2,000 | | 50 | 100 | 100 |
| al-'Izziyāt | 60 | 600 | 1,900 | 750 | | 200 |
| al-Qayqub | 3,000 | 11,000 | 8,293 | 1,000 | 211 | 250 |
| Khūlān | 20 | 4,000 | 2,000 | 350 | | 100 |
| Ayn Lalī | 4 | 1,000 | 200 | 15 | 150 | 50 |
| al-Qubba | | 15,120 | 21,500 | | 1,600 | |
| al-Abraq | 300 | 8,500 | 4,000 | 800 | 1,100 | 1,000 |
| Martūba | 30 | 6,000 | 10,000 | 200 | 50 | 150 |
| Ra's al-Hilāl | 20 | 4,500 | 500 | 30 | 150 | 50 |
| Makīlī | 70 | 3,000 | 4,600 | 450 | | 600 |
| at-Tamīmī | 100 | 6,100 | 6,450 | 30 | 700 | 3,500 |
| Umm ar-Razam | 50 | 9,700 | 10,800 | 150 | 90 | 500 |
| Umm Hfayn | | 200 | 150 | 50 | 70 | 50 |
| al-Būmba | 25 | 1,000 | 1,000 | 500 | 300 | 250 |
| Totals | 4,139 | 95,570 | 74,343 | 4,915 | 5,531 | 8,700 |

Source: Doxiadis Associates, Eastern Muhafadat Inventory (Tripoli, 1966).
The Doxiadis figures are useful because they present data by
minor administrative divisions, but a word of caution is in order.
Nomads frequently attempt to conceal the true size of their herds
from government officials in order to avoid tax assessments. The
mobility of nomadic herds also reduces accuracy. Thus, many of
the above totals are informed guesses rather than precise enumerations and should be regarded as indicative not definitive.

and the marked preference exhibited for the taste of local, as opposed to imported, lamb, help to explain the almost mystical devotion of the Cyrenaican
bedouin to this animal.

But preference for the local Barbary sheep is based on more than an
appreciation of its symbolic value. Just as the goat is the most efficient converter of the maquis flora, so too is the sheep the best adapted exploiter of the
interior steppes. A grazer rather than a browser, the sheep is limited by its
selective eating habits to the seasonal grasslands of the interior. Although
sheep can graze on the young shoots of cut-over or burned vegetation and can
make use of some of the maquis species, inadequate supplies of annual grasses
make the upper terrace and northern scarps an unattractive area. Symbolically

significant as an obligatory source of meat for feasts and important as a means
of utilizing the steppe flora, sheep have other prized attributes. Its wool, though
coarse and of insufficient quality for export,[1] is the main component of domes-
tically produced tents and rugs. An efficient producer of meat as a percentage
of total body weight, the Libyan Barbary sheep also is a prolific milk-producer
and continues to yield milk forty to sixty days after lambs have been weaned.[2]
Moreover, the fat extracted from its tail is a highly regarded additive to butter.

Although sheep are more fragile than either goats or camels, they are
remarkably well adapted to the harsh local environment and are capable of existing without water when grazing on green winter grass. In the height of summer
sheep can survive on the most meagre pasture if they are watered every two or
three days. Moreover, because they move in bunches, sheep are easy to herd
in large numbers and thus require less labor than do goats or camels. One of
the Barbary sheep's few drawbacks is a certain stupidity and lack of independent
initiative; the fact that their follow-the-leader proclivities can result in disaster
in the more rugged areas is well recognized by the bedouin and for this reason
they are often herded in combination with small numbers of goats who act as
guides and leaders for their less intelligent brethren.

Cattle

The indigenous cattle are a shorthorn breed that first appeared in Egypt
sometime during the New Kingdom, replaced the local Hamitic longhorns, and
gradually spread westward along the North African coast.[3] Although small in
size, the Libyan shorthorn is well adapted to local conditions and exhibits a
remarkable ability to operate under circumstances that would be impossibly
debilitating to imported breeds. Valued most for its high milk yields, the cow
is also a source of motive power during the plowing season. However, because
of relatively high water requirements it is almost exclusively restricted to the
better-watered districts. Unable to browse on the maquis vegetation and requiring large amounts of water, particularly in summer, cattle play only a limited role in the nomadic regime. In almost every case, ownership of cattle is
restricted to the least mobile tribal segments and to individuals who have become

---

[1] Arnott, Report on the Improvement of the Sheep Industry, p. 6, regards
this as the only attribute of the local animal that needs major improvement.

[2] Ibid., p. 12.

[3] Faulkner, Report on the Improvement of Cattle, p. 16.

sedentarized. Many of the occupants of the former Italian farmhouses maintain a small herd of cattle, as do the most northern of the nomadic segments. However, no herd of cattle ever reaches a large size and they are never moved over substantial distances to take advantage of regional differences in the availability of pasture. Thus, cattle are numerically and economically less important than sheep and goats.

## Camels

In almost every attribute, the camel is the direct opposite of the cow. The camel is of outstanding importance to the Cyrenaican bedouin because it brings into reach areas that are too arid, too poorly vegetated, and too distant to be otherwise utilized. A rugged, durable, mobile animal, the camel is ideally suited to the arid steppe and desert environments of the southern fringes of al-Jabal al-Akhḍar. In winter, when the herbage is green, the camel does not need to be watered, while in the summer months it can withstand up to fifteen waterless days between trips to wells. Coupled with its low water requirements is its ability to eat thorny shrubs and salt-tolerant plants that are unpalatable to other animals.

Strong and of good size, the camel until recently was essential as a baggage and a plow animal. Most nomadic families own at least one camel for without its assistance in transportation and agriculture no nomadic family could hope to remain mobile. Despite its often nasty temper, the camel has a reputation for patience and endurance that enhances its value. Although its gestation period is about one year, nearly twice the length of time required for goats and sheep, the camel's superior adaptation to local conditions and its high milk production compensate for a lower reproduction rate.

## Other Domestic Animals

Horses and donkeys are also kept by the bedouin of Cyrenaica, but they are not grouped into herds or used for milking purposes. Nonetheless, they are important to the nomad. Donkeys provide much of the daily transportation needs of the nomadic or rural-sedentary family. Strong and durable, the donkey fulfills a variety of important roles. Women and children make use of it in gathering wood or in drawing water from nearby cisterns. Men frequently ride donkeys to the local periodic markets if the journey is of moderate distance and they do not anticipate bringing home large loads. Its function, in short, is that of a small-scale, short-distance baggage animal.

The role of the horse is more complex.  Whereas the donkey is a utili-
tarian animal for whom no sentimental attachment exists,  the horse is preemi-
nently a symbol of prestige.  Because the horse is demanding in its water requirements,  only men of relative wealth can afford to own it,  to feed it adequately,
and to deck it out in the ornamental harnessings essential to its proper display.
Although the horse is necessary for those sections specializing exclusively in
camel herding, [1] for most bedouin,  the horse attains its primary importance in
raiding activities or during the annual display of horsemanship that occurs when
each section makes a pilgrimage to the tomb of its lineage's patron saint.

Most bedouin encampments include a small number of additional domes-
ticates.  While dogs accompany the goats and sheep when they leave the encamp-
ment,  they never aid the shepherd in the actual mechanics of managing and controlling the flock.  Ferocious in aspect,  but timid when faced with a threatening
homo sapiens,  the dogs function as a deterrent to marauding wolves and as an
early warning system directed at approaching visitors or potential enemies.
Cats are another bedouin campfollower and tents are seldom without them.  The
feline propensity to hunt field mice that might do damage to grain or rugs is
much appreciated and ensures the family cat the benign neglect and semi-starva-
tion essential to the proper performance of its functions.  Finally,  chickens,
prized for their eggs,  are a common sight around coastal camp sites where
movement is limited.

Herd Size

The number of animals required to support a nomadic family at the subsistence level has never been accurately determined.  As Nicolaisen points out
in his study of the Ahaggar Tuareg, [2] it is extremely difficult to get a true picture of the size of nomadic herds.  Not only are herds often grazing far from the
tent,  but also the nomad may obscure the true figures in order to avoid paying
taxes or to qualify for government assistance.  In part the minimum herd size
depends on the types of animals being herded.  Although evidence from Cyre-

---

[1]The speed and mobility of the horse makes it possible to locate lost
camels.  Insights into the camel herder's life are offered by Younis Bu Saraya,
"The Shepherd of Camels and his Life in Cyrenaica, " in David S. Tillson, Community Development Studies in Cyrenaica ([Benghazi?]:  Area Development
Office,  USOM, 1959), p. 123.

[2]Johannes Nicolaisen,  "Some Aspects of the Problem of Nomadic Cattle
Breeding among the Tuareg of the Central Sahara, " Geografisk Tidsskrift,  LIII
(1954),  96-97.

naica is inconclusive, attempts have been made to determine this number in other parts of North Africa and the Near East.

For most sheep and goat herders fifty to sixty is the crucial figure, [1] although instances as low as twenty-five have been reported in North Africa. [2] Tribes relying exclusively on camels herd substantially smaller flocks. The British Admiralty estimated twenty milking camels per tent in northern Arabia, [3] while Sweet's informants suggested that eighteen would suffice if a few additional camels were available for baggage and riding purposes. [4] In areas where personal preference or environmental opportunities encourage nomads to engage in caravan trading and agriculture smaller herds suffice to sustain each family. [5]

In Cyrenaica the uniformly large-size herds dotting the landscape belie this principle. Given the substantial involvement of the bedouin in agriculture, it is surprising that the size of the average herd would be larger than for other parts of the Near East where direct involvement in agriculture is limited.

---

[1] For this estimate from the Iranian evidence, see Fredrik Barth, Nomads of South Persia (New York: Humanities Press, 1964), p. 17; for Somalia: I. M. Lewis, A Pastoral Democracy (London: Oxford University Press, 1961), p. 58; and in Algeria: Pierre Ferrand-Eynard, "Enquête sur le revenu de quatre tribus nomades de la confédération des Oulad Naïl," TIRS, XX (1961), 91-134.

[2] Robert Capot-Rey, Le Sahara français (Paris: Presses Universitaires de France, 1953), p. 254; Emile Dermenghem, Le pays d'Abel (Paris: Gallimard, 1960), p. 155.

[3] Great Britain, Admiralty, A Handbook of Arabia (London: H. M. Stationery Office, 1916), p. 77.

[4] Louise B. Sweet, "Camel Pastoralism in North Arabia and the Minimal Camping Unit," in Anthony Leeds and Andrew P. Vayda (eds.), Man, Culture, and Animals (Washington, D.C.: American Association for the Advancement of Science, 1965), p. 133.

[5] Small herds are reported for the Tibu, who are active caravaners and agriculturalists, by both Robert Capot-Rey, "Le nomadisme des Toubous," in UNESCO, Nomades et nomadisme au Sahara (Paris: UNESCO, 1963), p. 91, and Jean Chapelle, Nomades noirs du Sahara (Paris: Librairie Plon, 1958), p. 215, who gives only slightly higher totals. Similarly, low figures of 15 goats and 10 camels per tent are recorded for the Tuareg of the central Sahara by Capot-Rey, Le Sahara français, p. 265, and totals per tent of 25-40 sheep and goats and 15 camels are suggested by Théodore Monod, L'Adrar Ahnet (Paris; Institut d'ethnologie, 1932), p. 9. Small herds reflect the traditionally important role of the caravan trade in the Tuareg economy as well as the forced extraction of agricultural products stemming from their total domination of the oasis communities.

Kikhia reports[1] that the average-size herd among the bedouin is between 100 and
150 head of sheep and goats. Again, this is difficult to assess, for most of the
nomads questioned in the Lamlūda area respond by claiming one hundred sheep
or goats even in cases where the observable flocks were demonstrably in excess
of this number. In the sāḥil, where goats are the sole herd animal, flocks of
less than fifty or sixty are never seen, while in the south one hundred is the
minimum-size sheep herd that can be located.

This suggests that herds of less than fifty goats or one hundred sheep
are too small to justify the expense of herding and that they must be combined to
make up the requisite economic figure. It also indicates that these are the minimum sizes required to remain nomadic, since those who possess less than this
number seldom, if ever, migrate and are invariably engaged in another activity
as the primary source of their wealth. The same type of argument can be applied to camel herding where the average-size herd ranges between thirty and
sixty head.[2] These figures reflect subsistence conditions. Successful herders
may amass huge herds, and flocks of up to one thousand sheep and goats are not
unknown.[3] These are unusual instances and the typical situation is an average
herd of 100-200 sheep and goats or 30-40 camels; to fall below these figures is
to descend beneath the level of viability and to cease migration.

Herding Life Styles and Migration Patterns

The particular combination of animals herded by a nomadic family and
the rhythm of movement undertaken in any one year reflect a complex decision-
making process. The nomad must make the right decisions concerning when and
where to plant his crops, whether to move his animals in anticipation of the winter rains or whether to wait, what animals to sell, in what markets, at what
time, for how much, or whether he should retain them and hope for a better
price. He must know from past experience which areas can expect adequate
rainfall and which cannot, where water can be found and under what conditions of

---

[1]Mansour M. Kikhia, Le nomadisme pastorale en Cyrénaïque septentrionale (Aix-en-Provence: La Pensée Universitaire, 1968), pp. 218-19.

[2]Ibid., p. 245.

[3]Ibid., p. 218. This would be a very rich individual, but I have recorded
an extended family, strongly united around an authoritarian grandfather, that
owned a combined herd of 600 sheep, 300 goats, and 100 milking camels.

ownership and quality. He must determine, taking into consideration the particular advantages and failings of each kind of animal available, what animal species are best suited to his district.

Because the nomad is interested in survival, his basic concern is to
insure that enough animals will survive in any one year to enable him to continue
to migrate. In the face of an uncertain climatic regime, he must choose the mix
of animals needed to maximize both the potentialities of the local flora and the
possibility that his herd will be able to recover despite possible environmental
disaster. To develop the widest possible range of options, the nomad plants
grain, generally barley, in his section's territory and stores any surplus both
to relieve himself of dependence on sedentary agriculturalists and to ensure a
supply of straw and grain for his flock in drought conditions. He tries to herd
as many different types of animals as the local environment permits in order to
utilize all of the resources available. If possible, he resists pressures to sell
or slaughter his animals, often increasing his herd to almost unmanageable numbers during a succession of rainy years so that some of his animals will survive
a prolonged drought. Should a sale be necessary, only the minimum required to
make ends meet will be sold. There are, of course, reasons for selling animals
in non-drought years as herds become too large to manage or if market conditions are especially favorable. However, the capital earned generally is set
aside for eventual reinvestment in more animals.

Household production of carpets, saddle bags, and other items can be
seen in the light of resource maximization and investment. In a sense the wool
produced by a nomad's sheep represents a surplus product since the animals
must be sheared whether the wool is used or not. Once processed, the wool can
be converted into attractive carpets at low cost in either labor or materials.
Significantly, these non-pile carpets (hedma) seldom enter the economy; instead
they are stored in the family tent and only sold if the family's fortunes drastically decline.

Peters[1] contends that, while water supply exercises an ultimate control
over group movement, what makes otherwise baffling locational shifts truly
intelligible are intersectional relationships. While migration to certain areas
is essential if claims to land and water are to be asserted or maintained, excessive emphasis on this important aspect of bedouin life minimizes the ecological rationality of the vast majority of the migrations undertaken by the Cyrenai-

---

[1] Peters, "Sociology of the Bedouin of Cyrenaica," p. 35.

can bedouin.  In balancing such factors as potential environmental resources, characteristics of the various species available for herding, the variability and uncertainty of the climatic regime, and the technology at their disposal, the bedouin of eastern Cyrenaica have evolved a sensible cultural adjustment.  This can be visualized in eco-system terms with each tribal component adjusted to the resources of a particular ecological niche but with all components of the system linked to each other by social and kin relationships for purposes of mutual support.

Goat Herders of the Coastal Plain

The number of tertiary sections herding only goats is relatively small. Usually they are confined to the coastal plain and in most instances are members of marābtīn tribes, although this latter generalization is less valid for western Cyrenaica.  In addition to goats small numbers of cattle are kept, but in every sense they are a minor concern.  The cow is present because it is able to utilize the spring water at the foot of the lower scarp or near the coastline, but it is curtailed in numbers because few areas of grassland are available.

The seasonal rhythm of life in the sāhil is defined not by pastoral movements but rather by the agricultural calendar, for while the population is traditionally nomadic in culture and economy, it is not very mobile.  Coastal pastoralists seldom shift their herds inland.  Their entire life is spent on the coastal plain and their goats graze on limited stretches of maquis vegetation around their tents.  Because the sāhil flora is unsuitable for large numbers of sheep, camels, or cattle, only goats can be kept.  Moreover, since the coastal vegetation supports sufficient goats to maintain a family and rainfall dependability is relatively good there is neither rationale nor pressure for movement to higher elevations. Thus, although natural highways in the form of wadi beds cut through the lower scarp and provide potential access to the upper terrace, there is little reason to utilize them and instead the sāhil operates in isolation from the interior.

Barley is the major crop of the coastal plain and the periodicty of its planting and harvesting gives shape and substance to the coastal regime.  Sowing does not begin until after the first rain.  This usually takes place in late September, although should the rains arrive later planting is delayed.  The amount of land available for agriculture is limited and is restricted to small alluvial fans and terraces along or at the mouth of northward-draining wadis or to the few districts where the sāhil is wide enough to permit the formation of broad wadi bottoms, or shallow, enclosed soil pockets.  During Italian administration, attempts were made to develop the best coastal locations at Ra's al-Hilāl and al-Aṭrūn as showcase settlements for native Libyan farmers, [1] oftentimes recruited from those tribesmen, frequently marābṭīn, who supported the colonial authorities. Some of the marābṭīn tribesmen whose tribal territory comprised the sāḥil undoubtedly participated in this settlement plan, but many of the settlers were brought in from outside the coastal plain. In this sense these prestige settlements, localized in the best agricultural areas and thus alienating them from the traditional coastal economy, tended to compete with and ultimately impoverish the sāḥil goat-herding economy.

Both the barley and wheat planted in the sāḥil, in contrast to the agriculture of the new settlements, is grown without irrigation. Only the caprice of the rainfall regime determines the ultimate yield, but, since precipitation is usually high in the headwaters of the wadis, a nominal output can be expected in all but the worst years. The harvest, which habitually begins in May or June and is rapidly completed, forms the endpoint to the yearly cycle. Because a seasonal movement of tents and herds to various pastures is essentially non-existent, changes in location are made on an ad hoc basis and cover only limited distances. Fouling of the tent site by domestic animals plays a major role in such small-scale shifts, and coastal life has a more timeless and leisurely aspect to it then nomadic activities elsewhere in the jabal.

The somewhat precarious nature of the coastal economy is also related to the seeming aversion on the part of Tarakī and Manṣūr tribesmen to exploit the potential piscine resources of the nearby Mediterranean. Despite living almost their entire lives within a stone's throw of the sea, coast dwellers never engage in either subsistence or commercial fishing activities and many of them have never tasted fish. Although water supplies are available in adequate quantities, the constraints imposed by the narrow coastal plain and the moderate amounts of vegetation that can be supported on it and on the lower scarp keep herd size small. In every sense the standard of living capable of being supported in the sāḥil under these conditions is low, perhaps explaining why the saʿādī allowed the marābṭīn to retain possession of the coastal plain.

Sheep and Goat Herders of the Jabal Terraces

Herding practices change as soon as one reaches the lower terrace. Although the majority of the tribesmen on the lower terrace belong to marābṭīn

---

[1] Adolf Kaempffer, "Libyen in Aufbau," in Reichskolonialbund, 40000 Siedeln in Libyen (Munich: Paul Wustrow, 1940), p. 49.

tribes, elements of the noble lineages also become prominent. Coupled with the
more frequent appearance of saʿādī lineages is the expanded importance of sheep
herding. Goats remain the largest proportion of the herds, but sheep begin to
figure in the nomad's calculations. Because access to the interior is assured
either through contiguous tracts of tribal land or by the presence of relatives
and genealogical affiliates south of the jabal crestline, it becomes possible to
invest in sheep as a means of economic improvement and as a mechanism whereby risk is spread over the maximum number of options. The existence of more
clearings in the maquis plus greater water supplies means that cattle can also
be kept with advantage, thus adding further diversity to the herding economy.
Moreover, the natural advantages of higher rainfall and suitable agricultural
soils means that cereal cultivation takes on increased importance. Substantial
numbers of horses, donkeys, and camels also are kept to supply baggage and
draft animals for agricultural operations and for transportation.

The result is a complex nomadic adjustment. Because this includes a
substantial involvement in cereal production it has often been described as "semi-
nomadic"[1] but to do so obscures the issue. Practitioners of a mixed sheep and
goat nomadism engage in more limited seasonal movements than their compatri-
ots on the southern dip-slope and on occasion may not move at all. But their
reliance on agriculture in no way reduces the nomadic quality of their life style;
rather it represents the special adjustment needed to optimize the potentialities
of the natural environment.

The seasonal cycle begins with the onset of the autumn rains. The exact
date changes from year to year, but generally occurs in late September or early
October. Planting of barley and wheat is the first concern and cannot begin until
the rains have dampened the ground sufficiently to make ploughing and seed survival feasible. Since each section possesses its own stretch of territory in the
upland districts it has at its disposal land that is eminently suited to barley and,
depending on proximity to the highest rainfall areas along the upper scarp, wheat
cultivation. Little clearing of the maquis for agricultural purposes is undertaken, since most grain is planted in fields that have been in operation since
Greco-Roman times.

The population of the lower terrace, possessing relatively well-watered

---

[1] See the general outline of the "semi-nomadic" sheep and goat regime
sketched in Evans-Pritchard, The Sanusi of Cyrenaica, particularly pp. 34-38,
and in Y. T. Toni, "Social Mobility and Relative Stability among the Bedouins of
Cyrenaica," BSGE, XXXVI (1963), 113-36.

land, plants a higher proportion of wheat to barley and, because uncultivated areas are covered with a maquis vegetation, keeps far larger numbers of goats than sheep. Advantage is taken of the relatively abundant water of the lower and upper terraces by herding small supplemental herds of cattle and by seldom, if ever, leaving the tribal territory. Sheep, when owned, are seldom present in their own home area and instead are entrusted to shepherds or to relatives who live farther south in more suitable grassland districts.

For those tribal sections living closer to the fringes of the maquis the autumn rains demand important decisions. Their herds comprise a far larger proportion of sheep and, if the maximum benefit is to be derived from them, they must be moved to seasonal pasture further south; this in turn requires decisions on where to shift the sheep and when. At the same time, there are issues pending concerning ploughing. All of the nomads living on the fringes of the maquis plant wheat and barley in those portions of their tertiary section's territory assigned to them by agreement and tradition, but they must determine how much land to plough relative to anticipated yield as well as the balance to be maintained between wheat and barley.

Generally each family plants two or three qanāṭīr (sing. qinṭār; the equivalent of just under 45 kilograms) of wheat and a similar quantity of barley, although these proportions have changed. In the past, barley, because of its ability to survive drought, was the preferred grain and wheat was restricted to the best-watered districts. Today the cultivation of wheat has expanded in response to the bedouin's improved economic condition and the government's aid programs and an avoidance of barley has developed.[1] One of barley's original advantages was that it could be fed to animals, but today this has given barley a reputation as the poor man's grain or worse. Informants are reluctant to admit that they are growing and eating sha'īr (barley) and not qamḥ (wheat).

Whether the entire family, goats and sheep together, move south depends in part on how much land is planted in the jabal. Should they decide to plant the maximum amount available and should their neighbors make similar decisions, only limited grazing will be conveniently obtainable in the jabal and shifting a majority of the herds will be essential. If less land is planted in grain, correspondingly greater amounts of pasture will be accessible and a numerically reduced migration becomes possible. The particular balance between pasture

---

[1] I. Abu Sharr, Report to the Government of Libya on Crop Agronomy and Improvement in Cyrenaica (Rome: FAO, 1962), p. 9, was one of the first to note this developing preference for white wheat rather than dark barley flour.

and plough in this case accurately reflects the bedouin's assessment of crop
yields and precipitation totals that can be expected.

There is an additional facet to the agricultural component of the bedouin
economy. The southward-draining wadi beds and shallow depressions between
al-Makīlī and Zāwiyat al-ʿIzziyāt are capable of producing spectacular crops of
barley whenever there is adequate rainfall. Bedouin claim that if rainfall is high,
yields of one hundred fold regularly occur in the south while ten to twenty fold is
usual in the jabal. But whereas the jabal yields are predictable and certain, the
southern depressions are a risk environment. Except in the most favorable locations, one or two good years in ten, the diametric opposite of conditions in the
jabal, is the best that can be expected.

The decision to plant in the south is based on a subtle, impressionistic
assessment of the chances of getting good yields coupled with early scouting
reports on the rainfall and run-off conditions at the foot of the dip-slope. If the
decision to plant is made, some of the men, together with a few camels and
horses for baggage and plowing, will leave in early October to plant in the section's traditional southern district. In recent years tractors, rented by a group
of neighboring families, have made an appearance in the south and have expanded
the bedouin's ability to plough more in the marginal districts. As much land as
possible is planted taking into consideration available seed and an appreciation of
the amount of return anticipated given past experience in the area. Since family
subsistence supplies are assured by grain grown in the higher elevations, sowing
in the south is a speculative endeavor designed to increase available capital.
The grain used as seed could be hoarded against future deficits or sold in the
local markets or to the government, but returns from the small quantities available for sale in this way would be limited.

Investment in this type of agriculture is not unlike speculative stock market operations where proper selection of an issue with rapid growth potential can
reap spectacular returns. The risk involved is one that all investors share, but
it is balanced by the assured "blue chip" grain production in the north. Variability in rainfall conditions plus the government's surplus purchase policy ensures
that surplus produced in one area will not be duplicated widely and cause a market glut and depressed prices. Capital gained by speculative agriculture is reinvested in animals which offer the sole source of power and prestige in the traditional regime.

Land tenure problems can be a major issue, for ownership of both grazing and agricultural resources in the south is vague. Generally speaking, the

Ṭariq ʿAzīza forms the dividing line between ownership in land to the north of the trail and possession of wells and cisterns to the south. Theoretically one can graze and plant anywhere in the south without regard to ownership rights since bedouin claim that it is free to all. This is distinctly different from the situation in the upper terrace where permission must always be asked before planting by strangers is permitted. But in practice tradition determines to a great extent where a particular section will graze and plant. When questioned, members of Ait al-Khādim, Ait al-Farkh, and Ait Rakhama from the Lamlūda area invariably mention the same group of wadis and depressions to the north, east, and south of al-Makīlī; movement to other areas is an exceptional response to radically different environmental conditions. Within the general zone of concentration around al-Makīlī families favor certain areas, although the precise choice in any one year is based on the availability of grazing. In the past the choice of area to plant was constrained by considerations of security, for only what could be defended could be effectively utilized. For this reason movement to the south was always undertaken by groups of people commonly, but not exclusively, genealogically defined who were willing to protect each other's mutual interests. In recent years the extension of governmental authority has reduced insecurity in the pre-desert, but this has had an unexpected outcome. Rather than favoring free access to southern agricultural zones it has led to attempts to regularize ownership of the potentially most valuable areas. Increasingly, tin sheds for grain-storage are being built to establish claims to certain areas based almost exclusively on traditional patterns of land use.

The October barley planting in the south is followed by a return northward of the men. This is completed by early November in time to plough and plant at the most favorable period in the upper terrace. The traditional picture of the lazy, anti-agricultural bedouin is belied during this period by the intense activity that takes place. Long days are spent following the plough and the bedouin show " . . . a burst of energy which one would hardly credit."[1] The reason for this enthusiasm is quite clear; in the traditional regime amassing grain is one of the ways to assemble enough capital to buy animals and thus achieve an independent position. Once the ploughing is completed, a southward movement of the herds can be contemplated.

This southward oscillation of the flocks takes place in December when the herbaceous vegetation is at its best. With the heavy agricultural work com-

---

[1] Peters, "Sociology of the Bedouin of Cyrenaica," p. 41.

pleted, the annual grasses appearing, surface water readily available for human consumption, enough moisture present in the vegetation to make watering the stock unnecessary, and the ewes at the peak of their milk production, the winter season is a prosperous one for the bedouin. The generalized pattern of movement for the sections in the Lamlūda area is presented in Figure 14. In good years this involves movement to the areas around al-Makīlī and Zāwiyat al-ʿĪzziyāt where the southern agricultural fields are also located.

The cartographic pattern of this movement resembles the constricted oscillatory nomadism described elsewhere for the mountains of Northern Africa and Southwestern Asia, [1] but with significant differences. Although migration is between two separate and distinct zones seasonally defined, it is not constricted by the relief of the jabal into narrow migration corridors. The need to funnel through narrow passes or travel along deep valleys is eliminated in al-Jabal al-Akhḍar because the general relief is gentle enough to allow essentially free movement. None of the southward-draining wadis are large enough to offer a barrier to communication and herders are able to move in flexible fashion cross-country to their destination. Moreover, in other tribal territories throughout the Near East the mountain areas are elevated enough to assure adequate summer and winter pastures, but in Cyrenaica provision must always be made for much more long distant movement in drought years to reach subsidiary zones with adequate pasture and water. For the Lamlūda sections this area has traditionally been Dafna, the portion of Marmarica extending from Ṭubruq to the Egyptian frontier. [2] From 1960 to 1966 most of the herders in the Lamlūda area shifted their herds, not to the balṭa zone around al-Makīlī, but to Dafna. As soon as conditions improved in the traditional pastures, the al-Makīlī area was revisited on a regular basis.

Finally, agriculture complicates the migration pattern of sheep and goat nomads. Most nomads are content to rely on the activities of sedentary communities for agricultural supplies, but Cyrenaica's sheep and goat herders raise their own. The extent of the agricultural component and its importance relative

---

[1]For a discussion and classification of pastoral nomads on the basis of their migration patterns see Douglas L. Johnson, The Nature of Nomadism (Research Paper No. 118; Chicago: University of Chicago, Department of Geography, 1969).

[2]The discussion in Kikhia, Le nomadisme pastoral en Cyrénaïque, pp. 268-77, of irregular displacements of herds and tents in response to fluctuations in climatic conditions in Marmarica and Barqa al-Hamra points out the frequency with which departures from the "expected" pattern can take place.

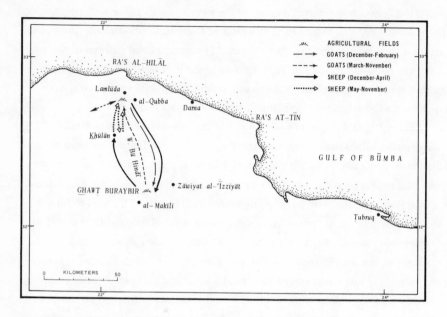

Fig. 14.--The generalized seasonal movements of sheep and goat herders of the Lamlūda area.

to sheep herding determines whether or not the entire family accompanies the flocks southward. In those families where agriculture is of major importance, the goats and the family tent often remain in the north while shepherds take the sheep southward. Where family wealth as represented by sheep are more important, sheep, goats, and the tent all head toward the interior while a member of the family remains behind to guard the fields. This contrasts with most practitioners of vertical nomadism where agricultural pursuits fail to enter into their calculations and the entire family and its flocks move as a unit. Today these generalizations are changing as more and more nomads become stationary and the practice of hiring shepherds grows.

The costs involved in hiring a shepherd are high, one sheep or goat per month for every ten herded plus a contribution of basic food stuffs and cigarettes being the average price for a Libyan shepherd.[1] An additional method employed by

---

[1] The high price for indigenous shepherds, who receive a premium for their knowledge of local herding conditions, is frequently avoided by hiring Egyptian shepherds at half the cost. Often illegal immigrants, many of these shepherds are drawn from the Awlad 'Alī tribe. Their relationship to the jabal

sedentarized bedouin is to leave their sheep in the care of client sections. Since only the sa ʿādī possess direct access to land and water resources, the arrangement is customarily of mutual benefit. In one such case that I recorded, a member of Ait al-Khādim paid a Mnifa client one young lamb for every ten fully grown sheep herded during the winter and a monetary fee of £L 1 per sheep per month during the summer. The Mnifa tent group also received the right to use the cistern owned by the Khādimī, although if the water ran out it would cost the Mnifa up to £L 90 to rent a similar well for the remainder of the summer. While the cost to the sheep owner was high, it was not exorbitant. Not only could he seek employment in the modern economy without having to abandon his animals, but also the sale of just one sheep per month would pay for the cost of summer shepherding. Since the winter shepherd fees are more than met by the natural increase in the herd, the arrangement is an advantageous one for both parties. The high cost and limited supply of shepherds also favors the development of exchange mechanisms whereby a brother or father remains in the upper terrace with the goats and cows and guards the fields while another brother or son combines the two flocks of sheep and undertakes the migration. Neighbors may enter into similar arrangements which always are based on mutual exchange of favors and services rather than monetary payment.

The southward oscillation lasts until April, although frequent departures from this rule occur. If grain is planted in the south, this is harvested in March. Although still cut by hand in the traditional way, this is not a lengthy operation for the size of the plots is always limited. Once cut, threshed, and winnowed, the grain is either transported northward to be stored in tin barak or Greco-Roman tombs (ḥaqfa; pl. ḥiqāf), or is left behind in kāf (storage pits scooped into the ground). Movement north is rapid and begins as soon as the southern harvest is completed. The tent and the subsistence goat herds return rapidly, while the sheep follow gradually in order to extract the maximum benefit from the withering steppe flora.

Once late April or early May arrives the majority of the sheep and goat bedouin are back in the jabal and engaged in the grain harvest, an activity that continues through most of the summer. Herds stay close to the tents and watering points. Some of the heaviest work of the year must be done by the men during this period in raising large quantities of water by hand every two or three days from the wells and cisterns for the animals.

---

tribes and their economic utility as low cost labor helps to explain the protection, assistance, and employment extended to them.

Concentration of the herds near the spring line dramatically increases the grazing pressure on the vegetation. Water requirements restrict animals to trips of one or one and a half days from the watering points. Long-term over-grazing results and contributes to the introduction of unpalatable species, the removal of plant cover and subsequent erosion, and a general deterioration of the environment. Short distance movements of sheep and goats away from the spring line continue throughout the summer; goats move northward to take advantage of the maquis shrubs and sheep shift to the south to graze on the withered remains of the annual steppe grasses or on the stubble of the barley and wheat harvest. As the summer progresses, cisterns become depleted and attention focuses on the major springs with accelerated localized pressure on the available fodder. Chaff and straw from the barley harvest gradually become increasingly important in the animals' food supply and the nomad begins to anticipate the resumption of the coming autumn rains. Once rain recurs, the yearly cycle of ploughing and planting and of southward migration begins again.

Although the long term pattern of movement involves an oscillation between the upper terrace and the balṭa at al-Makīlī, considerable variation is possible in response to differing yearly conditions. This point is illustrated by Figure 15 depicting the movement of one family of Ait Rakhama in 1969-1970. Initially the typical pattern for the area was followed, for once the grain planting was completed by early December the entire family with its animals moved to the Ghawṭ Buraybir north of al-Makīlī where it had planted a small barley patch. Heavy rains fell in the al-Makīlī area in early autumn and, although the promise of winter-long pasture was not to be fulfilled by additional precipitation, the grazing attracted nomadic families from as far away as Ṭubruq in the east and Ajdābiya in the west.

Extensive planting of grain in the north contributed to the decision to move all of the flock south, but the concentration of competing flocks from throughout Cyrenaica proved more than the pastures in the Buraybir area could accommodate. As a result, the father, his wife, youngest son, and divorced daughter returned north after only three months bringing the goats, but leaving his married son in the south with the sheep. The barley planted in the south failed to receive the requisite spring rains to reach maturity and eventually was written off as a total loss. This was not a complete disaster since it provided some grazing for the sheep and was adequately protected by a larger than normal investment in jabal grains. The eldest son remained in the south through April, although as the pasture slowly withered he withdrew gradually up the Wādī ar-

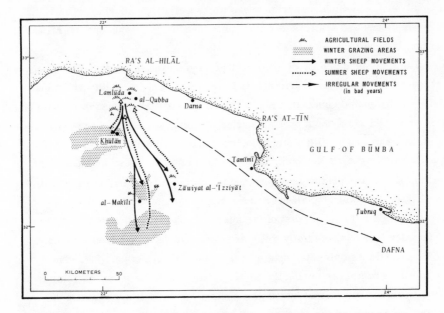

Fig. 15.--The movement pattern of a nomadic family from Lamlūda, 1969-1970.

Ramla to the watering point of Khūlān. With no harvest in the south to delay him, he returned in late April to the family center east of Sīdī Bū Dhraʿ to help with the northern harvest which continued for most of the summer.

It is important to note that departures from the normal sequence of movements are more common than are the typical and expected regular patterns. This is not surprising, for al-Jabal al-Akhḍar, despite its relative richness in the pastoral sense, is still a marginal zone experiencing climatic instability. Regularities can be observed if the cartographic representations of a large number of years are superimposed, but in any one year the pattern and rhythm of the response may be quite different. Flexible response within a framework of seasonal regularity and traditional habits explains the migration pattern at the family scale in any one year.

Sheep, Goat, and Camel Herders of the Dip-slope

A similar cycle of north-south oscillation is practised by the nomads of the dip-slope. As a function of increased aridity the composition of the nomadic herds changes and the importance of camel herding increases. Whereas in the

more northerly portions of al-Jabal al-Akhḍar the camel is useful only as a baggage and transport animal, in drier areas its capacity for enduring drought and
thriving on thorny and scattered pastures enhance its value as an integral part
of the family economy.

The increased aridity of the dip-slope also means that intensified emphasis is placed on owning fixed and inalienable watering points. Although Evans-
Pritchard's oft quoted generalization that north of the Ṭarīq ʿAzīza ownership of
land is practiced while south of it ownership of wells is the rule[1] is oversimpli-
fied, it does express a valid distinction between the two zones. With precipitation more precarious in the south, firm and inviolable possession of assured
water supplies is the primary concern and life would be impossible without it.
Each tertiary section living all year in the steppe owns a cluster of wells and
cisterns that form the focal point of the migration pattern and the basis of its
summer survival. These family wells are exclusively private property and can
be used by outsiders only after obtaining permission and paying a fee. The
issue is not a crucial one during the winter for the water needs of migrants from
the upper terrace can be met by surface pools. As a result pressure on the
wells that must support the southern tribes through the summer is reduced.

Since the requirements of goats, sheep, and camels are all different
with respect to their vegetation preferences, ability to withstand drought, speed
of movement, and economic value the various species are herded separately
during most of the year. This complicates the seasonal migration cycle and
large amounts of labor are required to perform widely separated herding and
agricultural chores.[2] Part of the bedouin preference for male children can be
understood in terms of the need for shepherds. Since one nuclear family can
provide the requisite labor pool for only a relatively short time, a variety of different methods, including the common herding of animals by brothers or other
members of an extended family, the acceptance of impecunious individuals into

---

[1]Evans-Pritchard, The Sanusi of Cyrenaica, p. 36. Many privately-
repaired wells and cisterns in the north are not available to the general public,
while many parts of the semi-arid and arid steppe capable of producing an agricultural crop are claimed by tertiary sections. Similarly, there are numerous
cisterns in the steppe that were re-opened with public funds and are available to
everyone.

[2]Emrys L. Peters, "Aspects of the Family among the Bedouin of Cyrenaica," in M. F. Nimkoff (ed.), Comparative Family Systems (Boston: Houghton
Mifflin & Co., 1965), pp. 139 ff., reports that among the camel-herding Barāʿasa
sections immediately to the west of the ʿAbaydat nine children, unequally divided
among males and females, is the ideal size for a family.

the herding group to bolster the labor supply, or the establishment of client relationships with single marābṭīn families or entire marābṭīn sections, [1] contribute
to a rectification of the labor imbalance. The amount of movement demanded
when operating mixed herds is considerable but it is only recently, under the
pressure of modern technology and in the rarefied atmosphere of an oil-boom
economy, that the most demanding species, the camel, requiring rapid movement over wide areas by individual shepherds or small portions of the family
especially during the dry season, has begun to lose its importance as more lucra-
tive ways of earning money become popular. The description below, drawn from
the experience of a family with mixed herds, has increasingly less importance in
reality as camel-herding in the more marginal areas is abandoned.

The seasonal migration pattern of the mixed-herd nomads is circumscribed by the same Mediterranean regime that controls the other nomadic adjustments of northern Cyrenaica. The yearly cycle begins with the ploughing
and planting of grain in the broad, flat wadi beds near the family watering point.

Once the sowing operations are completed, movement begins with each
herd following a separate orbit (Figure 16). The camels always move independently of the goats and sheep and so require a separate shepherd. The normal
movement of camels is southward beyond Zāwiyat al-ʿIzziyāt as far as the Wādī
al-Mra. Conditions in 1965 illustrate the variable distances covered by these
movements since localized rainfall in a group of wadis a few kilometers south of
the family wells encouraged a reduced oscillation.

Every spring the camels are shifted to the al-Fatāyaḥ plain on the lower
terrace south of Darna where thorny vegetation on the edges of the agricultural
area offers suitable grazing. Since in spring the annual grasses of the south
begin to dry up, this movement to al-Fatāyaḥ is an important supplement to the
available grazing resources in that it reduces pressure on the perennial thorn-
shrub species that must support camels during the summer months. During the
winter and spring there is no need to water the camel at the family wells as there
is enough moisture in the flora to meet its requirements. The frequency of contacts with the family center during this period is limited and the shepherd's food
needs largely are supplied by camel milk. Periodic visits by other members of
the family enable them to partake of this seasonal resource as well.

---

[1] Peters, "The Tied and the Free," pp. 180 ff., indicates the crucial importance of these relationships in the political sphere and the complications that
can result when a succession of bad years reduces the local resources below the
level necessary to support both the noble and client lineages.

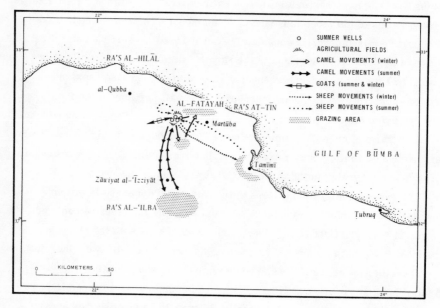

Fig. 16.--The seasonal migration pattern of a sheep, goat, and camel-herding family, 1964-1965.

In summer the camel is watered at five to fifteen day intervals.  This greater resistance to drought makes it unnecessary for the camel to stay in the immediate vicinity of the wells.  After being watered the camels are taken south in the direction of Zāwiyat al-'Īzziyāt, grazing on the thorny and perennially green sidr (Zizyphus lotus) shrubs along the way and heading for the district of Ra's al-'Ilba.  A few days heading south, a couple of days there, and a short period to cover the distance back to the wells constitutes the summer pulsatory movement.

Since sheep cannot eat thorny shrubs, and goats only can move a day or two away from the well, the camel is invaluable in utilizing the perennial vegetation to the full.  In this respect the camel was a way of utilizing marginal resources as well as of taking out an insurance policy against the kind of drought that might destroy the sheep and goats; the camel's superior adaptation to the arid steppe meant that it was certain to survive the worst imaginable conditions. However, the rigors of herding the camel, the constant movement required, and the recent expansion of other ways of insuring against drought, whether by government assistance programs or by funds earned by family members participating directly in the oil economy or in one of its related activities, has caused a decline in the importance of camel herding.

Goats are kept near the family tent because their milk and meat comprise the family's basic subsistence. In recent years this has meant that they do not move more than ten kilometers from the well center as an increasing preference for keeping the tent localized has become apparent. The normal pattern is to drive the goats out to graze each day in the charge of a young boy and to return to the tent each night. Such limited movement is clearly related to the goat's superior ability to exist on an impoverished vegetation making it unnecessary to shift to areas where the annual grasses are in the best condition.

Ironically, sheep, which are most sensitive to pasture and general environmental conditions, are the animals that often have to move the greatest distances and show the least regularity in areas visited. As a general rule they are moved to whatever area has the best rainfall. This means a basically north-south oscillation to the balṭa zone around Zāwiyat al-ʿIzziyāt, but in bad years the sheep may travel considerable distances to reach adequate pasture. In 1965 this meant a journey to the Tamīmī area, although in past years it might mean travelling no further than Martūba or as far away as Dafna. In winter drinking water is not a major factor in the localization of sheep, for they find all that they require in the annual vegetation, but in the summer they frequently must be brought to the well.

The result is a concentration of overlapping watering cycles at the summer wells, with sheep being watered every day or two, goats every two or three days, and camels at intervals of eight to fifteen days. The consequent pressure on the local herbage can reach staggering heights, and if the pasture appears to be severely inadequate there is always the option of moving the sheep further north toward the spring line into areas controlled by genealogical affiliates.[1] However, there is a serious problem associated with sending sheep to summer pastures in the jabal. Drās (Thapsia garganica), a conspicuous element in the maquis flora, is reputed in local lore to be poisonous to those animals that have not grown accustomed to it during the winter and spring. Whether an immunity to Drās is developed by those herds remaining in the jabal that is not shared by

---

[1]The mother's brother often plays a major role in aiding relatives in times of drought and it is the need to maintain relationships that provide security against environmental fluctuations that explain the frequency of marriages into neighboring tertiary sections. For the full range of situations in which the mother's brother tie can be activated see Peters, "Aspects of the Family," p. 135.

flocks grazing in the south or whether the northern flocks by means of their exposure to it in the winter acquire a food avoidance mechanism is unclear. But, as Peters points out, [1] the practical implications for the bedouin are considerable, for at an early stage in the winter they must make an assessment of the carrying capacity of their wells for the summer months. If the water supplies appear insufficient, then the sheep must be sent to the jabal at an early date so that they can learn in good time to avoid Drās. Failure to make this decision by spring means that the jabal is effectively denied to the southern sections as an alternative should their cisterns and wells run dry. In recent years the practice has been for the family tents to remain in the immediate vicinity of the wells with the goats while the sheep are entrusted to the care of shepherds. In the past it was more the accepted practice for the tent and the goats to move along with the sheep, but with the day-to-day labor supply no longer drawn exclusively from the family this is not essential.

Camel Herders of the Balṭa Zone

Only a small percentage of the total number of pastoral nomads in eastern Cyrenaica are exclusively herders of camels. A few sections of the Shīyyahīn, ʻAwakla, Ghaytḥ, Rfad, Mnifa, and al-Qaṭʻān specialize in camel herding but they are a distinct minority in the nomadic community. Erroneously described as "true" nomads by some observers, [2] they seldom appear in the jabal and have only a limited interest in agriculture. Unlike the camel-herding nomads of western Cyrenaica, who rely on annual trips to the oases of Awjila and Jalū for their agricultural supplies, [3] the ʻAbaydat camel sections lack access to an interior oasis. Instead they make two or three trips to the coastal market towns where needed supplies can be procured. If sheep are owned by camel nomads, they are entrusted to shepherds who move the animals in whatever direction is necessary to find suitable pasture.

While the tent usually does not stray far from the balṭa zone, the camels, guarded by men from the family wherever possible, pulsate out into the arid steppe and desert fringes during the rainy season (Figure 17). The Wādī al-Mra

---

[1] Peters, "Sociology of the Bedouin of Cyrenaica, " p. 20.

[2] Toni, "Social Mobility and Relative Stability among the Bedouin of Cyrenaica, " p. 121, is only one of the many who err by identifying camel nomadism as the "true" or "pure" variety.

[3] Peters, "Sociology of the Bedouin of Cyrenaica, " p. 10.

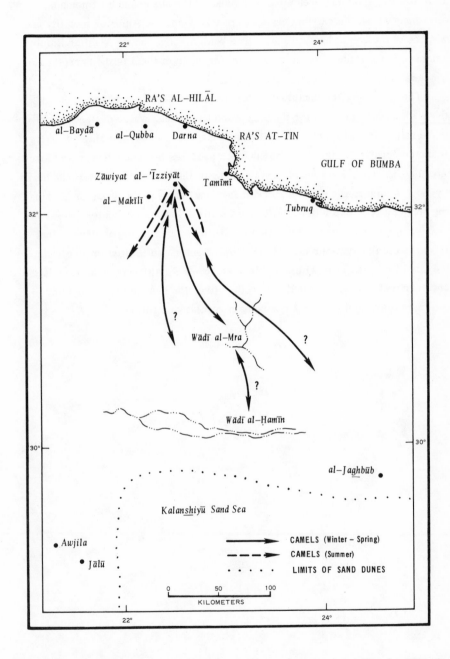

Fig. 17.--The seasonal migration pattern of a camel-herding family, al-ʿĪzziyāt region.

forms the focus of the winter migration, but these movements are much less constrained to particular areas than are those of the sheep and goat nomads. Sheep cannot reach the extreme southern pastures and the superior mobility and endurance of the camel has full play. The Wādī al-Mra and the Wādī al-Hamīn are the southern limits of pastoral activity for south of them is the barren Kalan-shiyū sand sea.

The camels of the southern pastoralists spend from eight to ten months in the Wādī al-Mra district for the vegetation has enough water content in winter to make return trips to the balṭa wells unnecessary. But by late May or early June the desiccation of the extreme southern pastures becomes severe and forces a return northward. With vegetation in the balṭa insufficient to support the herds throughout summer, the camels move at frequent intervals between the grazing in the south and the water in the balṭa zone wells. Just as the routes followed in the winter are flexible and reflect the distribution of available pasture for that year, so too is the summer migration, albeit much more limited in time and space, tied to those areas with suitable pasture. Yet, although an area visited in one year may not be revisited for another five, the overriding rhythm and pulsation of the camel herder's life remain regular and rational.

# CHAPTER III

## MARKETS IN THE NOMADIC MILIEU

## OF EASTERN CYRENAICA

Given that nomads, by virtue of the frequent movements necessitated by their way of life, theoretically are unable to produce themselves many essential material possessions and foodstuffs and that each of the nomadic life styles described in the preceding chapter possesses deficits and surpluses directly related to the characteristics of the ecological niche to which they are adapted, it follows that some mechanism of trade or raid is required to make up deficiencies. Moreover, the teapots, sugar, salt, tea, metal implements, weapons, grain, and other items essential to a smoothly functioning nomadic economy can be obtained only from people whose stationary habits favor their production.[1] However, these sedentary farmers and merchants, because they are tied to a relatively fixed location, are unable to dispose of enough grazing resources to produce all of the meat, milk, wool, leather, and other animal products required to balance their diet and provide raw materials for local craft products. In such a state of mutual interdependence, a system of interchange of the products produced by each community should be a prominent part of the traditional economy. Throughout much of North Africa and the Near East this need for exchange is met by a system of periodic markets where the agricultural and craft products of a sedentary society are available for sale to a nomadic community that has its animals and their products to offer in return.

Yet the importance of the market as an institution has varied considerably through time and three main periods characterizing marketing patterns can be discerned. Since the twelfth century Cyrenaica has been dominated by a nomadic lifestyle. During this extended nomadic era only a few urban centers, particularly Darna in the eastern and Banghāzī in the western Jabal al-Akhḍar,

---

[1]The case for nomadic reliance on material produced by sedentary society is presented by Xavier de Planhol, "Small-scale Industry and Crafts in Arid Regions," in E. S. Hills (ed.), _Arid Lands_ (London: Methuen; Paris: UNESCO, 1966), pp. 273-85.

retained their ancient vitality; these served as market centers for the bedouin.
In the traditional nomadic regime infrequent trips, usually no more than two or
three yearly, were made to the market towns for supplies.[1] The basic characteristic of nomadic livelihood during this period was its self-sufficiency in basic
foodstuffs and its lack of dependence upon the small sedentary population for
dietary staples.

Following an interlude of Italian colonial domination, during which severe
dislocations in bedouin economic and political life took place, a system of periodic markets sprang up. These markets met at small rural villages that had
crystallized around Sanūsī zawāyā or former Italian agricultural centers.
The periodic suq flourished for two decades, from the end of World War II to the
mid-sixties, but in many villages it now has died out completely. The description that follows is based on contemporary observation of surviving suqs, some
of which retain considerable vigor, in an attempt to assess the importance and
the impact of the periodic market on bedouin life. The third and most recent
era is still in the process of emergence, yet its salient characteristics seem
clear. The periodic market, save for certain remnants, has collapsed under the
pressure of transportation improvements and the economic boom induced by the
discovery of oil. In its place has emerged a larger number of moderately sized
higher-order centers challenging the preëminence of Darna and Banghāzī. These
centers now are supported by a lower level network of village centers that were
absent in the pre-Italian bedouin economy.

## Traditional Marketing Arrangements

### The Preëminence of Darna

One of the striking features of the post-Hilalian settlement pattern of
Cyrenaica was the limited importance of settled urban and village life. Although
conclusive documentation is lacking, urban life seems to have disappeared almost totally throughout Cyrenaica during the interval from the first appearance

---

[1] A similar pattern of infrequent trips to market, particularly during the
rainy season, has been described by Marguerite Dupire, "Trade and Market in
the Economy of the Nomadic Fulani of Niger (Bororo)," in Paul Bohannan and
George Dalton (eds.), Markets in Africa (Evanston: Northwestern University
Press, 1962), especially pp. 354-56. The Fulani seldom involve themselves
directly in agricultural activities so their situation is somewhat different from
that of the Cyrenaican bedouin. However, E. H. Winter, "Livestock Markets
among the Iraqw of Northern Tanganyika," in Bohannan and Dalton (eds.), Markets in Africa, p. 460, notes the complete absence of any system of inter-tribal
markets or exchange in the mixed pastoral-agricultural economy of the Iraqw.

of the Banī Hilāl and Banī Sulaym in A. D. 1046 to the revitalization of urban life
by Andalusian refugees and Tripolitanian merchants after A. D. 1500. Even
after the urban revival, the number of urban places was far less than during the
high point of Greco-Roman settlement and the population in every case was
greatly reduced from that of earlier eras. Settlement at Banghāzī ceased alto-
gether and the city owes its contemporary prominence to its selection in A. D.
1635 by the Ottoman administration as their headquarters in eastern Libya.
Darna remained a viable settlement only because a small group of Andalusian
Muslim refugees chose to settle there after the fall of Granada in A. D. 1492.
In the interior, both al-Marj (ancient Barka) and Qayqab (ancient Agabis) are
important today because the Turks placed forts in those two locations. Many
places now prominent in the rural settlement pattern pass unmentioned as population centers in either the early travel accounts or in the first Italian census.
Even in those places where local tradition recalls the existence of shops and
houses in rural villages during the early years of the twentieth century, the numbers involved are invariably small. Qayqab was typical of such villages during
the last years of Turkish rule and had only two shops and hardly more houses.

In almost every case, these settlements are inhabited by a population
excluded from bedouin tribal structure. Only six per cent of the Darnese population was composed of 'Abaydat or affiliated marābṭīn in 1922, while in Banghāzī, out of a total population of 22, 740, only 2, 460 represented any of the
various Cyrenaican tribes;[1] the remainder were Turks, Misuratans (twice as
numerous as the 3, 320 member Italian community), various urban Tripolitanians, Arabs from French North Africa, Albanians, Cretans, Jews, Maltese,
and Armenians. At Ṭubruq the 560 inhabitants were drawn entirely from urban
Cyrenaican and Tripolitanian tribes, Cretan Muslims, and Jews.[2] In Marsā
Sūsa 300 of the 710 town dwellers[3] were Muslim refugees from Crete and less
than half of the total population was composed of 'Abaydat, Hasa, or Darsa, the
tribes living adjacent to the town. Approximately two-thirds of Tulmaytha's
inhabitants were without lineage affiliation with the Cyrenaican tribes.[4] Only in
the case of Shaḥḥat (Cyrene),[5] where two-thirds of the population was of local
origin, and al-Marj,[6] where the tribal background of many of the inhabitants is

---

[1] de Agostini, Le popolazione della Cirenaica, p. 426.

[2] Ibid., p. 440.                [3] Ibid., p. 439.

[4] Ibid., p. 441.                [5] Ibid., p. 438.

[6] Ibid., p. 436.

vague, do local tribesmen outnumber the alien merchants and artisans from
Darna, Banghāzī, and the Tripolitanian cities.

The small number and limited size of towns and villages in Cyrenaica,
the scanty total of rural shops and shopkeepers, and the infrequent contacts
between nomad and farmer are explained by the history and ecology of the eastern jabal. First, there are few sharp distinctions between the two livelihood
modes in rural Cyrenaica. Almost all pastoralists, with the exception of the
camel-herding bedouin in the extreme south, plant grain either in the summer
or winter pasture areas or in both. Similarly, all farmers keep at least some
animals. In Darna substantial numbers of goats and sheep are owned by urban
merchants and farmers and are driven out daily to graze in the surrounding
sāḥil or along the Wādī Darna. The result is a system in which agricultural and
pastoral activities are inextricably mixed so that large deficits or surpluses of
grain and animals seldom occur in geographically discrete areas. Clear distinctions between groups based on the exclusive production of certain agricultural and animal products are infrequent and regularized exchange patterns are
not mandatory.

The nature of the seasonal regime also contributed to infrequent market
trips on the part of the bedouin and made a network of rural periodic markets
or villages unnecessary. Once the winter rains began, pastoralists moved into
the predesert zone south of al-Jabal al-Akhḍar. During this period it was unusual for herders to return to the more elevated portions of the jabal. Rather,
all food supplies and other necessities of daily life were carried with the family
during its moves or were stored in subsurface granaries. Since day-to-day
needs were simple, most purchases were obtained only a few times each year.
The major period during which this contact between nomad and merchant could
take place was the summer when the nomad had withdrawn from the interior
steppes to the coastal upland in close proximity to the cities.

Moreover, the products that nomads had to trade, sell, or exchange
were only seasonally available. Animals, the major item that any nomadic
society has to offer to settled people, were usually sold for slaughtering purposes in spring. This is the annual period when more young lambs are available
than can be expected to survive the rigors of the summer. The seasonal nature
of available local supplies of meat is illustrated from a contemporary prospective by the figures for animals officially slaughtered in Darna during 1969 graphed
in Figure 18.[1] This is the first year for which statistics are available that dis-

---

[1]It should be kept in mind that these figures only reflect animals butchered

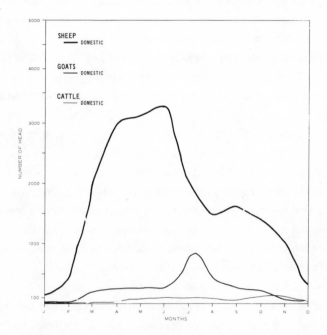

Fig. 18.--Animals slaughtered in the Darna municipal slaughter house, 1969 (unpublished municipal figures).

tinguish between native and imported animals and the graphed curves of local and alien species show a markedly inverse relationship. From March through June when sheep are in greatest supply the imported sheep component of the total number of animals slaughtered declines to negligible proportions. The tremendous discrepancy between consumption of sheep and that of either domestic or im-

at the official municipal facility. Animals purchased alive in the funduq for family consumption can be slaughtered privately and this practice is particularly common during the main Islamic holidays. I am particularly indebted to Dr. M. Hassan, the Department of Agriculture Veterinarian of Darna, for making these statistics available.

Seasonal fluctuations in the slaughtering of various species has also been noted for Banghāzī by S. Mukorji, A. Yamani, and Abdelsalam Hawaiw, "Seasonal Movement in the Consumption of Meat in Benghazi," Dirassat (The Libyan Economic and Business Review), V (1969), 81-92.

ported goats and cattle is an expression of the Cyrenaican preference for lamb in general, and the local variety in particular. It also reflects a deep-seated conviction that lamb is the only suitable meat for ceremonial occasions.

To cite another example, wool is sheared in April or May at which time much of the surplus above domestic needs for rugs, tents, saddle bags and so on is sold to village or urban merchants. In both instances mentioned above the availability of the products that the nomad has to sell is seasonal in nature and it does not require numerous trips to market to dispose of them. The same is true of supplies of butter and buttermilk, for they are in greatest quantity in winter and spring when the nomad is furthest away from the potential urban markets.

Thus, throughout the Turkish era Darna was the dominant market center for the bedouin population of Cyrenaica east of the Wādī al-Kūf, as was Banghāzī for the western half of the country. The seasonal nature of the nomadic regime, the limited availability of marketable products in the bedouin economy, and the low level of demand for luxury products made smaller market centers super-fluous. Throughout this period the bedouin consumer came to the merchant population concentrated in the town. Tea, sugar, coffee, and other luxury items were acquired during these infrequent market trips which were concentrated generally in late spring when wool, hides, and animals were most readily avail-able for sale or in late summer when preparations were underway for the winter migration. Jewish merchants played a prominent role in this trade with the bedouin. Certain families tended to monopolize the import of goods desired by the bedouin or the export of their animals and animal products.

Darnese merchants were particularly active in the export of live animals, sending them to Crete, Malta, and mainland Greece. This was a very impor-tant outlet for the less mobile bedouin of the eastern jabal, since the alternative was a long overland journey to the market in Alexandria. It is important to note, however, that in the traditional economy animal sales in the Alexandria market were of special importance as a mechanism for upward social and economic mobility. Anyone with capital to invest, be he urban merchant or wealthy tribes-man, purchased animals for resale at a profit in Egypt. Local tribesmen whose herds of sheep prospered in a succession of good years would, after the herd attained an unmanageable size, march the surplus overland to Egypt and sell it for a profit. Taken partially in trade goods, such as coffee, rice, and cotton cloth, and in coin, these profits would then be utilized to purchase more animals with which to begin the cycle anew. Several successive successful trips would suffice to make a man wealthy. At this point the accumulated capital would be lent, in return for at least one half of the profits, to other aspiring entrepreneurs with a knowledge of animals, but a shortage of funds, who desired to follow the same route to fame and fortune. Although climatic fluctuations causing herd depletions would tend to retard the process of capital formation through animal sales, economic advancement utilizing this mechanism remained the major means of upward mobility until the post-independence and oil boom era.

The Extent of Self-Sufficiency in
the Traditional Nomadic Milieu

An additional factor historically reducing the importance of the market as a medium of exchange is the relative self-sufficiency of each secondary level segment in basic foodstuffs. The potential resources of al-Jabal al-Akhḍar are subdivided among the tribal segments in such a way that each secondary level segment has its tertiary sections located at different points along the ecological gradient from coast to desert. Although each tertiary section may have certain deficits, the secondary level when viewed as a whole ideally has a balance in all agricultural and pastoral necessities. For example, the location of the 'Awayda Ait Madī in the lower and upper terrace areas where agricultural possibilities are relatively good but where goats are the only animals that can be raised in large numbers leaves them with certain deficiencies. The most marked of these is inadequate numbers of sheep; since the goat is basically a family subsistence item, valued for its milk and hair, and sheep are the major source of capital formation and the obligatory food for special guests and for feast occasions, the deficit must be overcome.

This is accomplished by a complex pattern of trade and debt relationships that are comprehensible within the context of the genealogy, but which operate outside the network of the periodic markets. Because the other 'Awayda families of 'Abd Allah, Maḥmūd, and Jābir al-Mabrūk possess a strip of territory running from north of Qayqab to Khūlān and have access south of Khūlān to seasonal grazing resources suitable for sheep and camels, they are able to raise a surplus of these animals. These same sections, especially those elements that spend all or most of their time in the semi-arid zones of the southern slopes, are vulnerable to drought-induced deficiencies in their grain supply. An ecologically conditioned instability in the economy of the bedouin is the result. Despite a large amount of self-sufficiency in foodstuffs during periods of moderately good environmental conditions, disaster can and does strike suddenly, while social obligations for marriages, circumcisions, funerals, and other obligatory feast occasions place additional strains on available family resources. No one family living in a particular zone can be sure that it will have enough to provide for all eventualities and so, despite pressures to retain goods within the group by preferential parallel first-cousin marriage, a significant number of marriage ties are created between groups in different zones.[1] These ties of marriage and kinship create patterns of obligation that can be activated in time of need.

The herder whose flocks have been wiped out in a drought may appeal to his maternal relatives for assistance, either in the form of new animals that may be owed him as dowry or as a loan to be repaid at some future time, or he may seek work with them as a shepherd until such time as payments for his services enable him to rebuild his decimated herd. The tribal segment whose grain crop has been destroyed may appeal for help to relatives living in more favored ecological niches. Should pasture fail in one area, recourse can be had to the grazing areas of genealogically affiliated groups. An invitation to a wedding or a funeral carries with it the obligation, should one be the possessor of abundant flocks, to bring a gift, be it a lamb, ewe, or goat, to aid the family sponsoring the celebration. Such gifts are remembered and a form of one-up-manship operates, for the man who can top the presentation of a sickly four year old goat with a fat two year old ewe on some future occasion, gains prestige and status. Conversely, one who fails to measure up in such situations of mutually obligatory gift exchanges becomes shamed in the eyes of his friends and relatives. Generosity has its rewards, just as stinginess has its built-in dangers.

In this way surpluses of grain in one area are coupled with deficits in certain types of animals, while an excess of camels and sheep above subsistence needs may well be linked with a net deficiency in grain supplies. By utilizing marriage and kinship ties tribal affiliates living in differing ecological zones are able to maintain a rough balance. This is not to contend that all exchanges take place outside a commercial market context. Animals, wool, grain, vegetables, fruit, and a variety of manufactured products were and still are bought and sold in both the rural periodic markets and in the permanent aswaq (sing. suq) of Darna, Baydā', and Banghāzī. But commercially-oriented activities are only one part of the overall system and one cannot understand the functioning of the whole without realizing the importance of extra-market exchanges.

The few merchant shopkeepers in the incipient rural villages also had an important role to play. Often related to the tribesmen of the immediate vicinity,

---

[1] Peters, "Some Structural Aspects of the Feud," pp. 274-75.

they functioned as a source of credit for anyone unwilling or unable to look to relatives for assistance.  Trust was the keynote of the system and merchants were willing to give merchandise on credit, knowing that the individual would pay back shortly.  In a system where everyone is genealogically comprehensible, there is no difficulty with credit ratings.  Although aid funnelled through the medium of kin relationships was the most common mechanism for providing assistance, the role of the rural shopkeeper should not be overlooked.

Unlike many nomadic groups, who rely on settled peoples for their agricultural supplies, [1] the bedouin of Cyrenaica grow their own grain.  Far from carrying a stigma, plowing operations are a matter of great interest precisely because grain surpluses sold in the urban areas are viewed as an easy way of amassing capital to invest in animals.  These incentives contribute to the development of the region's characteristically mixed agricultural-pastoral life style. At the extremes of environmental variation, either in the harsh and marginal fringes of the desert or in highly variegated mountainous areas, ecological conditions encourage highly articulated specialization.  This concentration on particular resources underlies life style differentiation and helps to stimulate patterns of exchange.  However, in more mediocre conditions, particularly where environmental instability and risk are present, more balanced patterns of activity characteristically are developed as a means of extracting maximum benefit from available resources.

Because bedouin produced both animals and grain themselves, they were self-sufficient in dietary staples.  Barley in particular was important in rural cooking and formed the basis of kisk-ksu (the local cous-cous). [2]  In rural diet, vegetables were only of minor importance, their utilization was seasonal, and store-bought staples were minimal.  This ability to do without foods now considered essential extended to items that today have an all-pervasive place in the local culture.  Coffee was not introduced by the Turks until the middle and late

---

[1] The Kababish of the Sudan are typical of nomadic tribes that do not grow their own grain.  In this instance animals are sold as advantageously as possible and the proceeds utilized to purchase grain and other essential items.  For discussion of this point consult Talal Asad, The Kababish Arabs (London: Hurst, 1970), pp. 30-31 ff.  Philip C. Salzman, "Movement and Resource Extraction among Pastoral Nomads:  The Case of the Shah Nawazi Baluch, " Anthropoligical Quarterly, XLIV (1971), 185-97, provides a contrasting example of nomads directly exploiting a multiplicity of resources.

[2] Abdel Kareem Ballu, "Libyan Food Habits, " in David S. Tillson, Community Development Studies in Cyrenaica ([Banghazi?]:  Area Development Office, USOM, 1959), pp. 69-72 (mimeograph), has an interesting discussion of the differences between urban and rural and Tripolitanian and Cyrenaican cuisine.

nineteenth century, while tea did not become popular until the British mandate period;[1] in both instances the cost was too great for everyday use and it was reserved for ceremonial occasions. Instead, halīb (cream) and laban (butter-milk) were consumed in season or herbal brews served as substitutes. Sugar was rare and usually was replaced as a sweetener by honey raised by more set-tled elements of the population. Given the gusto with which tea and sugar are consumed by Libyans today, and the important social role played by the tea-drinking ceremony, it is difficult to imagine how people were able to function in the past without these commodities.

Food was not the only item in which the nomadic family was self-suffi-cient. Many basic items required for daily use were fabricated by the family itself as consideration of the material inventory of a bedouin family reproduced in the Appendix makes clear. Because the family from whom the inventory was drawn has recently become sedentarized, they possess a wide range of items that the normal migrating household could not carry. However, since large-scale sedentarization is a recent phenomenon, most former bedouin retain the possessions required for their nomadic mode of life and so admirably demon-strate the rapid transition process that is taking place.

A large number of such essential items as strips of woven material for the tent roof, woolen cloaks (jard), various bags and nets for transporting or storing goods (hawīyya, hamaddīyya), rugs (hidma), and ropes (hubal) were made from the wool and hair of the family's flocks. A number of items that once were homemade are now purchased in the local suq or in Darna. A repre-sentative sample would include the farsh and machine woven straw mats replac-ing the hidma and homemade mats, aluminum serving and washing bowls (layyān) substituting for the wooden qaṣ‘a, [2] jerry cans (birmīl) instead of the goatskin qarba and shakwā, while hemp and manila ropes depose the hubal. Other prod-ucts traditionally purchased in the area's markets also suffer attrition in the face of mass produced imports, with bulghar giving way to plastic sandals, char-coal fire-pots yielding to gasoline stoves, maghraf, mihqin, and qaṣ‘a losing ground to the knives, spoons, plates, and plastic pitchers of occidental table

---

[1] A. Leriche, "De l'origine du thé au Maroc et au Sahara," Bulletin de l'Institut Français de l'Afrique Noire, XV (1952), 731-36, indicates that tea was also a late introduction elsewhere in North Africa.

[2] Peters, "Aspects of the Family among the Bedouin of Cyrenaica," p. 123, says that most of these wooden bowls were imported from south of the Sahara. While this is logical, given the trade contacts of many of the southern camel-herding tribes, enough timber existed in the jabal to make local manufac-ture conceivable as well.

etiquette, and the string of camels that carried the family's baggage becoming redundant as transportation shifts to surplus Land Rovers.

Significantly, the largest number of items purchased in the suq traditionally have been metal tools manufactured in Darna and cotton cloth imported from Egypt, both of which have been largely replaced by imports from further afield. The bewildering array of gadgets now available to the bedouin are purchased in increasing quantities as a consequence of oil-induced prosperity (to be discussed in Chapter VIII), but they are all peripheral to the traditional nomadic life style. Only a few items of clothing, some tools and metal implements, and certain items of conspicuous consumption such as jewelry and dowry boxes, in themselves analogous to capital investments, were needed at infrequent intervals from the urban markets. These items could be purchased, either directly or indirectly, by the sale of animals either in Darna for local consumption or for shipment to Crete and Malta or in Alexandria after overland movement through the Marmarican steppe. Thus, before the impact of westernization and modernization most items essential to the bedouin could be obtained or produced by the family from immediately available resources.

## Periodic Markets and the Impact of Modernization

The period immediately following the expulsion of the Axis Forces from Libya in 1943 instituted a process of extremely rapid change in the daily lives of Cyrenaicans that has continued with accelerating force down to the present day. One of the most important of these changes was a shift in the traditional pattern of marketing activity. In place of the time-honored system in which a limited number of trips each year were made to a distant market center, a system of weekly markets meeting in rural villages rapidly took root. The periodic market proved to be short-lived. It yielded after 1960 to new arrangements better adjusted to oil-generated prosperity and to widespread adoption of technological innovations such as the motor car. However, it was a central feature of Cyrenaican life during the twenty years that it flourished.

## Inception of the Periodic Market System

Several factors played a role in creating conditions conducive to the development of the periodic suq. Increased demand for western products generated by contact with Italians, Germans, and British was one. Coupled with increased demand was the opportunity to open new shops, for with the departure of the Italian administration restrictions on the number of stores that could be

operated were removed. Anyone with a small amount of capital was able to buy
a few goods and construct a make-shift shop. Many bedouin, already accustomed to such "untraditional" activities as raising grain, and urban dwellers
took advantage of the new possibilities that the lack of restrictions on merchants
seemed to offer. Coupled with this was a feeling that social prestige could be
gained by operating a shop; it was a profession that more uncouth bedouin could
not understand and therefore was intrinsically of value. The result was a proliferation of small shops in both the cities and the countryside.

Transportation improvements were also considerable both immediately
before and during the Second World War. The enhanced security that followed
the end of hostilities, the improvement in the road system to meet military
needs, and the increased availability of cars and trucks all made travel easier
and quicker than at any time in the past. The benefits of transportation improvements did not accrue equally to all. Initially they were confined to those urban
dwellers, largely merchants, already in possession of enough capital to purchase automobiles. Although in the past merchants were able to make a living
waiting for customers to come to them, it now was possible to increase potential profits by traveling into the countryside to meet prospective consumers.
Merchants in Darna and other major cities were quick to take advantage of increased demand and improved transportation and came to the rural villages on
certain days to buy from and sell to the local population. A series of periodic
market centers rapidly developed, and were visited in a regular cycle by the
centrally-based urban merchants.

Markets in Cyrenaica are always a village phenomenon, initiated, organized, and controlled by urban merchants or rural shopkeepers. This is simply
another way of saying that periodic markets are invariably associated with a
dispersed, but settled, subsistence agricultural population. Although subsistence agriculturalists rarely engage in the exchange of basic foodstuffs in such
local aswaq, it is their specialization in non-essential products such as eggs,
fruit, or craft items and tools that represents a motivating force in periodic
market development.[1] The association of periodic markets with settled agricultural communities is a significant feature, for subsistence oriented agriculturalists were never an important part of the last six hundred years of Cyrenaican
history. The rapid, but ephemeral, flourishing of a weekly suq system occurred
at precisely the time when much of the Cyrenaican population became more

---

[1]See Marvin W. Mikesell, "The Role of Tribal Markets in Morocco:
Examples from the 'Northern Zone,'" Geographical Review, XLVIII (1958), 498.

sedentary in its habits as tribesmen began to reoccupy the agricultural properties abandoned by the Italian settlers.

Unlike other parts of North or West Africa, at no time were periodic
markets held in the open country; villages preceded markets in Cyrenaica,
whereas in Morocco[1] and in Yorubaland[2] they have often grown up around the
site selected for the periodic market. Their focus invariably was the village
centers that had been constructed as part of Italian demographic colonization
schemes. These sites generally were locally rich agricultural areas and summer watering points that had previously been important centers in the bedouin
economy. The Sanūsī zawāyā (sing. zāwiya) erected at Umm ar-Razam, Martūba, Bishāra near al-Qubba, Shaḥḥat, and al-Fā'idīyya, all subsequently important as market centers, are an expression of their economic and tribal importance.[3] The market day for each village differs (see Figure 19), Shaḥḥat's
being held on Friday, Qayqab's on Saturday, that of al-Baydā' on Sunday, al-
Fā'idīyya's on Monday, al-Qubba's on Tuesday, Martūba's on Wednesday, and
Umm ar-Razam's on Thursday. These markets are visited on successive days
by the mobile merchants, the same group of businessmen appearing with predictable regularity in each market at seven day intervals.

Organization and Importance of the Suq

In its physical lay-out the periodic market clearly indicates that it is a
secondary development in the rural villages. It is always held in a funduq located at some distance from the permanent shops in the village center (Figure 20).

---

[1]Walter Fogg, "Changes in the Lay-Out, Characteristics, and Functions
of a Moroccan Tribal Market, Consequent on European Control," Man, XLI
(1941), 104-5.

[2]B. W. Hodder, "Some Comments on the Origins of Traditional Markets
in Africa South of the Sahara," Transactions, Institute of British Geographers,
No. 36 (1965), p. 99, where resting spots along trade routes formed the nuclei
for the growth of markets and subsequently of villages.

[3]For the location of the zawāyā of various Islamic orders before the effective establishment of Italian military control over the interior, see Governo
della Cirenaica, Confraternite mussulmane e templi delle diverse religioni in
Cirenaica (1:800,000; Sheet No. 10; 1922). As Evans-Pritchard, The Sanusi of
Cyrenaica, pp. 70-84, has stressed, an important criteria in selecting the location for a zāwiya was the cohesiveness of the tribe involved. For this reason
sites near the boundary of two or more sub-tribes were most desirable so that
the mediatory role of the order in tribal conflicts could be more readily carried
out. Although the order's functions were not specifically economic, it did engage in a number of economic activities.

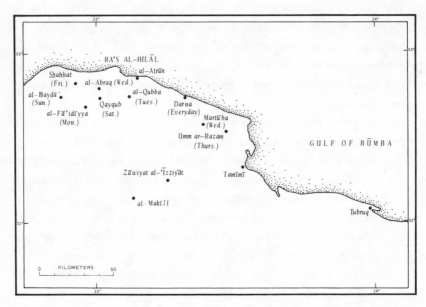

Fig. 19.--Villages and periodic market centers of eastern Cyrenaica

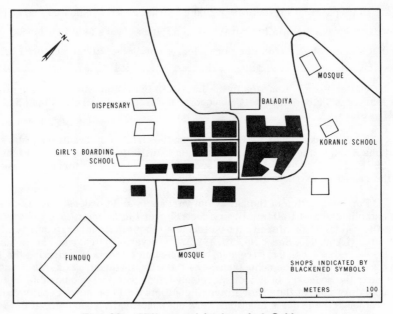

Fig. 20.--Village and funduq of al-Qubba

The shops that form the nucleus of the village line the main street; these shops
cater to the everyday needs of the village and the surrounding population. Their
position in the center of the village is a visible indication of their daily importance. The funduq, on the other hand, is nearly always located on the outskirts
of the village, a symbolically appropriate site for the primary meeting place of
nomad and sedentary.

The funduq is a square or rectangular open space enclosed by a high wall.
Usually built at government expense, the funduq can only be entered by a single
massive gate, an arrangement that facilitates the work of the government tax
collector who sits beside it and levies a five piastre duty on every animal sold.
The internal organization of the funduq is equally unpretentious. Only at al-
Qubba is there a series of seldom used concrete booths along parts of two of the
enclosing walls. All other fanādiq lack shop arrangements, although the al-
Baydā' funduq does have a tin roof along one wall that provides shade for some
of the merchants. Most of the vendors using the market prefer, even when
there is space available in booths, to spread their wares on the ground where
they can be examined by prospective customers. Despite the absence of internal
subdivisions in the funduq, similar products are sold in distinct areas (Figure 21).
Thus, vegetables are sold in one corner, usually near the entrance where the
crush of potential buyers is greatest. Clothes, shoes, hardware, and sundries
are grouped in poorly defined clusters, and animals are concentrated along the
shadiest wall.

Although the majority of the crowd in any market is composed of settled
people from the local area with a sprinkling of nomads, the dominant figure is
that of the urban merchant. There is more than mere symbolic separation in
the geographic aloofness of the funduq and the village shops. The merchants who
frequent it are always from outside the town; it is unusual for local shopkeepers
to display their goods in the funduq, although their stores are always open during
market day. The periodic suq thus serves as a point of contact, not only between
the nomad and the farmer, but also between rural and urban life styles.

The visiting urban merchants are engaged in competitive selling with
their local counterparts. Not only are the prices offered in the funduq lower
than those prevailing in the village, but also the goods offered for sale duplicate
items available in local shops. This price differential is recognized by villagers
and from their point of view represents one of the most attractive features of the
funduq. Vegetable prices are particularly illustrative of the funduq-town dichot-
omy. A sample of the prices charged for the most common vegetables on suc-

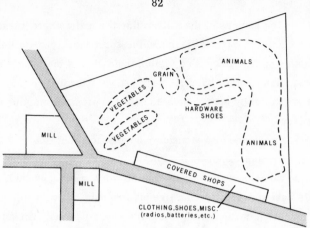

Fig. 21.--The internal organization of al-Bayḍā' funduq

cessive days in the suq and in town stores reveals a nearly 100 per cent rise in cost for most items (Table 2). Given a range of this magnitude, most buyers at the suq attempt to purchase sufficient vegetables with good keeping qualities to last until the market meets again. This has led to hard feelings between local and Darnese and Banghāzī merchants, with local shopkeepers often demanding protection. Since many of the Darnese merchants brought, and still bring, tea, sugar, coffee, and other dietary staples as well as cloth, tools, shoes, and vegetables, they directly undercut their village competitors.

TABLE 2

PRICE COMPARISON BETWEEN FRESH VEGETABLES
IN AL-QUBBA SUQ AND AL-QUBBA TOWN
(prices in piastres/kilo)

| Item | Price in Suq | Price in Town Shops |
|---|---|---|
| Green pepper | 10–15 | 24 |
| Onions | 3–5 | 8–10 |
| Tomatoes | 8–10 | 10 |
| Potatoes | 5 | 10 |
| Watermelon | 6–7 | 12 |
| Mint[a] | 2 | 5 |
| Lettuce | 5 | 12 |
| Bananas | 15 | 15 |
| Red pepper | 10 | 16 |

[a]Sold by the bunch.

In the traditional regime spring was the most common time for animal sales in the Darna market and animals were often driven there for sale. The development of the periodic suq meant that animals could be purchased year-round in the rural areas if trucks were used to transport them to market. Merchants attending the suq specifically to purchase animals for shipment to urban markets were not in direct competition with village shopkeepers, but they did pose a threat to the rural entrepreneurs, who often were village merchants with a small amount of surplus capital available for investment. Rivalry of this sort was most intense early in the rainy season, since rural speculators required the better part of the winter and spring to move their investment on the hoof to Egyptian markets.

The relative importance of the village periodic market is difficult to assess. In its hey-day it completely dominated the economic life of its immediate area; indeed, most of an average family's weekly cycle revolved around it. At a time when transportation improvements had not as yet begun to affect the average citizen, it frequently was impossible to reach the market site in one day's travel. Often the day before the suq was spent traveling to it, and, if the gathering was a large and exciting one, it might not be possible to leave the suq early enough to reach home on the same day. Thus, up to three days could be consumed either traveling to, participating in, or returning from the suq. Most of the remaining days in the week would be spent preparing for the coming market. The vitally important decisions concerning what to buy and sell in the periodic market had to be made in the setting of a complicated and difficult environment that requires complex decisions about anticipated future conditions of rainfall and pasture that might affect one's very chances of survival. By this measure, the suq loomed large in the daily and weekly life cycle.

At the height of its prosperity each market attracted people from a radius of approximately thirty kilometers. This figure is mentioned by informants as the maximum distance that they were willing to travel to a market before the advent of the automobile. Yet markets in the eastern jabal are located much closer together than a hinterland of this size would suggest. This is related to the arrangement of tribal territories in theoretically mutually exclusive strips.

Market centers tend to be associated with particular tribes or subtribes and are utilized largely by the tribe in whose territory they are located. Thus the Hasa tribal territory has two market centers, one at Shaḥḥat serving the northern part of the territory and one at al-Fā'idīyya which is frequented by Hasa tribesmen living along the southern slopes of the jabal. The 'Abaydat tribe, with a large territory and numerous subdivisions, has a number of markets. These usually are found at points where the territory of two or more tribal subsections comes in contact. al-Qubba is the headquarters of the tribe and many tribal sections have land adjacent to it. Qayqab is on the boundary of the 'Awakla and Ghayth sections; in fact, local tradition maintains that the north-south street leading to the Turkish castle is the dividing line between the two groups. Umm ar-Razam is the center for the Ait Mzayn and the Ait 'Abdul Karīm sections while the town itself was settled and developed by the Ait Haj Bubakr section of the Manṣūr subtribe. Thus, at least in the 'Abaydat territory, tribal market centers are always shared by more than one section.

However, at any one time a number of different groups are usually present at the periodic suq. Although the core of any market is composed of itinerant merchants from the major cities and tribesmen from the local segments, strangers from farther afield are invariably present. Since anyone can, in practice, graze wherever he wants, there always are members of other tribal sections present in another section's territory and trading in its market simply because it is closer than the market they would traditionally frequent. Other less regular visitors may appear from greater distances because rumor or reputation may extol the virtues or the better comparative prices of another section's suq. Simple curiosity or the desire for greater variety also might prompt a visit to a more distant market.

Thus, each periodic market center had a three-tier zone of influence, a feature which still survives in those markets, such as al-Qubba, that retain their vitality today. At any one time the vast majority of those present in the suq would be local tribesmen living within ten kilometers of the suq, a figure that delimits the effective trade area of the small villages that have emerged in the eastern jabal. Merchants came from greater distances, some from their base at Darna, others, particularly fresh vegetable merchants, from Banghāzī. The number of merchants present at a suq and the distance traveled to reach it were an accurate measure of the market's importance. Tribesmen from neighboring sections represent the third level. Only these less frequent and less numerous visitors would come from the thirty kilometer hinterland.

Many of the functions performed by the periodic markets are non-economic, and the importance of the market far exceeds its influence in the quantity of goods bought and sold. Most inter-tribal disputes are settled by tribal councils that meet on the market day. At the same time, intersectional feuding is also apt to develop due to tensions over problems being arbitrated as well as due to the presence of mutually antagonistic families and sections. Nearly all medical care is obtained on the market day, unless the illness is serious enough to justify a special trip to the doctor. The transaction of any government business that a tribesman has, be it the payment of taxes, the collection of pensions or other social services, or the settlement of police problems are handled on the once weekly trip to the village.

Still more important are the market's social functions. It serves as a center for the solidification of social and political contacts and for the exchange of news on a wide range of topics. It is an ideal place to meet friends and the amount of handshaking, ceremonial greeting, and animated discussion that takes place at the height of activity on a suq day is impressive. Frequently people come, not to buy, but to see their friends, to greet them, to exchange gossip, and to be seen by them. The market also serves as an important center for innovation. Often people are more interested in seeing what is new and different in the merchant's collection than they are in purchasing it. Social activities associated with the market can be so important that previously many individuals who lived quite close to the market came the night before. Guests would stay with village relatives or in small hotels run by widowed women or single men. Cafés catering to loungers were also a feature of the market and the night before the suq often was spent in a round of visiting and card playing. One function that the market did not serve was religious. Never as religiously ostentatious as townsmen, visits to a mosque or the tomb of a marābit were not an important part of the bedouin's rationale for attending the suq.[1]

Emerging Marketing Relationships

It is ironic that the same forces that gave rise to periodic markets have been instrumental in destroying them. Transportation improvements after World War II made the periodic market system possible; continued improvements post-1960, now financed by increasing amounts of oil revenue, reduced the viability of most of the periodic markets. Accelerated investment in upgrading roads has resulted in an abrupt decline in travel time. A comparison of driving times between Darna and al-Gubba illustrates the change. In 1945 the trip used to take four hours in one direction; in 1970 it was possible to cover the

---

[1] This is a significant departure from northern Morocco, where the economic radius of a suq is closely related to the religious radius of influence of the saint associated with it. See Walter Fogg, "The Suq: A Study in the Human Geography of Morocco," Geography, XVII (1932), 263.

same distance in forty minutes.

Coupled with the improvement in both quantity and quality of paved roads
has been a dramatic increase in the number of cars and trucks imported into
Libya (Table 3). Today many Libyan families possess a car or truck and those
who do not have direct access to motor transport have little trouble flagging
down a passing vehicle for the trip to the market. Moreover, relatively inexpensive scheduled bus and unscheduled taxi service is available along the major
roads between the main towns and this has greatly facilitated internal communication.

TABLE 3

NUMBER OF MOTOR VEHICLES IN LIBYA, 1959-1964

| Year | Trucks | Buses | Taxis | Private Cars |
|------|--------|-------|-------|--------------|
| 1959 | 1,072  | 310   | 335   | 13,919       |
| 1960 | 9,099  | 326   | 371   | 17,154       |
| 1961 | 10,670 | 354   | 375   | 19,747       |
| 1962 | 12,533 | 482   | 477   | 23,274       |
| 1963 | 14,994 | 507   | 829   | 27,879       |
| 1964 | 17,592 | 516   | 1,390 | 33,575       |

Source: Kingdom of Libya, Ministry of National Economy, Statistical Abstract 1964 (Tripoli, 1965), p. 17.

The result has been a rapid decline in the importance of the rural periodic market. Neither the Martūba nor the Umm ar-Razam markets meet any
longer. The periodic suqs in Shaḥḥat, al-Fā'idīyya, and Qayqab have been
reduced to purely local significance. Many of the shops in the rural towns,
whose numbers reflect enterprises that were usually open only on market day,
have closed their doors permanently. Merchants from Darna no longer visit the
periodic markets to buy animals and livestock sales have declined drastically.
Government revenue from other sources has increased so dramatically that at
most markets the animal tax is no longer collected. Most animal sales now
occur in the municipal markets of the coastal cities to which the animals are
brought by truck.

In general none of the small local markets today attract visitors from a
distance of more than ten kilometers. Indeed, during the winter it is unusual
for Qayqab to attract more than fifty men to the suq, a number that is insufficient to justify opening the funduq. More people attend the market during the

summer when the nomadic sections are closer to the upper terrace.[1] This seasonal difference in market attendance is visually evidenced not only by the total
number of individuals present but also by the percentage of women visitors.
Throughout most of the year the surviving markets are a masculine institution,
but during the summer months the attendance of women conspicuously increases.[2]

Almost invariably these women are from nomadic families temporarily
resident in the vicinity of the market. Their activities include buying food and
selling charms, perfumes, personal adornments, zatar and other spices and
herbs collected in the countryside, as well as surplus wool or goat hair. Village
women do not attend the suq; their husbands or older sons make the weekly purchases. Thus, the relative proportion of women present is a reliable indicator
of the size of the nomadic component in any market.

Historically, the bedouin made infrequent trips to Darna during the year
to procure the limited range of goods desired and no lower strata of intervening
intermediate markets in the countryside was required. In a situation where the
impetus for the indigenous internal development of periodic markets was lacking,
such development had to await the impact of an outside force to generate momentum toward modernization.

In Cyrenaica the crucial role of transportation technology in giving birth
to the periodic market system should be noted. Not until the development of a
modern road system and the establishment of security in the rural areas after
World War II, were favorable conditions created for the development of periodic
markets distant from the major urban centers. While these rural periodic markets exhibited little geometric regularity,[3] they did establish a marketing hier-

---

[1] J. F. Troin, "Observations sur les souks de la région d'Azrou et de
Khénifra," Revue de Géographie du Maroc, No. 3-4 (1963), p. 114, reports that
the suq at Bekrit is open only during the six summer months when the Beni
Mguild are present in the upper elevations of the Middle Atlas with their herds.
This is an analogous, albeit more extreme, parallel to the seasonal pattern in
Cyrenaica.

[2] The different social role of women north and south of the Sahara is indicated by attendance at market. In Yorubaland, markets are almost entirely a
woman's preserve and B. W. Hodder, "Rural Periodic Day Markets in Part of
Yorubaland," Transactions and Papers, Institute of British Geographers, No. 29
(1961), p. 153, reports that only rarely do men attend. For a contrasting male
dominance in East Pakistan, see Ahmen H. Patel, "The Rural Markets of Rajshahi District," Oriental Geographer, VII (1963), 144.

[3] Unlike the Chinese market systems studied by G. William Skinner, "Marketing and Social Structure in Rural China," Journal of Asian Studies, XXIV
(1964), 3-43; XXV (1965), 195-228, 363-99, which have developed a geometric

archy. It no longer was necessary to travel to Darna to purchase items of domestic or foreign origin, for these goods now came direct to the bedouin consumer through the courtesy of the itinerant merchant. Initiated after 1945, the periodic market system exhibited symptoms of immaturity similar to the still evolving market centers of Ankole described by Good. [1] Yet so fast-paced was the impact of modern technology that before the periodic market hierarchy could be well established, road development, the increased availability of the motor car, and a recentralization of trading functions into a slightly increased number of major centers has destroyed the raison d'être of the periodic market.

Whereas the traditional market arrangement was a two point system focused on Darna and Banghāzī, this has given way to a two echelon organization (Figure 22) in the eastern Jabal al-Akhḍar. Darna no longer is the paramount market center as rival market towns have blossomed at the oil port of Ṭubruq and the planned federal capital of the ex-royal government at al-Bayḍā'. These three towns fulfill both local market needs and less frequent market requirements of a wider district. Although the periodic market system now largely is defunct, the former suq towns survive as trading centers catering to the market needs of their surrounding local territory. al-Qubba remains something of a special case; as the center of government for the surrounding local sub-district and as the traditional center of the ʿAbaydat tribe, its population is growing and its periodic suq retains considerable vitality. These smaller villages and towns, including the interior centers of al-Makīlī and Zāwiyat al-ʿIzziyāt, now provide the lower-order daily market functions that were absent in the traditional system.

This change can perhaps best be illustrated by a recent interview with a farmer from al-Abraq. When asked to indicate where and how often he went to the suq, he mentioned trips to al-Abraq roughly once every three days, to al-Qubba about two times a month, to Darna possibly once a month, and to al-Bayḍā' at somewhat less frequent intervals. More expensive items, for example clothes, are usually purchased in Darna rather than al-Qubba because the al-Qubba shops frequently charge twice the price of the same item in the Darna suq. This illustrates two interesting points.

---

regularity after an evolution of several thousand years, both the periodic market system and the presently emerging market relationships are too recent to exhibit a discernible geometry.

[1] Charles M. Good, Rural Markets and Trade in East Africa: A Study of the Functions and Development of Exchange Institutions in Ankole, Uganda (Research Paper No. 128; Chicago: University of Chicago, Department of Geography, 1970).

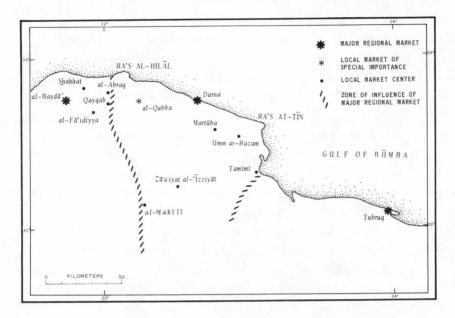

Fig. 22.--Contemporary market centers in eastern Cyrenaica

First, the role of the local village in meeting the needs of the population in its immediate area is growing. Every day is suq day for shops are always open and there never is any difficulty about acquiring bread, tomato paste, or sundry other items. Today the local market center emphasizes a different set of functions than it did previously, for, in the relatively affluent post-petroleum age, people buy many more non-local items than at any time in the past. Many of these purchases, from cans of Nestle's milk and bags of macaroni to jars of pepper paste and cans of tuna fish have become staples in the daily diet. What has died in the face of prosperity, sedentarization, improved transportation, and rural to urban migration is the entire rationale for the subsistence-oriented periodic suq. At the present time staples are usually bought at the local village, but more expensive items are sought elsewhere.

Second, Darna is no longer the dominant regional center. In the western part of the ʿAbaydat area, al-Baydāʾ has developed as a viable alternative to Darna. The decision to create a new federal capital on the site of the Grand Sanūsī's first zāwiya resulted in an influx of population and the development of a more active suq. This more lively market has attracted visitors from the Hasa

and western 'Abaydat areas. al-Makīlī illustrates these changes. Largely controlled by nomadic tribesmen of the 'Awakla and Ghayth subsections, the al-
Makīlī region's normal trade outlets, particularly for animals, were via the
periodic markets at Qayqab and al-Qubba to Darna. But the development of an
alternative market in al-Bayḍā', with prices equivalent to those of Darna, and
an opportunity to eliminate the merchant middlemen of al-Qubba and Qayqab,
has sharply reduced the number of sales by al-Makīlī natives in Darna. Significantly, most of the al-Makīlī people bring their animals for sale on non-market
days, since on Sundays the animal market is swamped by local sellers. Just
how much the republican government's desire to reduce investment in al-Bayḍā'
and transfer federal ministries back to the major urban centers will affect the
prosperity of the suq remains to be seen, but it is likely that any reduction in
the population of al-Bayḍā' will have an adverse impact.

Two other centers on the jabal have also managed to increase in size and
influence, although Darna still remains the predominant influence in the eastern
jabal. al-Qubba, because it is the center of a number of tribal groups, occupies
a position in a fertile farming area, and is roughly mid-way between Darna and
al-Bayḍā', attracts people from an area of greater than ten kilometers. al-
Abraq, which in the past lacked a periodic market, has developed a very local
suq meeting on Wednesdays. But only al-Qubba's shows any promise of exerting
more than strictly local influence.

In essence, the situation has reverted to a status somewhat analogous to
that existing before the growth of periodic markets. In certain respects Darna
has increased the area of its influence, for nearly everyone between al-Abraq
and Tamīmī comes to Darna for market purchases at least monthly rather than
the traditional two or three trips per year. Even in the areas around al-Abraq
and Qayqab where people have recently been attracted to al-Bayḍā' suq, traditional ties with Darna remain strong. Many people who go to al-Bayḍā' on several Sundays a month also go to Darna on other occasions, attracted, no doubt,
by the better shops and more interesting and lively covered suq which al-Bayḍā'
lacks. Darna's regional dominance has been challenged in recent years both by
al-Bayḍā' and by Ṭubruq and the animal funduq of the latter in particular has,
thanks to large-scale truck transportation, become an important outlet for the
sale of the eastern jabal's animals. But the underpinnings of both are somewhat
suspect, al-Bayḍā' because its growth was heavily dependent on royal favoritism
and Ṭubruq because of its almost total reliance on the oil industry now that the
royal palace and the British military at al-Adam are no longer potential sources

of employment. Only al-Qubba among the smaller centers in the eastern jabal appears to have retained a viable periodic market; the others are mere vestigial remnants of their former importance. Thus, although challenged by the rival towns of al-Baydā' and Ṭubruq, Darna remains the dominant market center in the eastern Jabal al-Akhḍar.

CHAPTER IV

PRE-ROMAN SETTLEMENT HISTORY

The model of a self-sufficient, mixed pastoral-agricultural life style
analyzed in the preceding chapters represented a successful cultural adaptation
because it possessed access to the full range of resources of al-Jabal al-Akhḍar.
However, those resources located in the better-watered upland districts easily
could support a sedentary farming community. Although a combination of dry
farming of cereals and herding of animals historically has been a common method of extracting a livelihood from the Cyrenaican environment, the balance
between animal husbandry and agriculture in any indigenous culture's economy
has varied. Instances of total internal stability between the two components are
rare. Farmers and herders have coexisted in Cyrenaica because the natural
environment offers possibilities for the development of each. This coexistence
frequently has been a strained and violent one, for to a considerable extent both
groups are in competition for access to land and water. The relative balance of
power between the two livelihood modes is exemplified by the repetitive advance
and retreat of the frontier of agricultural settlement. This theme of competition,
when viewed within the framework of the ecological model developed earlier,
serves to elucidate the settlement history of Cyrenaica and the fluctuating fortunes of the two livelihood forms.

The Libyan Berbers

When the first Greek settlers arrived in 639 B. C. they found, not an
unoccupied and virgin land, but rather a viable and largely self-sufficient nomadic Berber culture called "Libyan," a vague designation given by the ancient
Egyptians to anyone living west of the Nile. Grouped into three main tribal confederations, [1] the Thehenu immediately west of the Nile, the Lebu in southeastern Cyrenaica, and the Meshwesh in southwestern Cyrenaica, the Libyan tribes

_____

[1] Oric Bates, The Eastern Libyans: An Essay (London: Macmillan, 1914),
pp. 47-51. Bates' series of maps depicting changing tribal distributions as reflected in the writings of ancient authors are especially valuable.

possessed a mixed economy that achieved a rough balance between herding and agriculture. In striving to develop their economy and care for and increase their herds, the Cyrenaican tribes had access to the full range of resources found in al-Jabal al-Akhḍar.

This resource base was the same in its general characteristics as that found in Cyrenaica today. There is no evidence to suggest that any long-term climatic change has taken place in the eastern Mediterranean since the end of the last subpluvial around 2,500 B.C., although, obviously, short-term fluctuations can be expected in a climatically marginal zone. Any change that has occurred has been at the level of the micro-climate as a result of human and animal interference.[1] Although the precise composition of the flora of Cyrenaica in the initial Greek contact period is not known, the broad outline of the vegetation as presented in the classical authors parallels contemporary conditions. Both Strabo[2] and Pliny[3] divide Cyrenaica into four zones along a north-south axis beginning with a forested and fertile zone along the coast, shifting to a band suitable only for the production of grain and incapable of supporting trees, moving to a strip noted for its concentration of silphium,[4] and finally reaching the desert proper. A similar zonation is echoed in the works of Diodorus[5] and the banding of climatic and floral tracts corresponds closely to the pattern of maquis, subhumid steppe, arid steppe, and desert found in Cyrenaica today.

---

[1] For the stability of climate in the Near East in historic times, consult Karl W. Butzer, Studien zum vor- und frühgeschichtlichen Landschaftswandel der Sahara (Wiesbaden, 1958), and idem, "Environment and Human Ecology in Egypt during Predynastic and Early Dynastic Times," BSGE, XXII (1959), 43-87; the evidence indicating human modification of the environment is reviewed by Rhoads Murphey, "The Decline of North Africa since the Roman Occupation: Climatic or Human?" AAAG, XLI (1951), 116-32.

[2] Strabo Geography 17. 3. 23.

[3] Pliny Natural History 5. 5.

[4] The identification of silphium is uncertain since the species has disappeared completely from Cyrenaica. Speculation centers on various species of Ferula or Thapsia but remains unresolved. The plant was important to the Cyrenaican Greeks because it had medicinal utility. Systematically exploited, silphium was eastern Libya's major export crop until over-zealous extraction virtually eliminated it by the first century A.D. For further discussion see Steier, "Silphion," in August Pauly et al., Paulys real-encyclopädie der classischen altertumswissenschaft, 2nd series, III A, 1 (Stuttgart: J. B. Metzlersche, 1927), columns 103-14.

[5] Diodorus Siculus Library of History 3. 50. 1-4.

Knowledge of Libyan utilization of al-Jabal al-Akhḍar is based either on cryptic references to them in Egyptian hieroglyphics or by analogy from contemporary Libyan bedouin culture. It is certain that they balanced animal husbandry and agricultural pursuits.[1] Even at this early date Bates professes to see a distinction between the components of the Libyan tribal confederations.[2] Those tribes living close to the coast were postulated to be more agricultural, raising crops as a subsidiary activity to their more important pastoral concerns, and, because they occupied the better watered and more fertile portions of the jabal and had to return to the higher elevations for the grain harvest, they moved over shorter distances. Their more mobile brethren, living further south on the dip-slope and concerned less directly with agricultural activities, were able to travel over greater distances in search of pasture. This view reflects a valid distinction concerning the relative degree of mobility that undoubtedly existed in the Libyan community, but it should not be overemphasized. Because the camel had not been introduced into North Africa at this early date,[3] sheep and goats were the major components of the herds. Unable to exploit the far-distant desert reaches, the Libyan Berbers would have been unable to move seasonally into the most arid areas. All of them would have been restricted in their movements by their agricultural concerns. Thus, differences in mobility would be in degree rather than in kind and would reflect only minor variations in a common pattern of mixed agricultural and pastoral endeavors.

Moreover, Berber reliance on agriculture would have been even greater than in contemporary Cyrenaica because, before the arrival of Greek settlers, the option of obtaining products necessary to the nomadic genre de vie from a sedentary urban population was nonexistent. Unable to subsist solely on the products of their herds, lacking a settled population with which to trade for agricultural products, and devoid of the diversification in animal possessions

---

[1] Strabo Geography 2. 5. 33. notes for the post-contact period that both the Marmaridae and the Nasamones tribes "already" had mastered the art of farming. Given the absence of a sedentary agricultural population and the difficulty of nomadic existence without an assured grain supply, the rapid adoption of agriculture by the Libyan tribes as related by Strabo reflects a previous intimate familiarity with farming on the part of the nomadic community before the arrival of the Greeks.

[2] Bates, The Eastern Libyans, pp. 91-93.

[3] For a review of the evidence dealing with the natural history, domestication, and dispersal of the camel and its slow spread from Egypt to the remainder of North Africa, see Marvin W. Mikesell, "Notes on the Dispersal of the Dromedary," Southwestern Journal of Anthropology, XI (1955), 231-45.

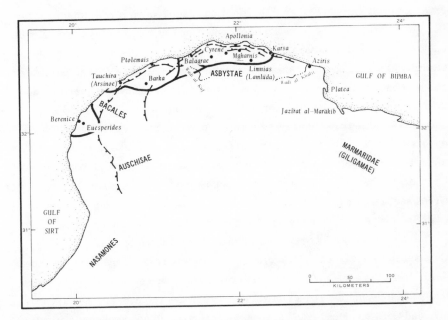

Fig. 23.--Cyrenaica, 631-96 B.C. Sources: Chamoux, Cyrène sous la monarchie des Battiades, Goodchild, Tabula Imperii Romani: Cyrene, and Herodotus, The Histories.

needed to stimulate trade between the various components of the nomadic community, all Libyans had to have access to enough land to grow a subsistence supply of grain and to provide pasture for their animals. This, rather than any genetic inability to withstand the rigors of the cool Cyrenaican winter as suggested by Goodchild,[1] explains the dispersed pattern of land use typical of the pre-Greek population.

Not only do the Berbers appear to have been self-sufficient in foodstuffs, but also there is no archaeological evidence to suggest that they made up for the absence of an indigenous urban population by engaging in trade with Bronze Age Minoan and Mycenean merchants. Belief in the existence of such trade was first expressed by Evans,[2] but his conviction was based on the short sailing distance

---

[1]Richard G. Goodchild, Cyrene and Apollonia: An Historical Guide (2nd ed.; [Shahat?]: Department of Antiquities [Eastern Region], United Kingdom of Libya, 1963), p. 8.

[2]Arthur Evans, "The Early Nilotic, Libyan, and Egyptian Relations with Minoan Crete," JRAI, LV (1925), 199-228.

between Crete and the area around Darna[1] together with some indications of cross-cultural exchange of artistic traditions and clothing styles rather than on firm evidence within the boundaries of contemporary Libya. The possibility of trade contacts with southern Europe as well as the more likely prospect of ties laterally along the Mediterranean coast with Egypt also recently has been raised, [2] although material evidence for trade of either type is scanty. A variation on the theme of trade as a crucial factor in the Greek colonization of Cyrenaica was advanced by Milne[3] who contended that the Assyrian conquest of Egypt, by virtue of its disruption of the normal flow of trade down the Nile and the consequent diversion of traffic through the western desert oases, inspired the foundation of Cyrene. Chamoux forcefully rejects this position, [4] and maintains that only after Greek settlement had produced a local urban population as a pole of attraction could the long desert detour be justified economically.

Three objections to trading opportunities as a motivation in founding Cyrene can be advanced. First, the clearly stated reason for the Therean decision to seek the advice of the Delphic oracle was a succession of famine years that made a population reduction via emigration desirable. [5] Second, any extensive and well-developed trade across the desert would be extremely difficult if not impossible without the camel, which as previously noted, did not become common west of Egypt until after the first century A.D. Finally, a recent archaeological survey of potential trading sites along the northern coast of Cyrenaica failed to reveal any material evidence for trade contacts between Greeks

---

[1]Strabo Geography 10. 4.5, for example, states that the sailing distance for vessels of his day between Crete and eastern Cyrenaica was two days.

[2]C. B. M. McBurney, "Libya's Role in Prehistory" (unpublished MS from the Libya in History conference; Banghāzī: University of Libya, 1968), p. 7.

[3]J. G. Milne, "Trade between Greece and Egypt before Alexander the Great," Journal of Egyptian Archaeology, XXV (1939), 177-83.

[4]François Chamoux, Cyrène sous la monarchie des Battiades (Paris: E. de Boccard, 1953), pp. 60-61. Chamoux's main objections to Milne's hypothesis are as follows: (1) desert routes were too insecure at this time for successful commerce; (2) there is no mention of trade via this desert route in Archaic Greek texts; (3) Egyptian grain was the major export of interest to the Greeks and there were not enough exotic products to justify the long detour through the western desert; (4) Cyrenaica was founded as an agricultural settlement not as a coastal trading site; and (5) Cyrenaica is not the logical natural outlet for a trans-Saharan route.

[5]Herodotus The Histories 4. 150-53.

and Libyans before the initial Greek settlement.[1] The fact that the Therean settlers first acquired a guide in Crete before departing for Libya[2] indicates that Cretans were familiar with its existence but no more. Their knowledge could as easily have been gained by fishing as by trading expeditions. In the absence of trading contacts, it must be assumed that the native Libyans produced all of the implements and tools they required, and the possibility that an oasis in the interior of the country supplied trade goods and agricultural products is unlikely and untenable.[3]

Blessed with a relatively rich resource base, possessing free access to the water and grazing resources of the entire jabal, and unfettered by direct competition with a predominantly sedentary agricultural society, the ancient Libyans must have been prosperous. Certainly they were powerful. However, even at this early date their primary contacts were with Egypt, rather than with Tripolitania and the rest of North Africa, and a drift of tribal fragments from the Cyrenaican plateau toward the Nile, as well as raids into the Delta, characterized the pre-Greek period. Periodically, large coalitions would form around successful leaders and pose a threat to the agricultural civilization of the Nile. Perhaps these raids and occasional conquests filled a gap in the nomadic economy by making available in the form of booty items that could not be produced by the nomadic society itself.

The first recorded conflict between Libyan tribes and the Egyptians took place during the Third Dynasty,[4] and a series of raids and Egyptian military reprisals continued sporadically during succeeding centuries.[5] Libyans living

---

[1] Theresa H. Carter, "Reconnaissance in Cyrenaica," Expedition, V (Spring, 1963), 18-27. Although Sandro Stucchi, "Prime tracce tardo-minoiche a Cirene: i rapporti della Libya con il mondo egeo," QAL, V (1967), 19-45, has since published evidence from Cyrene suggesting that Minoan trade with the eastern Jabal al-Akhdar was a reality, this view has been challenged by John Boardman, "Bronze Age Greece and Libya," ABSA, LXIII (1968), 41-44. Boardman believes that Stucchi's finds represent sixth century B.C. pottery styles or jewelry introduced after the Greek settlement. The existence of Minoan island gems at Cyrene and Tokra in Boardman's opinion reflects their continued popularity among the early settlers despite their lack of fashion elsewhere in the Greek world.

[2] Herodotus The Histories 4. 152.

[3] Speculation that an undiscovered oasis on the edge of the Sahara served as the Libyan urban center is advanced by Carter, "Reconnaissance in Cyrenaica," p. 27.

[4] Bates, The Eastern Libyans, p. 211.

[5] Alan Rowe, A History of Ancient Cyrenaica (Cairo: Institut Français

along the borders of Egypt were also able to penetrate in a more subtle form via recruitment into the Egyptian army. Organized tribally under the leadership of their chiefs, they were often given grants of land along the fringes of the Delta where they settled down and became Egyptianized in manners and customs but managed to preserve their ethnic identity. Whenever the power and authority of the central regime declined, they and their kin beyond the frontier posed a serious threat to the stability of the settled community.[1] On at least one occasion an Egyptianized Libyan family drawing on such semi-sedentarized military castes for its support was able to attain supreme power in Egypt and found the Twenty-Second Dynasty, foreshadowing the problem that Greeks, Romans, and Byzantines were destined to experience in attempting to settle and control the Cyrenaican plateau.

## Archaic and Hellenistic Cyrenaica

Initial Colonial Ventures

Greek settlers first appeared along the eastern coast of Cyrenaica in 639 B.C.[2] A combination of drought, famine, and overpopulation induced the inhabitants of the island of Thera to consider the establishment of a new colonial enterprise in order to reduce pressure on the resources of their homeland. Directed by a Delphic oracle to build a city in Libya the colonists, led by a Theran named Battus and assisted by a Cretan guide, landed first in the Gulf of Bumba. Their initial assessment of the potential of the Libyan coast for settlement was unfavorable, and the pioneers attempted to return to Thera. When permission was refused categorically[3] another attempt to settle along the coast

---

d'Archéologie Orientale, 1948), pp. 4-7; Bates, The Eastern Libyans, pp. 210-28; Chamoux, Cyrène sous la monarchie des Battiades, p. 51, suggests that at least one Pharaoh, Rameses II, was forced to anticipate later Roman and Byzantine practice and construct a limes zone as far west as al-Alamayn in order to combat these raids.

[1]Chamoux, Cyrène sous la monarchie des Battiades, particularly pp. 56-58.

[2]A number of legends are associated with the foundation of Cyrene and a widely divergent series of dates for the initial settlement are suggested as a result. Most authorities follow the account given by Herodotus and date the actual establishment of Cyrene some eight years after the initial settlement attempt. For a review of the various colonization traditions and a determination in favor of Herodotus see Chamoux, Cyrène sous la monarchie des Battiades, pp. 69-91.

[3]The limitations on the right of return, more severe than was usually the case in colonial ventures, is interpreted by Alexander J. Graham, Colony and

was made and the first two years of colonial life were spent on the island of Platea. [1] The location of the first settlement site somewhere in the Gulf of Bumba generally is accepted, but the precise location is a source of controversy. Some have opted for Jazīrat al-Marākib (Seal Island) at the base of the Gulf of Bumba, [2] others have favored various small islets scattered about the gulf. However, the most likely spot, despite dating difficulties, [3] is not an island but rather a tombolo now tied to the mainland by a sand-spit on the eastern side of the Khalū (cove) al-Bumba.

When the settlement at Platea failed to prosper, it was shifted northwestward along the coast to a mainland site called Aziris. Located at the mouth of the Wādī al-Khalij, [4] the settlement remained there for six years until 631 B.C. [5] At that time, on the advice of friendly Libyans, the colonists again changed their location, this time moving away from the coast and into higher elevations. The main attraction for the new settlement was the higher rainfall of the mountain upland and the constant water supply furnished by a spring line near the crest of the upper escarpment. One of these copious springs, soon to become famous throughout the Greek world as the Fountain of Apollo, formed the primary focus of the new settlement at Cyrene. Here the colony established itself firmly and prospered.

---

Mother City in Ancient Greece (Manchester: University Press, 1964), p. 51, to be an indication of the seriousness of the over-population problem facing the Therans.

[1] Herodotus The Histories 4. 158.

[2] Amilcare Fàntoli, "Le isole del golfo di Bomba e le prime basi della colonizzazione greca in Cirenaica," L'Universo, XXXVII (1947), 1064.

[3] John Boardman, "Evidence for the Dating of Greek Settlements in Cyrenaica," ABSA, LXI (1966), 149-50. Only late Roman pottery was found on the site by Carter, "Reconnaissance in Cyrenaica," p. 24, but her identification of the surviving ruins as qusūr remnants is questionable. The site was so disturbed during the Second World War by the airfield and supply depot located there, as well as by the construction of dugouts and shelters for the troops, that positive identification probably always will prove elusive.

[4] Carter, "Reconnaissance in Cyrenaica," p. 24. The inland location due west of the modern town of Bumba suggested by Chamoux, Cyrène sous la monarchie des Battiades, p. 227 and endpaper map, is patently erroneous.

[5] This date is confirmed by the presence of Archaic pottery dated no later than 631 B.C. by Boardman, "Evidence for the Dating of Greek Settlements," p. 151. Boardman's identification of Hellenistic pottery from the fourth and third centuries B.C. suggests that settlement either continued on a reduced scale after the main body of settlers shifted elsewhere or that it was resumed at a later date.

Relations with the Libyan tribes in the initial colonial period were cordial, a common phenomenon in the early contact period of most colonial enterprises. Not only did the Libyans aid the Greek settlers by guiding them to a favorable site at Cyrene but also intermarriage between the two groups was frequent, apparently because only men composed Battus' initial following.[1] The extent to which intermarriage took place is demonstrated by the constitutional reform undertaken by Demonax of Mantinea after the death of Arcesilas II, for this document admitted to citizenship the children of a Greek father and a Libyan mother.[2] Only intermarriage on a considerable scale would justify making specific provisions for the admission to citizenship of a mixed-blood population. As Kraeling points out,[3] one small agricultural settlement was not an immediate threat to the economy of the nomadic Libyans. Indeed, the original Battiad settlement would be an advantage to the tribal community. Linked to the local clans by marriage, capable of producing the agricultural commodities and craft goods that nomadic pastoralists have little opportunity or inclination to fabricate themselves, the original settlers easily could be accommodated within the existing genealogical and economic structure without tension and conflict.

Growth of Greek Settlement

But this equilibrium lasted for only a short time, and the spread of agricultural settlement took place rapidly. Recent evidence suggests that expansion progressed most swiftly along the coast, with settlement at Apollonia, Ptolemais, Tauchira, and Euesperides in western Cyrenaica occurring in the last quarter of the seventh century B.C. or the first quarter of the sixth.[4] These sites appear

---

[1]See the translation of Cyrene's foundation decree in Graham, Colony and Mother City, pp. 225-26, which indicates that only sons of Theran families were selected for the colonial venture.

[2]A. A. Kwapong, "Citizenship and Democracy in Fourth-Century Cyrene," in L. A. Thompson and J. Ferguson (eds.), Africa in Classical Antiquity (Ibadan: University Press, 1969), pp. 102-3; Chamoux, Cyrène sous la monarchie des Battiades, pp. 138-42.

[3]Carl H. Kraeling, Ptolemais (Chicago: University of Chicago Press, 1962), p. 3.

[4]Boardman, "Evidence for the Dating of Greek Settlements," pp. 152-54. Evidence for these early dates was unearthed in an exceptionally rich votive deposit at Tauchira and published by John Boardman and John Hayes, Excavations at Tocra 1963-1965: The Archaic Deposits I (Oxford: Thames and Hudson), 1966.

to have been founded from the settlement at Cyrene rather than from a later secondary inland settlement at Barka as claimed in the account of Herodotus. However, the early coastal settlements were of uniformly small scale and none of them represented a threat to the stability and success of the Libyan pastoralists. This situation rapidly changed during the reign of Battus II ("The Fortunate" ca. 590-560 B.C.), for free land was offered by the king as an inducement to increased Greek immigration. Spurred by the support of a favorable Delphic oracle, the Greek population, which up to this point had remained relatively small, was increased dramatically by a fresh wave of colonists.[1]

The free land offered to this group of new pioneers was territory held by the native tribes and was essential to the smooth operation of their balanced agricultural-pastoral economy. Settlement began to spread both east and west along the upper and lower terraces from a focus around Cyrene, and much agricultural land was alienated to the sedentary population. Moreover, because the camel had not reached northern Africa, a nomadic society exclusively dependent on sheep and goats, and cut off from access to dependable drought-free agricultural land, would have an increasingly difficult time establishing a modus vivendi in the more marginal districts. Just how far into the interior or how much land was actually occupied by sedentary Greek agriculturalists is, in the absence of detailed archaeological surveys and excavations on small sites in rural areas, open to conjecture. However, field observations in the area east of Cyrene reveal some of the broad outlines of the developing settlement pattern. At least two of the major village sites, Lamlūda and Biyib, that form major foci of classical settlement in Figure 25 show unmistakable signs, by virtue of surface pottery and rock-cut tombs, of having been occupied at an early period. Similar rock-cut tombs near al-Abraq and Tīrt west of the cross-section and at al-Qubba to the east, as well as an inscription from Mgharnis,[2] suggest similar developments along the middle of the upper terrace. Unfortified farmhouses are more difficult to date, since most of them are overgrown by maquis vegetation and surface pottery is difficult to locate. Their construction probably occurred somewhat later than the village centers and represented a gradual filling in of the settlement pattern. Thus, the initial settlement of the colonial wave attracted by Battus II was concentrated in small rural villages that controlled the territory immediately adjacent to their sites but left the interstices free for use by the

---

[1] Herodotus The Histories 4. 159.

[2] Chamoux, Cyrène sous la monarchie des Battiades, p. 221.

pastoral tribes.  The threat of steady encroachment on the part of the settled
population, as much if not more than the actual territory initially occupied by
the Greeks, was resented by the Libyans.

As the settlement network grew, the pastoral tribes gradually were
excluded from access to the jabal and the coastal plain.  The stage was thus set
for an outbreak of hostilities on the part of the pastoral tribes whenever unsettled conditions resulted in a decrease in the strength and effectiveness of sedentary government.  Three such instances are known in the early history of Cyrenaica.  Libyan hostility was first expressed about 568 B.C. shortly after Battus II
encouraged a new wave of settlers.  The native tribes rose in revolt and received
aid from an Egyptian army, only to be decisively defeated by the Cyreneans.[1]
Although momentarily suppressed by Battus II, the antagonisms engendered by
the steady expansion of the settled population and the resulting alienation of the
land from pastoral to agricultural usage seethed beneath the surface awaiting
only an opportunity to burst into the open.  During the reign of Arcesilaus II
(ca. 560-550 B.C.), quarrels within the ruling family caused a number of
Arcesilaus' brothers to establish their own independent town at Barka with the
aid of the Libyan tribes.[2]

Throughout the early era of Greek settlement, the sedentary community
remained vulnerable to attack by the native Libyan tribes whenever internal governmental control broke down.  The collapse of the unifying royal authority about
450 B.C. illustrates the process.  With the removal of the Battiad monarchy a
confused series of civil wars broke out between the various cities as well as
between democratic and aristocratic factions within the cities.[3]  The tribes,

[1]Herodotus The Histories 4. 159; Diodorus Library of History 1. 68.1-5.
The discovery of vandalized Archaic statues and building materials in an ancient
quarry outside Cyrene may date from a nomadic raid in this period, although
destruction associated with the Persian expeditions of 515-514 and 483 B.C. is
more likely.  The material is analyzed by R. G. Goodchild, J. G. Pedley, and
D. White, "Recent Discoveries of Archaic Sculpture at Cyrene:  A Preliminary
Report," LA, III-IV (1966-1967), 179-98.

[2]Herodotus The Histories 4.161, claims that during an attempt to suppress
the Barkan dissidents the army of Arcesilaus II was lured into the interior and
defeated with some 7,000 heavily armed Greeks losing their lives in the process.
The magnitude of the losses on this occasion may well be exaggerated, but they
do indicate the seriousness of the defeat for the Greeks as well as the scale of
potential danger represented by a hostile nomadic community.

[3]Diodorus Library of History 14. 34.4-6.  For a general discussion of
this period as well as a compilation of the major classical sources dealing with
Cyrenaican history consult Arnold H. M. Jones, Cities of the Eastern Roman
Provinces (Oxford:  Clarendon Press, 1937), pp. 351-64; 484-87.

either on their own initiative or as allies of urban factions, intervened in the
fighting. At least one settlement, Euesperides, was so hard-pressed by "barbarian" attacks that its citizens encouraged any and all available Greeks to join
them.[1] Even the influx of a large number of Messenian exiles proved insufficient and only the fortuitous appearance of the troops and ships of Gylippus,
blown off course while sailing to Sicily in 414 B.C., enabled the Euesperitae to
defeat their assailants,[2] possibly in conjunction with troops from Cyrene.[3]

Status of Settlement in 440 B.C.

The location of the settlement frontier and the relative balance achieved
between the sedentary and nomadic populations for the period around 440 B.C.
was sketched by Herodotus and forms the basis of our knowledge of conditions
for the era.[4] The better-watered coastal districts were divided between the two
rival city-states of Barka and Cyrene. The subsidiary coastal centers at Tauchira and Ptolemais were tributary to Barka, Apollonia functioned as the port of
Cyrene and was politically subservient to it, and Euesperides in the far west
preserved a precarious independence from Barka by virtue of its loose alliance
with Cyrene. One can assume that the best and most suitable portions of the
coastal plain as far east as Karsa (but not as far as the mouth of the Wādī Darna)[5]
had been occupied by Greek settlers. A similar situation applied to the western
coastal districts with the exception of the tribal territory of the largely Hellen-
ized Bacales on the coastal plain between Tocra and Euesperides.

The southward extent of Greek territory is more questionable. Gaps
between the village settlements and between isolated farmsteads and villas in the

[1] Pausanias Description of Greece 4. 26.2.

[2] Thucydides History of the Peloponnesian War 7. 99.2.

[3] An inscription published in Supplementum Epigraphicum Graecum, IX, 77,
and quoted by Chamoux, Cyrène sous la monarchie des Battiades, p. 228, indicates that the strategos (general) of Cyrene played an important role in defeating
this nomadic incursion.

[4] Herodotus The Histories 4. 168-78. The same information is presented
in abbreviated form by Diodorus Library of History 3. 49.1, while the major
modern analysis of the Herodotian material is found in Chamoux, Cyrène sous la
monarchie des Battiades, pp. 225-29.

[5] Herodotus The Histories 4. 169, states that Cyrene's territory extended
eastward to the island of Aphrodisias and this island is identified by Chamoux,
Cyrène sous la monarchie des Battiades, p. 225, with the small rocky island off
the coast at Karsa.

interior undoubtedly existed and the archaeological remains visible today imply that settlement in the eastern half of the upper terrace did not extend south of a line connecting al-Qubba, Lamlūda, Tīrt, al-Abraq, and al-Baydā'. As Chamoux pointed out,[1] the curious grouping of rock carvings at Suluṇṭa, which exhibit clear signs of Hellenistic and Roman influence upon an indigenous art form, support the proposition the Greek settlement in the southern part of the upper terrace took place slowly. A system of isolated villages and large estates occupied by a rural aristocracy fits Mitchell's analysis of the political events of the reign of Arcesilaus III,[2] since it explains the power source for the aristocratic opposition to royal authority as well as some of the difficulties in chronology caused by Arcesilaus' extended campaigns to reduce the rural strongholds of his rivals.[3]

The tribal distribution of Herodotus reflects a situation that remained fairly stable into the Roman era. Both the Marmaridae (the Giligamae of Herodotus) and the Nasamones remained largely unacculturated and the names of these powerful tribal groupings became standardized designations for nomads of the interior. Inland from Cyrene and Barka were the Asbystae and the Auschisae. In both cases a large proportion of their prime summer grazing was lost to permanent sedentary agriculture, but enough agricultural land on the southern fringes of the upper terrace as well as sufficient water supplies along the southern spring line remained unexploited by the Greek colonists to permit a reasonably adequate, although admittedly more marginal, nomadic regime. Strabo's reference to the Cyreneans' ability to defend themselves against the barbarians who lived "above" them[4] carries both a directional significance, i.e., that the native tribes lived south of the centers of Greek colonization, and the implication that the nomads had not been pushed as yet off the highest levels of the upper terrace that lie south of Balagrae (al-Baydā') and Limnias (Lamlūda). More-

---

[1]Chamoux, Cyrène sous la monarchie des Battiades, p. 225. The unusual shape of some of the animal figures has led to speculation on the part of G. S. C. Hyslop and S. Applebaum, Cyrene and Ancient Cyrenaica (Tripoli: Government Press, 1945), p. 54, that the figures represent a sacred pig cult, thus following a comment by Herodotus that the Libyan woman of Barka refused to eat pork.

[2]B. M. Mitchell, "Cyrene and Persia," Journal of Hellenic Studies, LXXXVI (1966), 99-113.

[3]I. Noshy, "Arkesilaus III" (unpublished MS from the Libya in History conference; Banghāzī: University of Libya, 1968), pp. 14-20.

[4]Strabo Geography 17. 3. 21.

over, the nomadic tribes were held in check by their lack of military superiority over the settled population. The use of chariots by the citizens of Barka and Cyrene to follow raiders quickly and bring heavily-armed, fully-rested soldiers into battle was one of the salient characteristics of the sedentary Cyrenaican military forces.[1] The use of the chariot in Cyrenaica long after it had gone out of favor in other parts of the Mediterranean world attests to its effectiveness in meeting the nomadic threat.

## Ptolemaic Cyrenaica

Little is known from literary sources about Cyrenaica's history from 322 to 96 B.C. when it was ruled by the Ptolemaic kings of Egypt,[2] and even less information exists on nomad-sedentary contacts. Although considerable political turmoil resulted from Thibron's attempt to erect an independent kingdom in Cyrenaica[3] after the death of Alexander the Great and from various revolts during the early years of Ptolemaic control,[4] eventually Cyrenaica settled down to the status of a relatively prosperous backwater whose economic and political fortunes closely paralleled those of Egypt.[5]

There was only a limited expansion of the settled population and no really new cities were founded during the period. To be sure, Ptolemais, formerly the port of Barka, was given independent status, an ambitious city plan, and a wall, and became the headquarters of Ptolemaic control in Cyrenaica,[6] but this reflects an intensification of settlement at one point rather than an expansion into virgin territory. Indeed, there are suggestions that the inland town of Barka declined in importance, since later enumerations of the five towns of the Pentapolis fail to mention it. Apollonia was raised to separate status during consti-

---

[1] Aeneas Tacticus On the Defense of Fortified Positions 16. 14-15. For the full range of references to Cyrenaican chariots in the classical literature, see J. K. Anderson, "Homeric, British and Cyrenaic Chariots," AJA, LXIX (1965), 349-52.

[2] The scanty literary evidence is discussed by Jean Machu, "Cyrène: La cité et la souverain à l'époque hellénistique," Revue Historique, CCV (1951), 41-55, who concludes that between the independent spirit of the local Greek population and the ambitions of their governors Ptolemaic control was always somewhat precarious.

[3] Diodorus Library of History 17. 19.1-21.7.

[4] Ibid. 19. 79.1-4; 20. 41-42.　　　　[5] Kraeling, Ptolemais, pp. 7-8.

[6] Ibid., pp. 7-10.

tutional reforms in Cyrene about this time, [1] but this reflects a political development that merely recognized an accomplished physical fact. The location of Euesperides was shifted from the edge of a shallow inland lagoon to a more secure peninsula setting (beneath the site of modern Banghāzī) adjacent to a good harbor [2] and its name was changed to Berenice in honor of the wife of Ptolemy III Euergetes. [3] Similarly, Taucheira was renamed Arsinoe after another of the ruling family's females, [4] but the settlement remained unchanged despite the concession to dynastic egotism.

The main points of settlement during the period of Ptolemaic control continued to follow the earlier Archaic pattern of location along the coast, but it is unlikely that the decreased importance of Barka at the western end of the lower terrace reflects a decline in security for the rural population. The issue is complicated by the fact that the city walls at Cyrene, [5] Apollonia, [6] and Ptolemais [7] all date from the era of Ptolemaic control. But this coincidence in the periodicity of fortification does not demonstrate an increased security problem. It could reflect an attempt to regularize the urban situation by equipping the main urban centers with an essential characteristic of all cities. A similar

---

[1] Strabo Geography 17. 3. 20 mentions Apollonia as Cyrene's naval station, describes it as being a large city, and implies that it is independent politically at this period. For a discussion of the implications of this remark see Jones, Cities of the Eastern Roman Provinces, pp. 359-60.

[2] Richard G. Goodchild, "Euesperides: A Devastated City Site," Antiquity, XXVI (1952), 208-12, suggests that drying of the salt lagoon prompted the shift. Coins found by R. C. Bond and J. M. Swales, "Surface Finds of Coins from the City of Euesperides," LA, II (1965), 91-101, cannot be dated later than 258 B.C. which strongly suggests that the shift to the more coastal location took place before Berenice married Ptolemy III in 247 B.C. For a summary of the history of classical settlement at Banghazi, consult Richard G. Goodchild, Benghazi (Euesperides - Berenice - Marsa Ibn Ghazi) (2nd ed.; Cyrene [Shahat]: Department of Antiquities, 1962).

[3] Pliny Natural History 5. 5.          [4] Ibid.

[5] Alan Rowe et al., Cyrenaican Expedition of the University of Manchester, 1952 (Manchester: University Press, 1956), p. 29. Even in the acropolis area where one would expect to find fortifications of pre-Hellenistic date Goodchild, Cyrene and Apollonia, p. 52, failed to observe any earlier survivals.

[6] The wall at Apollonia can be dated more precisely to the last quarter of the fourth century B.C. or the early years of the third century. John G. Pedley, "Apollonia Excavations, 1966," Archaeology, XX (1967), 219-20, and Donald White, "Excavations at Apollonia, Cyrenaica: Preliminary Report," AJA, LXX (1966), 264.

[7] Kraeling, Ptolemais, p. 60.

argument explains the stationing of mercenary troops in Cyrenaica. While the evidence demonstrates the presence of two units of Nubian mercenaries at Ptolemais[1] and the introduction of Jewish military settlers into Cyrene and other cities in Cyrenaica,[2] there is no sign that this was necessary to reconcile the Greeks to Ptolemaic overlordship or to protect the Greek settlements from nomadic incursions. The reverse process of using Libyan Berbers in large numbers in the Egyptian Ptolemaic armies during Ptolemy IV Philopator's wars with the Seleucid monarchy also was practiced.[3] Since a number of the Cyrenaican recruits were used in the cavalry, they were probably recruited from the nomadic tribes. Libyans were also introduced to Greek infantry tactics at this time, for some 3,000 of them were armed like Macedonians and conscripted into the phalanx; significantly their leader was a Greek from Barka, the Cyrenaican town that traditionally had the closest ties to the native Libyan tribes. Tactical training of this kind could serve to improve the nomadic military potential in any future conflict with the settled population.

Although the land area devoted to agriculture did not expand dramatically during the Ptolemaic period and while the settlement of Jewish mercenaries and the construction of city walls indicates an increased concern for the security of the settled areas, the commercial and agricultural prosperity of the country remained at a high level. Despite the variability of the rainfall regime, the better-watered upper terrace produced reliable yields of grain and, at least in famine years elsewhere in the Greek world, surpluses were available for export. From 330 to 326 B.C. some 805,000 medimni[4] of grain were sent to famine-stricken areas in Greece.[5] Because this is one of the few available epigraphic references relating to yields and export totals for Cyrenaican grain, it is diffi-

---

[1] Rowe, A History of Ancient Cyrenaica, pp. 64-67.

[2] Josephus Against Apion 2. 44. Epigraphic evidence for the presence of Jews in the cities of Tokra, Barka and Cyrene is presented by Rowe et al., Cyrenaican Expedition, 1952, pp. 44-59, but a precise dating of their arrival, other than Josephus' statement that they were introduced by the Ptolemaic kings, is not available.

[3] Polybius The Histories 5. 65.5-8.

[4] The medimnus was a Greek dry measure equivalent to 52.53 litres or 1 1/2 bushels. Harry T. Peck, ed., Harper's Dictionary of Classical Literature and Antiquities (1962), p. 1023.

[5] S. Ferri, Alcune iscrizioni di Cirene, no. 3, quoted by W. W. Tarn, "Greece: 335 to 321 B.C.," Cambridge Ancient History (New York: Macmillan; Cambridge: University Press, 1927), VI, 448.

cult to generalize about the state of agricultural prosperity during the period. But given the generalized line of settlement advance in Figure 23, a surplus of this magnitude is consistent with the known extent of subsistence agricultural settlement during the period, provided that a series of climatically favorable years locally coincided with deficit conditions elsewhere in the Greek world.

Only two instances of hostility between the settled population and the nomads are recorded. Significantly, both incidents occurred at times when the stability of the local government degenerated. Cyrenaica's rulers were usually younger sons or brothers of the reigning member of the Ptolemaic dynasty in Egypt, and they occasionally indulged in attempts to usurp the royal authority using the political and military base represented by the Pentapolis. Two such abortive attempts are known and both were thwarted by a revolt of the Libyan tribes. The first such instance occurred in 274 B.C.[1] when Magas, the half-brother of Ptolemy II Philadelphus, launched an invasion of Egypt. His army successfully advanced along the coast into Egypt but was brought to a halt by a revolt of the Marmaridae in his rear before a conclusive engagement could be fought with forces loyal to the monarch. The second revolt arose out of the quarrels of Ptolemy VI Philometer, ruling in Egypt, and Ptolemy VII Euergetes II, controlling Cyrenaica, over the distribution of the dynastic inheritance.[2] Euergetes got his troops as far as the Egyptian frontier when a combined insurrection of the inhabitants of Cyrene and their Libyan allies forced him to abandon the project.

Two related points deserve emphasis in this context. The paucity of references to Cyrenaica in the literature and in particular to any numerous hostile contacts between nomads and sedentary Greek society supports the generalization that the post-Battiad Ptolemaic period was characterized by relative stability between the two groups. The best agricultural land was in the hands of the farming population, but not enough had been alienated to encourage hostile reactions on the part of the nomads. Similarly, Greek settlement was concentrated in a relatively limited area in the northern coastal districts and as such represented no immediate threat to the nomad. In the absence of a systematic campaign of agricultural expansion, the nomadic tribes were left to themselves and only appear as an effective intervening force in the settled community when its internal political arrangements deteriorate into chaos.

---

[1] Pausanias Description of Greece 1. 7.1-2.

[2] Polybius The Histories 31. 18.

CHAPTER V

CYRENAICA UNDER ROMAN AND BYZANTINE

ADMINISTRATION (96 B.C.-A.D. 643)

Although Cyrenaica was rather isolated throughout most of the Ptolemaic
era, its position relative to the rest of the Mediterranean world changed significantly as the millennium drew to a close. The drive of Roman military and
political power to dominate the Mediterranean did not ignore the Cyrenaican
Pentapolis. Gradually the region was incorporated into the Roman political
system and its subsequent history became tied inextricably to Empire-wide
developments. While the establishment of Roman control initially was accompanied by considerable chaos and uncertainty, subsequent reorganization during
the Empire re-established governmental authority and parallel trends throughout North Africa witnessed a massive expansion of agricultural settlement. Evidenced by an increased agricultural population, the settlement of military veterans, improved roads, the surviving ruins of farmhouses and villages, and the
construction of a coordinated defensive system, sedentary agriculturalists expanded into the interior. An expanding agricultural frontier and the nomadic
reaction to it forms the focus of this chapter.

Republican Chaos

Ptolemaic control of Cyrenaica ended in 96 B.C. when Ptolemy Apion,
the last ruler of an independent Cyrenaica, died and left the Pentapolis in his
will to the Roman people.[1] Reluctant to accept responsibility for the region, the
Senate assumed control only of the former royal lands and declared the cities to
be free.[2] The hesitation of the Senate to establish direct Roman authority over
the region resulted in a steady drift into economic decline and political chaos as
inter- and intra-city strife crippled effective local government.[3] The same con-

---

[1]Appianus History 17. 121.      [2]Titus Livius Summaries 70.

[3]The detailed account of Stewart I. Oost, "Cyrene, 96-74 B.C.," Classical Philology, LVIII (1963), 11-25, summarizes the meager available evidence
for the transition from local dynastic to Roman rule.

flicts, pitting democracies supported by the masses against tyrannies based on oligarchic factions of the aristocracy, that had characterized the end of Battiad rule followed the termination of Ptolemaic control.

On at least one occasion nomadic tribesmen interfered in Cyrene's domestic squabbles. This occurred when Aretaphila, a representative of the aristocracy who had been forced into marriage with a hated tyrant, arranged for his assassination. When his successor proved to be equally undesirable, she negotiated with a powerful tribal chief to intervene in the domestic urban crisis, seize the offending tyrant, and deliver him to his enemies. [1] Although further involvement of the tribes in the politics of the sedentary community is not recorded, this incident personifies the threat posed by the nomads whenever the balance of political power shifted substantially.

The disruptive effects of this period were still evident when Lucullus arrived at Cyrene in 87-86 B.C. while searching for naval support for Sulla. [2] The reforms that he instituted failed to improve the situation substantially. Local prosperity continued to decline, [3] piracy and raiding reached a level approaching open warfare, and a virtual reconquest of the province had to be undertaken by Cn. Cornelius Lentulus Marcellinus, a lieutenant of Pompey, in 67 B.C. [4] This pacification also failed to achieve complete success, and relations with the Marmarican tribes degenerated into open warfare. [5] This war began sometime before 15 B.C. and continued for an extended period, an entire series of campaigns under the direction of P. Sulpicius Quirinius being required before security was attained. It was not until A.D. 2 that peace and stability was once again fully restored. [6]

---

[1] Plutarchus Moralia 255-57.  [2] Plutarchus Lucullus 2. 3-4.

[3] Mikhail I. Rostovtzeff, The Social and Economic History of the Roman Empire (2nd ed.; Oxford: Clarendon Press, 1926), I, 308, and Kraeling, Ptolemais, p. 11.

[4] Joyce Reynolds, "Cyrenaica, Pompey, and Cn. Cornelius Lentulus Marcellinus," JRS, LII (1962), 97-103.

[5] An inscription found in Cyrene and published in Doc. Afr. Ital. Ciren., II, 1, no. 67, pp. 100-101, as quoted by Pietro Romanelli, La Cirenaica romana (96 a.C. - 642 d.C.) (Verbania: A. Airoldi, 1943), p. 77, celebrates the Roman triumph in this protracted war. See also Pietro Romanelli, "The Province of Crete and Cyrenaica," Cambridge Ancient History (New York: Macmillan; Cambridge: University Press, 1936), XI, 659-75, for events following the establishment of a Senatorial province in 74 B.C.

[6] The precise dates for the Marmarican wars of P. Sulpicius Quirinius are uncertain. The dating followed here is that suggested by Richard G. Goodchild,

It would be a mistake to regard the situation of the pastoral tribes as being desperate at this time. For although conflict between nomads and farmers was periodically violent during the Greek period and although it required substantial military effort to restore Roman control over the interior, the survival of the pastoral way of life was not basically in doubt. Access to the water and grazing resources of the jabal was still possible in A.D. 2. Rural settlement was sparse in the gaps between the major cities and along the southern dip-slope; sufficient open space was still available for pastoral use. Just how much land potentially was available for agriculture but unused is unknown since adequate dating is unavailable for the length of occupation in the smaller rural towns and villages, most of which are unexcavated in the archaeologist's concentration on the principal urban centers. However, it is clear that most of the agricultural population at the beginning of the Imperial period was distributed on the coastal plain, the north slopes of the jabal, and along the crest of the upper terrace in a pattern analogous to that of the Ptolemaic period. As yet sedentary agriculture had not pushed down the south slopes of the jabal into the subhumid and semi-arid steppe.

The nomad and farmer would not be in direct competition. The onset of the winter rains would find the nomad pushing out into the steppe with his herds using pasture that could not be converted to agriculture. This same move would remove the herds from areas being sown with grain and thus eliminate any temptation for the nomad to graze his flocks on the fields of germinating barley and wheat. Also the nomads would return to the jabal after the harvest and so would pose no threat to the continuity of agricultural life. The sedentary farmers, on the other hand, would not be able to pasture enough animals near their farms to threaten the nomad's summer water supply, since the expansion of a farmer's herd would be limited by his inability to move them over considerable distances to seasonal grazing. Only in times of severe drought would the nomad fail to migrate from the upper terrace in the winter and thus it was only in exceptional circumstances that the two groups were in close and competitive proximity throughout the year. As long as settlement did not spread across the upper terrace and down the south slopes of the jabal a certain degree of tenuous stability can be assumed, fractured only when unsettled conditions in the sedentary community seemed to offer attractive opportunities to supplement the nomadic economy with booty taken in raids.

---

Tabula Imperii Romani: Cyrene (Sheet H.I. 34; 1:1,000,000; Oxford: Society of Antiquaries of London, 1954), p. 9.

Imperial Period:  The Expansion of Agriculture

That the end of the Marmarican War found Cyrenaica in an impoverished condition seems clear from the low property requirements for jury duty stipulated in the Cyrene Edicts of Augustus dating from 7-6 B. C.[1] It is equally certain that the restoration of peace throughout the Mediterranean during the reign of Augustus did much to change this situation as a result of efforts to increase security, settle Latin-speaking veterans, and reorganize the financial and administrative system.

Settlement of Military Veterans

Considerable Imperial attention was focused on the province and, although the Greek character of the population persisted[2] and the development of strictly Roman architectural styles in both public and private construction proceeded slowly,[3] settlers with Latin names, possibly retired army veterans, begin to appear in the epigraphical material.[4] The actions and attitudes of many of these Roman settlers aroused the hostility of the indigenous Greek population and the Augustan edicts regulating the status of the two groups was the result.[5] Regular army troops also begin to appear with greater frequency in Cyrenaica during the

---

[1]Naphtali Lewis and Reinhold Meyer, Roman Civilization (New York: Columbia University Press, 1955), II, 37-38.  J. G. C. Anderson, "Augustan Edicts from Cyrene," JRS, XVII (1927), 33-48, briefly discusses the constitutional and judicial implications of the edicts.

[2]The admission of Cyrene to the wider Greek community through the influence of Hadrian despite the mixed blood of the population and the influx of Latin settlers after A. D. 117 is a case in point.  J. A. O. Larsen, "Cyrene and the Panhellenion," Classical Philology, XLVII (1952), 7-16.

[3]Evidence for the gradual appearance of non-Greek architectural forms in the major Cyrenaican cities is summarized by Sandro Stucchi, "First Outline for a History of Cyrenaican Architecture during the Roman Period" (unpublished MS from the Libya in History conference; Banghāzī:  University of Libya, 1968), pp. 1-11.

[4]Kraeling, Ptolemais, p. 12.  Inscriptions relating to the Imperial cult, with prayers in Latin, have been noted at both Cyrene and Ptolemais by Joyce M. Reynolds, "Vota pro Salute Principis," PBSR, XXX (1962), 33-36, and idem, "Notes on Cyrenaican Inscriptions," PBSR, XXXIII (1965), 52-54.

[5]That the Romans were not the only offenders and that the local Greeks were not above trying to escape their obligations by claiming a special tax-exempt status has been demonstrated by James H. Oliver, "On Edict III from Cyrene," Hesperia, XXIX (1960), 324-25.

first and second centuries A. D.[1] The presence of Syrian troops, probably cavalry, at Corniclanum (Ajdābiya) as early as A. D. 15[2] and units of legio III Cyrenaica elsewhere, both formations veterans of the Marmarican War,[3] served to stabilize the frontier and provide the security necessary for an expansion of agriculture. A concern for the financial arrangements of Cyrenaica as well as a desire to regularize agricultural settlement and land ownership resulted in a land survey of the royal estates instituted by Claudius and undertaken by Acilius Strabo around A. D. 55.[4] A similar instance of the regularization and division of the city lands of Apollonia by Vespasian about A. D. 74 recently has come to light[5] and reflects the long-term Imperial interest in and advancement of agricultural settlement as well as a desire to protect and augment governmental revenues.

Road Improvements

In conjunction with an expansion of the agricultural population, considerable care was devoted to improving and developing the major roads in northern Cyrenaica. Two types of roads existed in the Imperial period, those of official status, marked by milestones, and the smaller connecting links that serviced the agricultural population but lacked any administrative standing. Unlike the well-developed road network of the Roman provinces of Africa and Numidia,[6] Cyrenaica had only one road that appeared on the "official" route book of the empire.[7] This road forms part of the east-west highway along the North African

---

[1] The sketchy evidence for some of these units is summarized by E. Ritterling, "Military Forces in the Senatorial Provinces," JRS, XVII (1927), 28-29, many of them having served in the suppression of the Jewish revolt of A. D. 115-117.

[2] Richard G. Goodchild, "'Libyan' Forts in South-west Cyrenaica," Antiquity, XXV (1951), 140, and idem, "The Roman and Byzantine Limes in Cyrenaica," JRS, XLIII (1953), 67.

[3] Kraeling, Ptolemais, p. 16.     [4] Tacitus Annals 14. 18.

[5] Joyce M. Reynolds and Richard G. Goodchild, "The City Lands of Apollonia in Cyrenaica," LA, II (1965), 103-7.

[6] See Pierre Salama's study of Les voies romaines de l'Afrique du Nord (Alger: Gouvernement Général de l'Algérie, 1951) which uses the Peutinger Map of the third century A. D. to demonstrate the close correspondence between the Roman road system at the height of its development and the contemporary highway network.

[7] Konrad Miller, Die Peutingersche Tafel (Stuttgart: F. A. Brockhaus, 1962), Seg. VIII.

coast. In the Cyrenaican jabal it follows very closely the roadbed of the earlier Greek highway. Whereas Roman engineers usually pushed their roads through on straight lines overwhelming natural obstacles in the process, the Greek practice was to follow the natural contours and only in special circumstances was grading of the roadbed by filling or rock cutting employed. This is demonstrated by the main east-west highway in the upper terrace whose twists and turns were incorporated into the Roman route (Figure 24).

Cyrene was the center of the communications network for the eastern jabal and mileage figures for the official roads were measured from the city's central intersection. Only a few milestones have been found along the main routes radiating from Cyrene and these have been located north and west of the city; none has been found along the main routes running eastward across the study cross-section. The earliest milestones date from the reign of Claudius (ca. A.D. 45-46) and subsequent restorations from the reign of Trajan (ca. A.D. 100) using local legionary recruits and by Hadrian following the destruction caused by the Jewish revolt have also been discovered.[1] Recent construction activities at al-Baydā'(Balagrae) unearthed a number of mile markers, including one of Philip the Arab (A.D. 244-246);[2] all of the stones so far known date from the first, third, and early fourth centuries and are concentrated along the Cyrene-Apollonia and Cyrene-Balagrae routes. This is a major departure from conditions in Tripolitania where all of the known milestones date from the third century and represent the propaganda rather than the road-building efforts of Caracalla and his successors.[3] Although two milestones have been located beyond Apollonia,[4] the difficulties involved in bridging the numerous deep coastal wadis and the complete absence of other surviving remains make it unlikely that a coastal link from Apollonia to Darnis (Darna) existed.

---

[1] Richard G. Goodchild, "Roman Milestones in Cyrenaica," PBSR, XVIII (1950), 85-89.

[2] Richard G. Goodchild, "The Roman Roads of Libya and their Milestones" (unpublished MS from the Libya in History conference; Banghāzī: University of Libya, 1968), p. 16.

[3] Richard G. Goodchild, The Roman Roads and Milestones of Tripolitania (Discoveries and Researches in 1947) ([Tripoli]: Department of Antiquities, British Military Administration, Tripolitania, 1948), and idem, "Roman Roads of Libya," p. 6.

[4] Both of these date from the early fourth century. Goodchild, "Roman Milestones in Cyrenaica," p. 90.

Instead, the main routes of communication to the east of Cyrene ran through the upper terrace. Despite the absence of mile markers, the highway running from Cyrene to Darnis via Limnias (Lamlūda) can be followed on the ground for substantial distances. Long use has resulted in depression of the old roadbed below the surface of the surrounding farming areas and shallow cuttings through rock outcrops have enhanced the process. So too has the practice of installing curbing along the roadbed near the major towns, although no evidence to suggest a paved road surface outside the largest urban centers has come to light. Also a prominent feature of the roadsides, both near large cities such as Cyrene and on the outskirts of rural villages, are numerous tombs and sarcophagi. A form of conspicuous consumption sited to impress the passing traveler, they serve to facilitate the identification of the road's location. These features form the basic identifying marks of highway location except in areas where the wheels of Greek and Roman vehicles have cut into rock outcrops and left definite and conspicuous wheel ruts when exposed by erosion. Ruts of this kind are the primary indication of the side roads of the region for these lack the tombs, curbings, and depressed roadbeds of the major highways.

Although the upper terrace highway through Limnias carried the largest share of the daily agricultural traffic of eastern Cyrenaica, there is some doubt that it was the main Imperial route to Egypt. The Peutinger Map[1] indicates a course that bypasses Darnis, running from Agabis to Mandis and Paliuros. Goodchild identified Agabis with contemporary Qayqab and Paliuros with modern Tamīmī[2] but finds no clear signs of the actual course east of Agabis.[3] Goodchild correlated Qaṣr Karmusa on the modern Martūba-Qayqab road with Mandis,[4] but this correlation is based on the fact that it is the largest Greco-Roman ruin in the area rather than on the discovery of an inscription or other more conclusive proof. Goodchild's Gasr Carmusa is undoubtedly the contemporary Qubūr 'Īt aṭ-Ṭīra,[5] since it contains a sprawling assemblage of unfortified farm build-

---

[1] Miller, Die Peutingersche Tafel, VIII, 5.

[2] Richard G. Goodchild, "Graeco-Roman Cyrenaica," in F. T. Barr (ed.), Geology and Archaeology of Northern Cyrenaica, Libya (Tripoli: Petroleum Exploration Society of Libya, 1968), p. 31.

[3] Goodchild, Tabula Imperii Romani: Cyrene, map facing p. 16.

[4] Richard G. Goodchild, "Mapping Roman Libya," Geographical Journal, CXVIII (1952), 151.

[5] Goodchild's designation follows the place names used by Italian cartogra-

ings, now largely reworked into corrals, as well as two unusually large, somewhat crude, Greco-Roman mausolea. These are described as qūsūr (forts;
sing. qasr) by the local tribesmen but the designation is in error since no fortified structures are today observable in the area.

A cut-off from the Cyrene-Limnias-Darnis route is visible in the form of
a shallow depression running southeast from Ṣafṣaf, while a rutted junction
slightly further east at al-Abraq just southwest of the modern al-Abraq - Qayqab
road intersection with the main highway is exposed by surface erosion. Either
of these could be the departure point for the route to Paliuros, although Goodchild favors the former.[1] Beyond Agabis the roadbed is not as yet precisely
located. Its course probably was roughly analogous to that of the Martūba by-
pass (particularly if Mandis is assumed to be Qubūr 'Īt aṭ-Ṭīra) constructed
before and during World War II to avoid the sinuous climb up and down the lower
scarp at Darna and to circle south of the headwaters of the Wādī Darna. However, it is likely that this inland route will continue to defy discovery because it
may well have lacked the kind of formalized structure attained by the main upper
terrace route. Certainly no milestones have been found along it[2] and it is quite
possible that, rather than having the character of a great highway traveled by
heavily laden carts and chariots, it was instead a narrow footpath frequented by
caravans composed of beasts of burden. Such a route would be difficult to discover and the traces that it would leave would be no more definite than those
resulting from present-day goat paths.

If major highways are limited in number, the same cannot be said for the
non-official rural routes of eastern Cyrenaica. Whereas the official highways
run east-west, the unofficial roads exhibit a distinct north-south pattern. Un-
marked by milestones or by any form of paving or curbing, they are identified
by the numerous wheel ruts exposed along their course wherever erosion has
stripped off the surface soil. Several of these routes appear on the cross-section

---

phers. A Gasr el-Garmusa appears on United States, Army Map Service, Derna
(1:250,000; Sheet NI 34-16; Washington, D.C.: Army Map Service, 1955) which
is compiled from earlier Italian work. However, the detailed map of the area,
drawn from aerial photography and subjected to extensive field checking (Matār
Darnah [1:50,000; Sheet 3890 III; Washington, D.C.: Army Map Service, 1964]),
omits all reference to Gasr Karmusa. Despite a certain amount of resulting confusion, a correspondence in general location suggests that the two sites are in
fact the same.

[1] Goodchild, Tabula Imperii Romani: Cyrene, map facing p. 16.

[2] Goodchild, "The Roman Roads of Libya," p. 10.

(Figure 24) and additional examples can be found both to the east and west.

One such road runs east-west from the ruined village site at Biyib until it joins a north-south track that can be followed as it twists back and forth across the modern roadbed as far as Qaṣr ar-Raqayyiq at the foot of the second scarp. Although no wheel ruts can be traced beyond the upper scarp, Goodchild's belief that the road continued to the main highway at Limnias undoubtedly is correct. Another rutted track can be traced for roughly half the distance from Qaṣr Madīna to Qaṣr Raqayyiq and its continuation to the north-south track at that point can be assumed. Since the wadi bed at Qaṣr ar-Raqayyiq is the most gentle in the immediate area, it forms the most likely point at which to ascend the second scarp and probably was the main junction for tracks servicing the lower terrace to the west as well. The north-south orientation of streams draining into the Mediterranean and their deep incision into the lower terrace favors a similar pattern in the feeder roads and explains why the main routes of east-west communication were, and still are, concentrated in the upper terrace. Although no signs of communication by developed road could be discovered between the lower terrace and the Ra's al-Hilāl area, movement between the two zones could be maintained by pack animals if not by wheeled carts. This is particularly true of the Wādī Jirliblis where a footpath gives access today to the coastal plain.

Finally, wheel-rutted roads similar to those of the lower and upper terraces can be found in the dip-slope areas between Qayqab and Khūlān. In the Wādī al-Muʻaliq along one of the tracks leading to Khūlān from the northwest wheel ruts appear at several points and their depth and number indicate that the volume of traffic must have been substantial and that the route must have continued in use for a lengthy period. Roads in this area are more recent than those further north in the upper terrace and the presence of occasional lids from Roman period sarcophagi, coupled with the absence of Hellenistic tomb styles, indicate that during the Imperial period agricultural expansion and its associated wheeled vehicles began to push into the pre-desert zones.

The attention devoted by the Roman Emperors to the major highways supports the contention that agricultural expansion and increased governmental attempts to dominate the more marginal areas were characteristic of the first and second centuries A.D. The revolt in A.D. 85-86 of the Nasamones tribe, whose homeland was in the arid steppe environments of the Gulf of Sirt, was, in

---

[1]Goodchild, Tabula Imperii Romani: Cyrene, map facing p. 16.

the opinion of Dio, directly related to Roman attempts to extract monetary contributions from the tribe.[1] Their ultimate defeat and near, if not total, annihila-
tion by Cn. Suellius Flaccus, the governor of Numidia, when coupled with the
complete suppression of the Marmaridae during the reign of Augustus, established the peaceful conditions and state of sedentary military superiority over
the nomads that was an essential precondition for successful agricultural expansion into the pre-desert zones. This expansion probably also explains why silphium became extinct, since overgrazing in the steppe regions in which it grew,[2]
alienation of land to agriculture,[3] and overextraction[4] eliminated the wild species by the time Nero became emperor.[5] Eventually agricultural expansion
resulted in an organized system of frontier defenses designed to protect the settled population from nomadic attack.

## The Cyrenaican Limes

The steady advance of agricultural settlement involved both a filling up of
the plateau area and an expansion toward the steppe margin. This agricultural
development took place throughout North Africa, where Imperial policy favored
the expansion into pastoral areas in order to reduce the military threat posed by
nomadic tribes and to develop all potentially arable land.

Unlike many of the limes zones in Europe or North Africa, where fortified walls or interconnected zones of forts, walls, and signal stations often were
constructed,[6] Cyrenaica offered few natural barriers along which continuous

---

[1] Cassius Dio Cocceianus History 67. 6.

[2] Pliny Natural History 19. 15.

[3] Rostovtseff, Social and Economic History of the Roman Empire, I, 309.

[4] Chamoux, Cyrène sous la monarchie des Battiades, p. 263.

[5] However, silphium continued to be cultivated on a small scale in the gardens of the sedentary community until at least A.D. 400 where it is mentioned
by Synesius, The Letters of Synesius of Cyrene (trans. by Augustine Fitzgerald;
Oxford: University Press, 1926), p. 106. For a brief discussion of silphium
see above, n. 4, p. 93.

[6] The literature relating to Roman frontier organization is vast and, because its review is beyond the scope of the present work, a few examples must
suffice. For an overview of the complex system defending the Rhine-Danube
frontier see H. Schönberger, "The Roman Frontier in Germany: An Archaeological Survey," JRS, LIX (1969), 144-97. Research on Rome's Scottish frontier
is summarized by K. A. Steer, "The Antonine Wall, 1934-1959," JRS, L (1960),

fortifications could be developed. Instead, a system of defense-in-depth was organized analogous to the limes of Tripolitania[1] and eastern Syria.[2]

Two basic zones constituted the defensive system of the Pentapolis.[3] An inner zone of forts, located in the middle of the zone of densest agricultural settlement, ran along the main road that maintained communications between Ptolemais, Cyrene, and Darnis (Figure 25). A particularly intense concentration of defensive structures in and around the Wādī al-Kūf protected the central portion of the upper terrace west of Cyrene. Here the danger of nomadic penetration into the heart of the farming area, utilizing the wadi's broken terrain, was the greatest.[4] Most of these forts probably were defended not by regular troops, for the garrison of Cyrenaica was small, but by the farmers and local militia of the immediate area.

South of the inner zone additional forts were built near the 500-meter contour at the outer limits of agricultural expansion.[5] Forts in this southern tier were located to control access to the plateau along the beds of seasonal streams draining al-Jabal al-Akhdar. One such fort is Qaṣr Wartīsh (Figures 3 and 25) whose commanding local setting gives it a wide view over the surround-

---

84-93. The situation in North Africa was somewhat different for, as A. N. Sherwin-White, "Geographical Factors in Roman Algeria," JRS, XXXIV (1944), 5, has pointed out, mountainous areas were often bypassed by Roman agricultural settlement. Thus, islands of quasi-hostile territory, ringed by military posts, frequently were contained within the settled zones. Jean L. Baradez, Vue-aérienne de l'organisation romaine dans le sud-algérien: Fossatum Africae (Paris: Arts et métiers graphiques, 1949), has examined air photos of fortified frontier defenses and his work indicates that construction of wall systems was limited to areas most vulnerable to nomadic penetration.

[1] Richard G. Goodchild, "Roman Tripolitania: Reconnaissance in the Desert Frontier Zone," Geographical Journal, CXV (1950), 161-71.

[2] H. C. Butler, "Desert Syria, the Land of a Lost Civilization," Geographical Review, IX (1920), 77-108, is a good review of the ruins scattered throughout the Syrian steppe, while a systematic investigation of the region using aerial photography has been undertaken by A. Poidebard, La trace de Rome dans le désert de Syrie (Paris: Paul Geuthner, 1934), and by R. Mouterde and A. Poidebard, Le limes de Chalcis (Paris: Paul Geuthner, 1945).

[3] Pietro Romanelli, Il limes romano in Africa (Rome: Istituto di studi romani, 1939), p. 6.

[4] Goodchild, "Roman and Byzantine Limes," pp. 67-72.

[5] Goodchild, "Roman and Byzantine Limes," pp. 68-70; idem, Tabula Imperii Romani: Cyrene, pp. 15-16.

ing countryside. Goodchild believed that some of the forts in this outer region may have been begun by the Greeks, but in the case of Qaṣr Wartīsh such an attribution is doubtful. No Greek period pottery is observable on the site and its sloping exterior walls, with some of their surface plaster still intact, are Byzantine additions to an earlier, probably Roman, core. The defensive arrangements, which would force any attacker gaining access to the ditch to make a circuit of the fort before approaching the main entrance, are reminiscent of Goodchild's Gasr el-Heneia[1] near Ajdābiya, although by no means as elaborate. The absence of indications of Greco-Roman cultivation, despite the fact that the bedouin of the area are able to plant small crops of barley, and the large number of cisterns near the fort support the inference that Qaṣr Wartīsh was never important as an agricultural center but instead fulfilled primarily military functions on the extreme southern edge of the cultivated zone, although some animal herding as a supplemental activity may have been undertaken.

Additional posts at favorite nomadic watering points in the interior were sited to maintain surveillance of the pastoral population. One such post is known to have existed at Masūs in western Cyrenaica[2] and another is presumed at al-Makīlī where Islamic ruins are abundant but Roman surface remains are not so immediately obvious.[3] al-ʿIzzīyat, a Sanūsī zāwiya some twenty kilometers east of al-Makīlī, has a similar complex of Islamic ruins that predate the foundation of the zāwiya and its numerous cisterns, general location, and surviving remnants of arched vaulting suggest that it too may have been a small advanced post. The practice of placing forts beyond the settled zone in order to control both the local nomadic population and to protect the caravan traffic is well known from Tripolitania[4] and probably was duplicated in Cyrenaica also.

---

[1] Goodchild, "'Libyan' Forts in South-west Cyrenaica," p. 134.

[2] Goodchild, "Roman and Byzantine Limes," p. 68.

[3] Ibid., p. 72. Goodchild regards al-Bakrī's description of the Wādī Makhīl as being al-Makīlī beyond any reasonable doubt. However, doubt is justified, since the change in sound from Khā to Kāf is possible but not patently obvious. Thus, the similarity is suggestive, not definitive, and other sites, particularly Madīnat Bū Hindī a few kilometers north of al-Makīlī, are equally logical candidates for recognition by virtue of their more impressive and extensive ruins.

[4] Forts at Bū Nujaym, constructed in A.D. 200-201, and at al-Qaryat al-Gharbīya, dated to A.D. 230-235, have been reported by Richard G. Goodchild, "Oasis Forts of Legio III Augusta on the Routes to the Fezzan," PBSR, XXII (1954), 56-68, while a detailed investigation of Bu Ngem was undertaken by R. Rebuffat, J. Deneauve, and G. Hallier, "Bu Njem 1967," LA, III-IV (1966-1967), 49-137. The existence of a third century military garrison at Ghudāmis

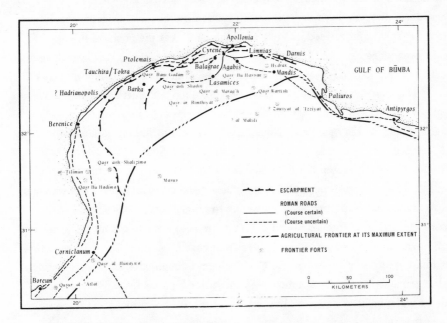

Fig. 25.--Agricultural frontier in the second and third centuries A.D.
Sources: United States Army Map Service, Libya (1:50,000), Richard G. Goodchild, "Boreum of Cyrenaica," idem, "'Libyan' Forts in South-west Cyrenaica,"
idem, "Roman and Byzantine Limes in Cyrenaica," idem, Tabula Imperii Romani: Cyrene, idem, "Roman Roads of Libya and their Milestones," and field
observations.

A number of ancient cisterns, now largely collapsed, also can be found
along the tracks leading south to al-Makīlī and al-ʿIzziyāt. Often conspicuous
because they support a richer flora than surrounding areas, these cisterns are
located well outside today's permanent agricultural areas. The considerable
time and effort required to hew them out of solid rock could only be justified if
they were officially sponsored and were designed to provide reliable watering
points for travelers moving between the agricultural zone of the high jabal and
the southern desert fringe. Goodchild's claim[1] that the Tripolitanian desert
forts were prestige structures designed to impress the bedouin is correct in
terms of the large scale of their construction; but this size is also a product of

was demonstrated by the publication of several inscriptions by Joyce M. Reynolds,
"Three Inscriptions from Ghadames in Tripolitania," PBSR, XXVI (1958), 135-36.

[1] Goodchild, "Oasis Forts of Legio III Augusta," p. 67.

their position on the most important caravan route across the Sahara.  In Tripolitania form and function were mutually reinforcing, but in Cyrenaica frontier
police duties of a more modest kind were the most that the posts in the al-
Makīlī area were expected to perform.  It is no wonder, then, that surviving
remains in this area are seldom more impressive than a few ancient cisterns.

The other access routes to the main jabal agricultural areas of the Pentapolis were blocked by extensive limes zones.  The system along the coast of
the Gulf of Sirt is the best understood.  An elaborate system of defensive forts
and fortified farmhouses occupied the area from Corniclanum (Ajdābiya) to
Berenice (Banghāzī) from the first century A. D. until the end of the Byzantine
era.[1]  This extensive limes effectively blocked potential raids by the Nasamones
tribe via the coastal plain and is analogous to the defensive systems along the
Saharan frontiers of Roman Algeria, where the areas most vulnerable to nomadic incursions were controlled by fortified zones.[2]  As yet there is no indication that the blocking limes around Corniclanum is duplicated in the area southeast of Darnis.  But such an inference is justified both by analogy from the
known development of such an organization in the Banghāzī plain and by examination of topographic maps for the Gulf of Būmba area.[3]  The coastal plain both
north and south of the Wādī al-Muʻallaq from Būmba to Tamīmī contains numerous sites that are labeled as ancient ruins.  Experience suggests that such ruins
are most likely to have been constructed out of stone, the approved Roman tech-
nique, since mud brick decomposes rapidly when not cared for properly.

However, building in mud brick was a common Islamic practice, and
structural preservation of ancient ruins in the coastal plain supports a Roman
origin.  In addition to the possibility that some of the sites might be Islamic in
origin, the more recent complication of Second World War involvement in the
area must be reckoned with.  Certainly the ruins surviving near the Būmba airfield are to be dated either to the Italian occupation or to wartime developments.
How far this is true of other parts of the coastal plain is unknown, for Tamīmī
was an important road junction during various stages of the fighting.[4]  However

---

[1]Richard G. Goodchild, "Boreum of Cyrenaica," JRS, XLI (1951), 11-16,
and idem, "Arae Philaenorum and Automalax," PBSR, XX (1952), 94-110.

[2]Louis Leschi, "Rome et les nomades du Sahara central," TIRS, I (1942),
52.

[3]United States, Army Map Service, at-Taḥīmī (1:50,000; Washington, D.C.:
Army Map Service, 1964).

[4]The Tamīmī area was a focus of several advances and retreats through

most of the actual combat and the development of defensive minefields and anti-
tank obstacles were concentrated either around and to the south of al-Qubba and
the Martūba-Qayqab road in the jabal or between 'Ayn al-Ghazāla and Bi'r al-
Ḥukayyim (Bir Hacheim) in Marmarica.

Moreover, subsistence farming is clearly possible in this coastal zone.
al-Jabal al-Akhḍar is not high enough to block the drift of eastward-moving
cyclones and to create a severe rain-shadow effect along the east coast; thus the
net effect is a gradual decrease in the quantity of rainfall in eastern Cyrenaica
rather than an abrupt transition to arid conditions. Rainfall still remains the
crucial limiting factor, and the close correspondence between the 100 mm. isohyet and the desert margins of ancient settlement around Tamīmī is an expression of this limitation. Under most conditions this limited quantity of water
would preclude dry farming. However, the water supply situation is alleviated
somewhat by a concentration of precipitation in the cooler winter months. This
increases crop growth prospects. Moreover, numerous wadis that drain the
eastern jabal reach the coast in the Būmba-Tamīmī region and provide a seasonally sporadic water supply. Dry farming techniques no more sophisticated than
those of the area's modern inhabitants would have been sufficient to sustain a
subsistence livelihood. Outcrop springs immediately behind the coastal dunes
also are a feature of the Tamīmī area and, although sometimes brackish, they
represent a significant contribution to local water supplies. East of Tamīmī the
amount of rainfall available decreases steadily and the opportunities for agriculture are limited. Thus, conditions east of Tamīmī were unsuitable for an extension of defensive farm settlements.

Settlement Phases: Ra's al-Hilāl to Sīdī Bū Dhra

The fortified farms and military posts described above protected the
Cyrenaican plateau during the early Imperial period. Dense agricultural settlement undoubtedly stopped before the 500-meter contour (Fig. 3) and, while favored spots further down the southern slopes of the jabal may have had military
garrisons, it would be a mistake to view continuous settlement as extending deep
into the interior.[1] Although the dating of settlement phases in the upper terrace

---

the steppe and desert. See Erwin Rommel, The Rommel Papers (ed. by B. H.
Liddell Hart; trans. by Paul Findlay; London: Collins, 1953).

[1] For example see Kraeling's map in Ptolemais, p. 34, which shows the
limes as a line from Corniclanum to Tamīmī. This obscures the issue by imput-
ing a greater extent to the settled area than it ever attained.

awaits a detailed survey of the construction period of the numerous small farm sites, some tentative conclusions can be advanced for the cross-section in Figure 24 and the areas immediately adjoining it. Two lines of evidence, the structure of farm buildings and funeral remains, contribute to a rough dating of the process of settlement.

The restored tombs on the lower terrace near the Biyib-Lamlūda road are of Hellenistic date.[1] Pottery discovered at Biyib is of Greek age. The style of the village's defensive wall and church indicate that it was occupied at least as long as the end of Byzantine rule. Indeed, its superb defensive setting makes it an ideal site for the survival of a Christian community following the Arab conquest. Rock-cut tomb chambers in outcrops north of both al-Abraq and Lamlūda (Limnias) suggest settlement no later than the fourth and third centuries B. C., while Hellenistic tombs at Mgharnis and Tīrt, Ptolemaic boundary stones near al-Marazigh,[2] and a Hellenistic period carved facade for the spring at al-Qubba imply early dates for the main centers of settlement in the upper terrace followed by a gradual expansion outward into the surrounding area. Adjacent to most village sites are Roman period sarcophagi; these attest to the continuity of settlement into the Imperial era. Most rock-cut tombs continued to be used by succeeding generations of the same family,[3] as did mausolea. The occurrence of Roman-style sarcophagi in areas between the early settlement centers and along the southern fringes of the settled area suggests that both a filling up of the plateau as well as a southward expansion characterized the Roman and early Byzantine eras. Two Byzantine period churches at Limnias and churches at several other coastal, lower terrace, and upper terrace sites east of Cyrene, together with numerous Byzantine fortified farms, suggest continued agricultural prosperity into the century preceding the Arab Conquest.

Evidence from farmhouse architectural styles is more difficult to utilize

---

[1] Hyslop and Applebaum, Cyrene, p. 49.

[2] Goodchild, Tabula Imperii Romani: Cyrene, p. 16.

[3] John Cassels, "The Cemeteries of Cyrene," PBSR, XXIII (1955), 1-43, believes that most tomb construction ceased after the third century B.C. This implies that population, at least in the Cyrene area, had stabilized and that most subsequent burials were in reused structures. This view is questioned by R. A. Tomlinson, "False-Facade Tombs at Cyrene," ABSA, LXII (1967), 249, who dates some tombs to the Augustan era and indicates that, because Greek stylistic traditions continued into the Roman period, tombs dated stylistically to earlier periods may have been constructed at later dates.

because detailed surveys of rural settlement are less common in Cyrenaica than in the Tripolitanian pre-desert.[1] Many surface remains are of Byzantine age and, in the absence of excavation, this veneer obscures evidence from earlier eras. Greek farm sites perhaps were unfortified and date from a period when security was greater and the need for a high level of defense was less. The next phase[2] probably involved the construction of farm complexes with rather large, well-shaped, rectangular blocks laid in regular courses. Most of these sites continued to be occupied in succeeding periods and in the Byzantine era a sloping talus or "batter" often was added to the exterior of the earlier perpendicular wall. Coursing and exterior corner jointing varies in quality from site to site, but distinctions between sites on the basis of the size of the stone and the quality of the coursing involved, with the poorer quality workmanship being assigned to later periods, is questionable. Variations could reflect simply the difference between sites benefiting from official support and those imitating the official style but lacking the governmental assistance necessary to defray the expenses involved in such additions.

Most fortified farms are located on low hilltops adjacent to farmed wadis or depressions or on easily defensible spurs of the escarpments. All have inter-visibility with several sites around them so that communication by means of fire or smoke signals, not to mention more sophisticated heliographic techniques, is conceivable.[3] Similar communications possibilities exist between the coastal plain and the upper terrace east of Cyrene with line-of-sight links from Limnias to Qaṣr Salīz on the crest of the upper scarp, to Qaṣr ar-Raqayyiq at the foot of the scarp, to Biyib or any one of a number of sites on the lower terrace, and from the fortified farmhouse on the crest of the lower scarp north of Sīdī Bū Barīq to the cluster of farmhouses on the fossilized coastal dunes at Ru'us al-Aslāb (from which site Apollonia is visible) west of Ra's al-Hilāl (Naustathmus). The greater number of these sites possess rectangular block cores with external Byzantine batter-style reinforcement. This argues in favor of an Imperial period

---

[1]A dating system based on the masonry construction techniques of Tripolitanian forts and fortified farmhouses has been developed by Richard G. Goodchild, "The Limes Tripolitanus II," JRS, XL (1950), 35-37. However, because Tripolitania was lost to the Vandals whereas Cyrenaica remained part of the Byzantine empire, the two provinces are not strictly comparable.

[2]This period is analogous to Tripolitanian Period I; ibid., pp. 37-38.

[3]White, "Excavations at Apollonia, Cyrenaica," p. 265, reports that an analogous system of signal stations, potentially linked by heliograph, connected Apollonia and Cyrene.

origin for many of the farm sites followed by a continuity in settlement in subsequent epochs.  Thus, the conclusion seems inescapable that the extent, level of integration, and effectiveness of the agricultural community in the Imperial period was greatly enhanced and as such that it posed a serious threat to and constraint upon the nomadic population.

Although Cyrenaica recovered from the disruption of a major revolt in A.D. 115-116, the fighting was not without its effects.  The revolt, launched by the Jewish population of Cyrenaica against their Greek neighbors, had both racial and political overtones; it was undertaken in response to persecution[1] and in an expectation of imminent messianic intercession.[2]  Casualties were high among both Greeks and Jews, although Greco-Roman authors exaggerated the magnitude.[3]  Nonetheless, extensive Imperial rebuilding efforts were required at Cyrene.[4]

The extent to which destruction was confined to the cities or spilled over into the surrounding countryside is a subject of debate.  At least one instance has come to light of a rural Jewish semi-military settlement at Ain Targhunia west of Cyrene dating from about A.D. 54-55.[5]  This settlement has a much

[1]Flavius Josephus Jewish Antiquities 16. 160-61.  The long history of Greek-Jewish hostility at Alexandria, where attitudes paralleled those of Cyrene, is reviewed by H. Stuart Jones, "Claudius and the Jewish Question at Alexandria," JRS, XVI (1926), 17-35.  An earlier Jewish revolt led by Jonathan of Cyrene proved abortive (Josephus The Jewish War 7. 437-52).

[2]Sh. Applebaum, "Notes on the Jewish Revolt under Trajan," JJS, II (1950), 26.

[3]Cassius Dio Cocceianus Roman History 8. 67. 421-23, claims that there were some 220,000 casualties.  Orosius Seven Books of History against the Romans 7. 12, describes Cyrenaica as being desolate and without inhabitants, while Eusebius Ecclesiastical History 4.2, mentions heavy Jewish losses when the rebellion was suppressed by Marcius Turbo in A.D. 117.  An analysis of the Jewish position in Egypt and Cyrenaica concludes that the result of the revolt was to substantially reduce, and in some cases annihilate, the Jewish community. E. Mary Smallwood, "The Jews in Egypt and Cyrenaica during the Ptolemaic and Roman Periods," in L. A. Thompson and J. Ferguson (eds.), Africa in Classical Antiquity (Ibadan: University Press, 1969), p. 131.

[4]The largest Jewish population and the majority of the fighting was concentrated at Cyrene and most of the major public monuments and temples were singled out for destruction by the rebels.  For the reconstruction of Cyrene, see P. M. Fraser, "Hadrian and Cyrene," JRS, XL (1950), 77-87, and E. Mary Smallwood, "The Hadrianic Inscription from the Caesareum at Cyrene," JRS, XLII (1952), 37-38.

[5]Shimon Applebaum, "Cyrenensia Ivdaica: Some Notes on Recent Research Relating to the Jews of Cyrenaica in the Hellenistic and Roman Periods," JJS, XIII (1962), 32.

wider significance in the context of nomad-sedentary relations than the racial/
religious character of its inhabitants might suggest. Its location along the southern spring line near the border between dry cereal cultivation and the semi-arid
steppe would be a major threat to the nomads. Large-scale settlement throughout this zone inevitably would result in a drastic reduction in the land and water
available for the nomad's combined agricultural-pastoral economy. The urban
Jews were strong enough to seize Cyrene and drive out the Greek inhabitants and
any substantial number of Jewish settlements in the rural areas logically would
have resulted in severe fighting and heavy losses there as well.

Applebaum[1] believes that food shortages and labor deficits at Cyrene suggest the possibility of serious rural depopulation. Repair work on the massive
Temple of Zeus, for example, was not completed until A. D. 172-175[2] and work
on other public monuments similarly was prolonged. Resettlement programs
were undertaken by encouraging a fresh influx of Greek settlers, by founding a
new city (Hadriane or Hadrianopolis), and by giving land to some 3,000 legionary
veterans. An inscription from Pamphylia[3] dated at the end of Trajan's reign
indicates that the question of resettlement was dealt with immediately, both from
a desire to insure firm central control of the region as well as to replace the
losses caused by the Jewish revolt.

The actual site of the legionary settlement is open to question as various
authorities favor Tokra, Cyrene, Apollonia, or several sites on the upper terrace east of Cyrene.[4] Agricultural operations in the stony Cyrenaican soil have
resulted in the accumulation of linear piles of stones along the property lines in
crude approximation of a centuriation system. One such area occurs on the
coastal plain west of Apollonia[5] and others on the upper terrace near Safsaf and

---

[1]Shimon Applebaum, "The Jewish Revolt in Cyrene in 115-117, and the
Subsequent Recolonization," JJS, II (1951), 178-79.

[2]Richard G. Goodchild, J. M. Reynolds, and C. J. Herington, "The Temple of Zeus at Cyrene," PBSR, XXVI (1958), 33.

[3]Reported by Applebaum, "Notes on the Jewish Revolt under Trajan," p. 27.

[4]A brief summary of the epigraphic evidence for the potential sites is reviewed by S. Applebaum, "A Note on the Work of Hadrian at Cyrene," JRS, XL
(1950), 87-90. The confusion derives from the ambiguity of the inscriptions
available, since it is difficult to determine whether the reference to Cyrene as
the site of the colonization implies the city or the entire district of Cyrenaica.
However, most authorities follow Goodchild, Tabula Imperii Romani: Cyrene
(1:1,000,000), in placing Hadrianopolis about halfway between Tokra and Berenice and identifying it with the legionary settlement.

[5]This, together with some vague and inconclusive epigraphic material, led

al-Qubba have led to speculation that they, rather than one of the large urban areas, might have been the foci of a settlement of veterans.[1] The irregular nature of these field lines, enclosing plots of varying sizes and not strictly parallel in alignment, argues against the rigid centuriation characterizing Roman agricultural settlements elsewhere. Instead, they may represent an adaptation to the cultural practices of the local inhabitants.

The fullest development of regular field lines occurs south of Limnias (Lamlūda). This suggests that these agricultural relics are relatively late in date and probably reflect a regularization of the land division under the second and third century emperors at a time when agricultural settlement was expanding to its limits. Field lines in these southerly portions of the upper terrace around Sīdī Bū Dhra are not nearly as massive as those of the central part of the upper terrace just south of Limnias. This implies that settlement was later and of shorter duration than that further north. Significantly, south of Sīdī Bū Dhra Greco-Roman settlement becomes restricted to the wadi edges and reflects the last stage of Roman agricultural expansion toward the semi-arid steppe. Most of the ruins between Sīdī Bū Dhra and Qaṣr Wartīsh are difficult to date, although the presence of a Roman sarcophagus top near Jabbana Bū Zāhiya on the track leading to Khūlān provides an approximately third and fourth century dating for maximum Imperial involvement in this region. The crude construction techniques employed in most of the southern sites together with their present ruinous condition suggests that they were occupied primarily by sedentarized nomads and that only the fortified post at Qaṣr Wartīsh[3] was an officially spon-

---

Alexander Fuks, "Aspects of the Jewish Revolt in A.D. 115-117," JRS, LI (1961), 99, to tentatively suggest Apollonia as the proper site for the Hadrianic colonization.

[1]Hyslop and Applebaum, Cyrene, p. 50, were the first to suggest a Hadrianic colonization scheme at Ṣafṣaf. For a discussion of the Greco-Roman cistern at Ṣafṣaf and its importance to the water supply of its immediate area see W. B. Fisher, I. R. Fraser, and D. W. Ross, "The Aberdeen University Expedition to Cyrenaica, 1951. Part III," Scottish Geographical Magazine, LXIX (1953), 28-29. However, Applebaum, "The Jewish Revolt in Cyrene in 115-117," p. 181, while continuing to support the idea of a veteran colonization east of Cyrene, adds the caveat that the rectilinear field lines could have resulted from the various Roman surveys of the public lands after the death of Ptolemy Apion.

[2]There is a possibility that some, if not all, of these straight field lines date from Ptolemaic land divisions. See John Bradford, Ancient Landscapes (London: G. Bell, 1957), pp. 214-15, reporting a personal communication with Richard Goodchild.

[3]See above, pp. 121-22.

sored settlement. West of the cross-section, where rainfall totals are greater, settlement extended further into the interior and pushed closer to the Balṭa zone at the foot of the dip-slope. However, east of Qayqab the 500 meter contour represented the outer limit of Greco-Roman agricultural settlement. Thus, following the termination of the Jewish Revolt of A.D. 115-117, restoration of the economic health of eastern Cyrenaica by urban reconstruction programs and expanded rural settlement was only partially successful and, while Cyrene and the rest of the Pentapolis did not experience an abrupt decline in prosperity, [1] it did sink gradually into a more chaotic and depressed condition paralleling a similar decrease in the vitality and effectiveness of the empire as a whole.

## Late Empire: The Nomadic Reaction

The cause of Cyrenaica's difficulties is unclear, but during the third century A.D. signs appear signifying a less effective defense of the plateau. Political turmoil elsewhere in the empire, increased nomadic raiding, fortification of farmhouses, and alienation of grazing land all bespeak changing nomad-sedentary relationships.

## Factors Contributing to Instability

Part of the problem must be seen in the context of larger empire-wide difficulties of frontier control. A series of debilitating struggles for the imperial throne, rather than a collapse of the frontier defenses, encouraged rival claimants to enlist barbarian forces as their allies and sponsor their introduction into the centers of the empire. [2] Increasing nomadic militancy and raiding

---

[1] Evidence for continued vitality at Cyrene is presented by Joyce Reynolds, "Four Inscriptions from Roman Cyrene," JRS, XLIX (1959), 95-101. An inscription from the Temple of Zeus ca. A.D. 175 describes Cyrene as the metropolis, or capital, rather than the mere polis or civitas that it was in Hadrian's reign. This indicates a considerable amount of government investment in and concern for the eastern Pentapolis and suggests a modest amount of resulting prosperity. See also Reynolds, "Vota pro Salute Principal," p. 33, and idem, "Notes on Cyrenaican Inscriptions," pp. 52-53, for the activities of procurators in early third century Cyrene.

[2] Gerold Walser, "The Crisis of the Third Century A.D.: A Re-interpretation," Bucknell Review, XIII (1965), 1-10, states this argument in a succinct form. For somewhat more detail A. Alfoldi, "The Crisis of the Empire (A.D. 249-270)," Cambridge Ancient History (Cambridge: University Press, 1939), XII, 165-231, is useful. A more broadly based review of literature dealing with the third century crisis is found in Gerold Walser and Thomas Pekáry, Die Krise des Römischen Reiches (Berlin: Walter de Gruyter & Co., 1962).

in response to the expanded agricultural settlement may well have been a major factor in eastern Cyrenaica. Although few campaigns against the nomads are recorded, an inscription from Cyrene indicates that an expedition was carried out by Tenagino Probus against the Marmaridae in the reign of Claudius Gothicus (A. D. 268-270), [1] after which extensive Imperial efforts were required to revitalize Cyrene. Although assistance in the face of nomadic incursions traditionally was drawn from Egypt, as was the case in Probus' anti-Marmaridae operations, an inscription at Ptolemais also notes the presence of a vexillation of Legio III Augusta. [2] Dated to the late third or early fourth century, this testifies to a serious crisis, otherwise unrecorded, requiring despatch of special assistance from the main garrison formation of the western half of North Africa to meet one of the series of difficulties that enveloped Cyrenaica after the middle of the third century. The shift of the capital from Cyrene to Ptolemais in Diocletian's reign reflects increasing insecurity in the interior as well as actual devastation caused by nomadic raids.

Also in the third and fourth centuries the development of fortified farmhouses became a prominent feature in the Pentapolis. [3] This type of defensive arrangement long had been a prominent feature in rural Tripolitania [4] and reflects Imperial interest in and support of defensive arrangements in the interior designed to protect the coastal urban centers. [5] Dry farming techniques sup-

[1] Richard G. Goodchild, "The Decline of Cyrene and Rise of Ptolemais: Two New Inscriptions," QAL, IV (1961), 92-93.

[2] R. G. Goodchild and J. M. Reynolds, "Some Military Inscriptions from Cyrenaica," PBSR, XXX (1962), 41.

[3] Richard G. Goodchild, "Farming in Roman Libya," Geographical Magazine, XXV (1952), 76-80.

[4] R. G. Goodchild and J. B. Ward-Perkins, "The Limes Tripolitanus in the Light of Recent Discoveries," JRS, XXXIX (1949), 81-95, and Goodchild, "Limes Tripolitanus II," pp. 30-38. In Tripolitania the reign of Septimius Severus saw the final consolidation of the limes system; the date in Cyrenaica was somewhat later.

[5] S. N. Miller, "The Army and the Imperial House," Cambridge Ancient History (Cambridge: University Press, 1939), XII, 20-21, states the traditional view that Septimius Severus' African origin explains Imperial interest in the military and civic affairs of North Africa. This position has been challenged by Richard M. Haywood, "The African Policy of Septimius Severus," Transactions of the American Philological Association, LXXI (1940), 175-85, who contends that Septimius' interest in North Africa, and in the process of settlement advance into and consolidation of marginal semi-desert and steppe areas, reflects a continuation of previous Imperial policy rather than a new departure.

ported a wide zone of _limitanei_ settlers, dwelling in fortified farmhouses along the wadis of the Tripolitanian steppe and engaging in subsistence agriculture, during the first four centuries A.D.[1]

In eastern Cyrenaica numerous Roman remains can be found in the dip-slope in environments analogous to those of the Tripolitanian pre-desert; these remains lack, in general, the same well-cut stone block construction character-istic of the quasi-military _limes_ settlements of Tripolitania or of the Cyrenaican jabal. Usually only a few rectangular stones are found serving as door jambs or as orthostats reinforcing poorly fashioned rubble stone walls that long since have fallen into ruin. The crucial point at issue is whether or not this repre-sents a movement of Greek and Latin settlers down from the jabal or a Roman-ization and sedentarization of the indigenous Libyan tribesmen. Actually both processes occurred simultaneously. There is obviously no way of determining from a superficial examination of the ruins, other than their poor original con-struction and the observation that a similar process seems to have taken place in the western coastal plain between Berenice and Boreum,[2] that bedouin seden-tarization was taking place. However, there is every reason to suspect, on the basis of similar processes in Tripolitania,[3] that as nomadic tribes gradually came into increased contact with an expanding Greco-Roman culture and tech-nology they adopted a more settled and agricultural mode of life. There would be no reason for these sedentarized nomads to give up animal herding to a marked

---

[1] See particularly Lady Olwen Brogan, "First and Second Century Settle-ment in the Tripolitanian Pre-Desert" (unpublished MS from the Libya in History conference; Banghāzī: University of Libya, 1968), pp. 1-6; Olwen Brogan and David Smith, "The Roman Frontier Settlement at Ghiza: An Interim Report," JRS, XLVII (1957), 173-84; R. G. Goodchild, "Roman Sites on the Tarhuna Pla-teau of Tripolitania," PBSR, XIX (1951), 43-77; David Oates, "The Tripolitanian Gebel: Settlement of the Roman Period around Gasr ed-Dauun," PBSR, XXI (1953), 81-117; J. M. Reynolds and W. G. Simpson, "Some Inscriptions from el-Auenia near Yefren in Tripolitania," LA, III-IV (1966-1967), 45-47; and J. B. Ward-Perkins, "Gasr es-Suq el-Oti: A Desert Settlement in Central Tripolitania," Archaeology, III (1950), 25-30.

[2] Goodchild, "'Libyan' Forts in South-west Cyrenaica," p. 144, believes that most of the crude defensive structures in this coastal area were built by local tribesmen heavily influenced by Roman culture.

[3] Olwen Brogan, "Henscir el-Ausāf by Tigi (Tripolitania) and some Related Tombs in the Tunisian Gefara," LA, II (1965), 55-56, maintains that inscriptions favor a punicized and romanized Libyan tribal population, rather than an intro-duction of Italian settlers, as the basis of agricultural expansion during the first three centuries A.D.

degree, since the potential for sending the family herds with hired shepherds or with still nomadic relatives would still exist. Rather, initially such a process would represent the localization of dwelling patterns and an intensification of the agricultural component of the mixed nomadic economy. Only at a later stage, when settled patterns of life and a dependence on agriculture had become more dominant, would animal herding and ties to nomadic elements be reduced.

Paralleling the process of nomadic sedentarization was a movement into the agriculturally marginal areas of a possibly small but nonetheless important body of colonists who posed a major threat to the survival of traditional nomadic livelihood patterns. The existence of mausoleum and temple styles at Mandis similar to those in the jabal, the construction of farmhouses analogous to the unfortified structures of the jabal, and the use of a system of check-dams to capture more effectively the limited wadi run-off argues that at least some of the settlers in the steppe areas were drawn from highly acculturated elements in the native tribal population if not from alien settlers. [1] None of these settlers could hope to live on agriculture alone; animal herding would be a necessary supplemental activity. Such herding would clash with the nomad's need for pasturage, particularly during the summer season when the southern pastures are most desiccated and the necessity for access to assured water and pasture near the spring line is most compelling. Since the critical factor in utilizing the southern pastures in the winter is the number of animals that can be successfully carried on the northern pasture through the summer, it is the summertime competition for grazing that would be the most important.

Equally crucial would be the agricultural activities of a settled community in the steppe areas. Unable to occupy large areas because of the shortage of water and of sophisticated irrigation techniques, steppe-fringe settlements concentrated along the wadi bottoms where the limited available rainfall was most concentrated as run-off. These areas were also the most crucially important for the nomadic population. Only in the northern wadi bottoms could they hope to grow barley with enough certainty about successful yields to organize a stable genre de vie. Forcible concentration on the depressions and wadi bottoms at the foot of the dip-slope, an area that is the site of speculative barley planting by the contemporary bedouin, would represent an extremely precarious

---

[1] The suggestion that the indigenous population, recruited from native legionary veterans and local townspeople who had been granted Roman citizenship, formed the cutting edge of the expanding sedentary community is advanced by L. A. Thompson, "Settler and Native in the Urban Centres of Roman Africa," in L. A. Thompson and J. Ferguson (eds.), Africa in Classical Antiquity (Ibadan: University Press, 1969), pp. 138-48.

and hazardous reliance on an unstable and capricious environment. Crop failures here are frequent and the consequences of several successive failures
would be of the utmost severity.

By A. D. 400 the main wealth of the settled population was considered to
be its herds of cattle, camels, and horses, not its agricultural products.[1] Yet
these herds never challenged nomadic survival, since employment as shepherds
for the settled population always would exist.[2] Moreover, the sedentary community's lack of mobility would reduce their ability to support large numbers of
animals through a series of bad years because long-distance movement of the
herds to suitable pasture was extremely difficult. Agricultural competition, in
contrast, was a much more serious irritant. Indeed, agriculture was the most
important source of conflict since the very wadis and areas along the southern
fringes of the upper terrace that were vital to the nomads were alienated from
use as a result of their occupation by settled folk. This eliminated part of the
nomadic economy, thus reducing its long-term stability. The net result would
be to encourage raiding as a mechanism to compensate for the lost agricultural
opportunities and to redress the balance.

Synesius and the Crisis of A. D. 400

In the face of increasing efforts to stiffen the frontier limes, both by a
southward expansion of agriculture and by the construction of more defensive
structures in the agricultural heartland, the level of nomadic raids rose correspondingly and reached a crescendo of violence during the lifetime of Synesius,
bishop of Ptolemais. The picture presented by Synesius shows the settled population thrown into a state of chaos and confusion by the raids of the Austuriani
tribes of the Gulf of Sirt from A. D. 395 to 413.[3] Apparently the army was in a

---

[1]Synesius Letters 130.

[2]A mosaic discovered at Oudna depicting a nomad (recognizable as such
because of his nearby tent) shepherding a farmer's animals suggests that employment of this type, with its corresponding monetary rewards and/or possibilities
for reestablishing a decimated herd, was not so farfetched. Thérèse Précheur-
Canonge, La vie rurale en Afrique romaine d'après les mosaïques (Paris: Presses
Universitaires de France, n. d.), p. 32. However, K. D. White, Agricultural
Implements of the Roman World (Cambridge: University Press, 1967), p. 11,
warns that Précheur-Canonge's attempt to characterize Roman North Africa's
life style solely on the basis of the evidence available in mosaics should be used
with considerable caution, since it is always questionable how accurate a representation of reality the mosaic is and how typical, taking into consideration the
accidents of discovery and survival, the scenes depicted really are.

[3]See, for example, the unsettled conditions described by Synesius Letters

state of considerable decay, the soldiers often on leave, discipline lax, rank
and advancement open to purchase, the lower ranks forced to present gifts to
their superiors, and the leadership weak and ineffectual, all abuses that the
government still was trying to correct one hundred years later.[1] Among the
numerous abuses legislated against by the Theodosian Code at least two were
directed at the peculations practiced by members of the military administration
of Cyrenaica and Marmarica. The first, sent in A.D. 417 to Vitalianus, Duke
of Libya, establishes heavy fines for the illegal purchase of successions to previously held offices[2] and points to the type of corruption in military command
centers that so frequently is the object of Synesius' complaints. A second decree directed to Nomus, the Master of Offices, ordered the dukes entrusted
with frontier defense to end corrupt solicitation of funds intended to support the
frontier soldiers and to cease expropriation of tax-free land specifically reserved for the personal use of the limitanei.[3] The decree refers to Libya as
one place among many where abuses of this type occurred; dated A.D. 443, the
decree makes clear some of the complaints that were rife among the inhabitants
of border regions and perhaps explains some of their lack of enthusiasm for
strenuous resistance to the enemies of the empire beyond the frontier. The
inefficiency, corruption, and ineffectuality of local administrative bodies is
illustrated by the growth of a quasi-feudal system of illegal patrons for villages
who, in return for village support, assist the local inhabitants to escape from
their obligations.[4] Extra-legal associations of this type develop when local
bureaucracies are so venal that resort to alternative protective devices becomes
necessary. Synesius in both a private capacity and in his position as a bishop
was forced to organize resistance to the depredations of Austuriani raid-

---

13, 59, 69, 95, 104, 125, 130, 132, 133. The exclusive dependence on this one
source for the period, however, should be kept in mind. Despite Synesius'
gloomy predictions, the country remained in Byzantine control, although con-
stantly threatened by nomadic attack, until the Arab conquest in A.D. 642.

[1] See the decree of Anastasius (ca. A.D. 500) first published in an incom-
plete version by W. H. Waddington, "Edit de l'empereur Anastase sur l'administration militaire en Libye," Revue Archéologique, XVIII (1868), 417-30, and
more extensively discussed by Gaspare Olivero, Il decreto di Anastasio 1° su
l'ordinamento politico-militareo della Cirenaica (Rome: Istituto Italiano d'Arti
Grafiche, 1933).

[2] Cth 8. 1. 16.                    [3] NTh 24. 3-4.

[4] The practice was well developed in Egypt and was legislated against in
an imperial decree of A.D. 395. CTh 11. 24. 3.

ers[1] and he records instances where other private citizens were forced to take independent action[2] in the face of the incompetence of the military and political leadership. Local leadership was at a distinctly low ebb and Synesius' verbal assaults condemning the venality, corruption, and self-seeking incompetence of many of the generals and governors assigned to the Pentapolis are memorable.[3]

A number of factors combined to make successful nomadic raiding a practical possibility. The internal decay of sedentary society and the violent nomadic reaction to the loss of pasture, water, and agricultural land to an expanding sedentary community are major parts of the picture and have been referred to above. Other ingredients are needed to complete the picture, for otherwise it is unlikely that the integrated defensive network of the jabal would have failed to halt the nomadic invaders. One factor contributing to internal disorganization was a series of earthquakes, the most serious of which occurred in A.D. 365.[4] The area around Cyrene was hit particularly hard, causing Ammianus to describe the city as "deserted" during the later part of the decade.[5] Another more localized earthquake struck the Cyrene area in A.D. 262,[6] perhaps

---

[1]Synesius Letters 107, 108, 125, 132, 133.

[2]See Synesius Letters 122 where a band of raiders was defeated by peasants led by the deacon Faustus and the priests of the church of Axomis.

[3]For example, Synesius' comments on the military abilities of Cerialis (Letters 24, 130) or his opinion of the governor Andronicus (Letters 57, 58, 72, 73). Daniel G. Bates, "The Role of the State in Peasant-Nomad Mutualism," Anthropological Quarterly, XLIV (1971), 109-131, argues effectively that in situations where farmers and nomads compete for access to the same resources, it is the relative power balance between the two communities, and particularly the role the state plays in adjusting relationships between the two groups, that is of crucial significance. An interesting instance of tribal intervention in political conflicts and in resource management decisions where the central government is weak is recounted by Amal Vinogradov, "The 1920 Revolt in Iraq Reconsidered," International Journal of Middle East Studies, III (1972), 123-39.

[4]Richard G. Goodchild, "Earthquakes in Ancient Cyrenaica," in F. T. Barr (ed.), Geology and Archaeology of Northern Cyrenaica, Libya (Tripoli: Petroleum Exploration Society of Libya, 1968), pp. 41-44; John G. Pedley, "Excavations at Apollonia, Cyrenaica: Second Preliminary Report," AJA, LXXI (1967), 146, sees evidence for the quake of A.D. 365 in the attempted but unfinished bath restoration at Apollonia. Work ceased about A.D. 390 when the danger from Austuriani raiding parties made it unsafe to use stone from the city's defensive wall to complete the repairs.

[5]Ammianus Marcellinus History 22. 16.4.

[6]Richard G. Goodchild, "A Coin-hoard from 'Balagrae' (El-Beida), and the Earthquake of A.D. 365," LA, III-IV (1966-1967), 208.

accounting for some of the devastation that needed to be repaired at Cyrene after the anti-Marmaridae campaign of Tenagino Probus in A.D. 268-270.[1] Later unrecorded earthquakes probably also affected the region and provide a partial explanation for the batter-constructed farmhouses, since the sloping external walls would buttress the original wall in the event of a further quake.

Internal dissension associated with the Arian heresy, whose foothold among the bulk of the Cyrenaican population was strong,[2] probably weakened the defensive arrangements of the plateau. It is also possible that many of the frontier limitanei, particularly when drawn from pastoral tribes that had submitted to the Romans or were located in exposed positions south of the main agricultural areas, developed a neutral attitude toward the nomads, with whom they may have been related, and permitted raiders to cross the frontier with impunity.[3]

C. H. Coster has suggested that the introduction of the camel into Cyrenaica about A.D. 400 and its rapid adoption by the nomads made them a formidable military threat for the first time.[4] Although this date is unrealistically late, the spread of the camel into North Africa is curious, largely because its adoption was so slow. Introduced into Egypt by the Persians during the sixth century B.C., knowledge of the camel preceded its appearance in the Delta by a considerable period.[5] The gap between the camel's entry into Egypt and its first appearance in a literary reference to the North African campaigns of Julius Caesar is a considerable one and is largely unexplained.[6] Indications that the

---

[1] Some of this repair work involved a new, improvised system of defensive walls at Cyrene. R. G. Goodchild, "Cyrenaica," LA, I (1964), 143.

[2] Henry Chadwick, "Faith and Order at the Council of Nicaea: A Note on the Background of the Sixth Canon," Harvard Theological Review, LIII (1960), 179 ff. P. Francesco Rovere, "Il Christianesimo in Cirenaica: origini-vicende-storiche-monumenti," Libia, III (1955), 43-52, reviews the history of Christianity in Cirenaica and indicates an elaborate diocesan structure incorporating many of the rural towns.

[3] Goodchild, "'Libyan' Forts in South-west Cyrenaica," p. 144 (following Synesius Letters 130) contends that it was the treachery of the limitanei, particularly the Macetae tribe, that permitted the series of nomadic incursions around A.D. 400. But note the objections of B. H. Warmington, The North African Provinces from Diocletian to the Vandal Conquest (Cambridge: University Press, 1954), p. 26, who feels that the self-interest of the frontier forces would preclude the possibility of treason.

[4] Charles H. Coster, "Christianity and the Invasions: Synesius of Cyrene," in Late Roman Studies (Cambridge: Harvard University Press, 1968), p. 246.

[5] Mikesell, "Notes on the Dispersal of the Dromedary," pp. 236-38.

[6] Ibid., p. 239, hints at a gradual spread westward through the southern

camel preceded the Romans into the Sahara precludes Imperial encouragement
as the motivating force in its introduction (although Roman development of security along the trans-Saharan caravan routes may have facilitated the camel's use
in commercial activities) led Demougeot to speculate that the camel may have
arrived in southern Tunisia during the first century A. D. simultaneously from
the central Sahara and along the coast of the Gulf of Sirt.[1] In Cyrenaica there
are suggestions that the last Ptolemaic rulers used the camel in the coast-wise
caravan traffic; a representation of the camel on a Roman coin from 39 B. C.
issued at Cyrene shows that it was familiar and important enough to serve as a
symbolic device on a monetary issue.[2]

The retarded adoption of the camel by the nomadic population of Cyrenaica is related to ecological factors. The Libyan Berbers concentrated on
sheep and goats as their herd animals while horses and donkeys met transportation and military needs. This was a satisfactory arrangement as long as access
to the upper terrace remained open. The assured grain yields of the jabal reduced the element of risk to the agricultural part of the nomad's economy, while
goats were efficient converters of the maquis shrub vegetation of the upper terrace and sheep exploited the grassland resources of the more arid south. With
all basic wants fulfilled, there was no need to herd the camel which was of potential utility as a converter of the most marginal pastoral areas outside the range
and exploitive abilities of the sheep and the goat. The slow spread of the camel
in Cyrenaica is not surprising. With Greek settlement largely confined to the
agriculturally better parts of northern Cyrenaica, resources adequate to support
the traditional nomadic regime were available.

Absence of motivation favoring adoption by the nomads of Cyrenaica, in
turn, explains the retarded progress of the camel across the North African
coast, since a large territorial gap would be created by the lack of receptivity of
the indigenous Berbers to the new animal. Since caravan trade either with Egypt
or sub-Saharan Africa was minimal, the camel's commercial applications in

---

fringes of the Sahara, while E. W. Bovill, "The Camel and the Garamantes,"
Antiquity, XXX (1956), 21, hypothesizes an unhealthy Nile valley climate and
adoptive resistance to the "novelty" of the camel as mechanisms blocking its
introduction into North Africa along a Mediterranean coastal route.

[1]Émilienne Demougeot, "Le chameau et l'Afrique du Nord romaine,"
Annales, Economies, Sociétés, Civilisations, XV (1960), 244-45.

[2]Ibid., plate facing p. 223 and p. 224.

Cyrenaica were not numerous. However, once Imperial policy promoted agricultural expansion and land was alienated from nomadic use, pastoralists increasingly were restricted to more marginal areas. Significantly, it is the settled or sedentarized portion of the population that appears as the first major user of the camel in domestic agriculture and transportation,[1] but its gradual spread to the nomads as agricultural pressure increased can be assumed. Restricted to the more marginal areas along the southern dip-slope, only large-scale adoption of the camel could ensure exploitation of enough pasturage to ensure a reasonable chance of survival in a high-risk environment.

The speed and mobility of the camel ushered in a period of nomadic military superiority at precisely the same time that internal confusion and decay sapped the vitality of sedentary society. Certainly the fact that Synesius[2] mentions that Austuriani hoplites were mounted on camelback and that in one raid 5,000 camels were needed to carry off their booty demonstrates that the camel played an important role in the effectiveness of the raiding parties even if the figures contain an element of exaggeration. On those rare occasions when able commanders led mobile cavalry units against the raiding parties success could be attained, but in Synesius' day this seldom occurred.[3] Thus, a passive attitude on the part of those entrusted with the defense of the province, widespread use of the camel to increase the mobility of raiding tribesmen, and the spreading disorganization of the local government, explains why the nomadic raids were so destructive in this period.

Byzantine Cyrenaica: Nomad-
Sedentary Equilibrium

Despite Synesius' gloomy prognostications, the Pentapolis' agricultural community survived. But by A.D. 400 its period of expansion was over and the nomad-sedentary frontier unquestionably stabilized and probably retreated in

---

[1] Olwen Brogan, "The Camel in Tripolitania," PBSR, XXII (1954), 126-31, indicates that not until the third century A.D. did the camel become a common component of tomb motifs in Tripolitania and a comparably late date seems likely for Cyrenaica also.

[2] Synesius, The Essays and Hymns of Synesius of Cyrene (2 vols.; trans. by Augustine FitzGerald; Oxford: University Press, 1930), II, 366.

[3] See Synesius' account (Essays and Hymns, II, 360-62) of the victory of Anysius and a small band of soldiers over a large raiding party, as well as the contrast between Anysius' character and ability to control his troops and the chaos existing among the local soldiery under previous commanders.

places. The major casualty of the era was city life, which declined in vigor and population. At Cyrene the urban area shrank. The Roman period forum, which once was near the heart of the city, was converted into a fortress on the outskirts of the contracted city while buildings between it and the old city wall were leveled to improve defensive visibility.[1] Similar conditions pertained at Ptolemais, where the Hellenistic city wall was abandoned and replaced by a series of forts and fortified houses interspersed with residential dwellings within the reduced urban area.[2] Despite indications that the urban population experienced a sharp decline, rural districts continued to flourish as the countryside gradually was transformed into a land of castles and fortified churches.[3]

Throughout the Byzantine period the nomads remained a constant threat, so emphasis on a defense-oriented rural settlement pattern is understandable. Although literary sources for the period are scanty,[4] it is known that attempts were made to control contact between the settled and nomadic populations,[5] presumably in order to restrict the flow of war material to the restless population of the steppe. Evidence attests to at least two further nomadic invasions, although the precise dating of these incursions is uncertain. The first, mentioned by Priscus Panites,[6] is a rather vague reference to a second appearance of the Austuriani sometime before A.D. 449.[7] Some fifty years later the Mazices

---

[1] J. B. Ward-Perkins and M. H. Ballance, "The Caesareum at Cyrene and the Basilica at Cremna," PBSR, XXVI (1958), 141.

[2] Kraeling, Ptolemais, pp. 26-27, 100-107.

[3] Goodchild, "Roman and Byzantine Limes," p. 73.

[4] Joyce M. Reynolds, "The Christian Inscriptions of Cyrenaica," Journal of Theological Studies, N.S., XI (1960), 284-94, catalogues twenty-five inscriptions, most of which date to the sixth century revival of the cities sponsored by Justinian. Reynolds suggests that the paucity of Christian epigraphy in the Pentapolis is a reflection of a local rural tradition of painting, rather than cutting, inscriptions on walls as well as a shift in emphasis in the settlement pattern from the urban centers to the countryside after A.D. 400.

[5] For example, the provisions regulating contact between merchants and nomads in the Anastasian decree (ca. A.D. 500) in Olivero, Il decreto di Anastasio 1º, XI.

[6] Priscus Panites, Frag. 14 in K. Müller, Fragmenta Historicorum Graecorum, IV (Paris: Ambrosio Firmin Didot, 1868), 98. I am indebted to Joyce M. Reynolds for this reference.

[7] Goodchild, Tabulae Imperii Romani: Cyrene, p. 9, accepts this date unequivocably.

tribe is mentioned as a disruptive influence, [1] although the exact date is uncertain; Romanelli [2] suggests A.D. 491 for the event while Goodchild [3] opts for A.D. 513. With the reign of Anastasius (A.D. 491-518) thus conveniently bracketed by the leading authorities, perhaps no more precision can be attained than to say that a date sometime during that monarch's rule is indicated. [4]

Unlike Tripolitania, which was lost to the empire after the Vandal conquest of the North African coast, the Cyrenaican Pentapolis never slipped from Byzantine control [5] and so did not play a central role in Justinian's attempts to regain the lost western provinces. But the fourth through the sixth centuries did see the construction of a number of fortified farmhouses and churches in the coastal areas from Berenice to Susa (Apollonia), a development that connotes insecurity induced by Vandal naval raids as much as it does the depredations of nomadic forays. A number of the coastal churches, particularly those of Ra's al-Hilāl (Naustathmos) and al-Aṭrūn (Erythrum), [6] date from the Justinianic era and represent lavish prestige displays on the part of Constantinople government. Equally interesting are the rural churches of the eastern jabal; numerous examples are found throughout the upper terrace of ecclesiastical structures constructed of local materials (devoid of the ornamentation of the coastal churches but with the same three-aisle basilica design) and heavily fortified with well-coursed, external-batter additions. Most of these churches form the nucleus of small village agglomerations and represent the community's largest and most defensible building available for fortification in an age of insecurity. The Christian mosaics of Cyrenaica date from the flurry of building and restoration that

[1] Joannis Anthiochenus, Frag. 216 in K. Müller, Fragmenta Historicorum Graecorum, IV, 621. This reference was provided by Joyce M. Reynolds.

[2] Romanelli, La Cirenaica romana, p. 170.

[3] Goodchild, Tabula Imperii Romani: Cyrene, p. 9.

[4] Joyce M. Reynolds, personal letter.

[5] Christian Courtois, Les Vandales et l'Afrique (Paris: Arts et métiers graphiques, 1955), map, p. 187.

[6] R. M. Harrison, "A Sixth Century Church at Ras el-Hilal in Cyrenaica," PBSR, XXXII (1964), 1-20. Helmut Sichterman, "Archäologische Funde und Forschungen in Libyen: Kyrenaika, 1959-1961, Tripolitanien, 1942-1961," Archäologischer Anzeiger, 1962, Heft 3, pp. 433-34, reports a private communication from Walter Widrig, the excavator at Erythrum. This surveys the excavation of one of the two al-Aṭrūn churches and recounts its destruction by fire (possibly during an Austuriani invasion?), subsequent reconstruction and fortification by Justinian, and final devastation after the Arab invasion.

characterized Justinian's reign in the rural churches as well as in the larger
cities, although the derivation of themes and techniques from conventionalized
mosaic traditions originating outside the Pentapolis means that little insight into
local conditions, other than the observation that their existence betokens a certain amount of prosperity, can be derived from them.[1]

Justinian's main emphasis was on restoring urban life, and the walls of
Tokra and Berenice were singled out for particular attention.[2] The aqueduct at
Ptolemais which had fallen into disrepair was reopened and the decline in population that had resulted from a reduced water supply was checked.[3] To what extent the Emperor's claim to have "brought back to it its former measure of prosperity" is justified is questionable, for Justinian's efforts did not include a return of governmental functions to Ptolemais. These shifted to Apollonia (or
Sozousa as it was known in the Christian period[4]) during the reign of Anastasius
about A. D. 500. It is in Apollonia that the palace of the dux, complete with private chapel presumed to have been used in swearing solemn oaths (particularly
important in granting safe-conducts to leaders of the nomadic Berbers), has
come to light.[5] However, the emphasis that Justinian placed upon providing a
defensive wall for the city of Boreum at the base of the Gulf of Sirt and upon
refortifying other structures in the region,[6] the source area of many of the
destructive nomadic raids in previous generations, shows that the nomadic
threat remained a very real one. Justinian's extension of Byzantine control
southward to include the oasis of Awjila denotes a slightly more forward policy
than that practiced by the Augustae, since it brought within the orbit of sedentary
authority agricultural areas of vital concern to the nomadic tribes of the Sirtic
desert fringes. However, with this one exception the Byzantine Sirtic frontier
thus occupied the same area that it did in the first century A. D., while that of
the eastern plateau had withdrawn closer to the level of Qaṣr Wartîsh.

---

[1]J. B. Ward-Perkins, "A New Group of Sixth-century Mosaics from Cyrenaica," Rivista di archeologia cristiana, XXXIV (1958), 190.

[2]Procopius De aedeficiis 6. 2.4-5.    [3]Ibid., 6. 2.9-11.

[4]Philip Ward, "Place-names of Cyrenaica," in F. T. Barr (ed.), Geology
and Archaeology of Northern Cyrenaica, Libya, p. 10. Ward's glossary of place-
names updates Goodchild's Tabula Imperii Romani: Cyrene, pp. 12-14, with
greater attention to an Arabized spelling of the various sites.

[5]Richard G. Goodchild, "A Byzantine Palace at Apollonia (Cyrenaica),"
Antiquity, XXXIV (1960), particularly pp. 254-55.

[6]Procopius De aedeficiis 6. 2.6-8, 12-13.

It is interesting to note that the cities mentioned by Procopius as having received assistance in Justinian's reign are all coastal sites and that they are all in western Cyrenaica.  No mention is made of Cyrene, Apollonia, or any of the smaller villages and towns of the eastern Pentapolis.  Just why this should be the case is uncertain, since the absence of literary sources can be interpreted as implying either decline in the eastern part of the jabal or sufficient prosperity to make government intervention unwarranted.  However, the large quantity of late Byzantine farmhouses, forts, and churches throughout the upper terrace suggests that the quality of rural settled life continued to be prosperous at least until the Arab conquest in A.D. 642.

CHAPTER VI

THE ARAB CONQUEST AND

THE HILALIAN INVASION

Sources for conditions in seventh century Cyrenaica are limited and this makes it difficult to isolate the factors which resulted in the rapid collapse of Byzantine resistance in the face of the Arab invasion forces led by ʿAmr ibn al-ʿĀṣ. This uncertainty is unfortunate because the initial Arab conquest, and the subsequent invasion by the Banī Hilāl tribes in the eleventh century, can be regarded as the culmination of a series of nomadic onslaughts which ultimately overwhelmed urban civilization in large parts of North Africa. Thus, an attempt to marshall the limited available evidence in an effort to understand conditions immediately preceding and following the Arab invasion is essential to comprehension of this chapter in Cyrenaica's settlement history.

The Military Conquest of
ʿAmr ibn al-ʿĀṣ and its Impact

When ʿAmr ibn al-ʿĀṣ led a small force of cavalry from Egypt into Cyrenaica during the summer of A.D. 642, his success was rapid, although not immediately total.[1] Barqa (the Greek Barka), a major town on the lower terrace in western Cyrenaica was ʿAmr's initial objective and it fell after only limited opposition. The governor of Cyrenaica and his supporters, described by Joannes as the "rich men of the province,"[2] abandoned the eastern portions of the jabal and retreated, together with the garrison of Apollonia (Sozusa),[3] to Tauchira

---

[1] The earliest Arabic account of the conquest of Cyrenaica is the cursory narrative of Ibn ʿAbd al-Ḥakam, Futūḥ Miṣr wa 'l-Maghrib (ed. by ʿAbd al-Munʿim ʿĀmir [Cairo, 1961]), pp. 229-30. ʿAbd al-Ḥakam, who died in A.D. 871, was a zealous, although occasionally uncritical, collector of traditions and later Arab historians relied heavily on his work. For his brief biography, consult C. C. Torrey, "Ibn ʿAbd al-Hakam," Encyclopedia of Islam, II (Leyden: E. J. Brill, 1927), p. 353.

[2] Joannes, Bishop of Nikiou Chronicle 120. 35.

[3] Excavations conducted along the south wall of the city in conjunction with

145

(Tokra). Here the remaining Byzantine adherents held out until a combined
naval and land expedition appeared in A. D. 645 to complete the conquest. With
Barqa as a base of operations, and with the benevolent neutrality of the Berbers
apparently assured, Arab control gradually was extended over the entire jabal.
Startling in its rapidity, overwhelming in its completeness, irrevocable in its
finality, 'Amr ibn al-'Āṣ' conquest requires explanation.

Causes of the Byzantine Collapse

Unsettled conditions in the Eastern Empire throughout the initial decades
of the seventh century offer partial insight into the problem. Political intrigue
in Constantinople ending with the murder of the emperor, Maurice, and the
struggle during A.D. 609-610 for the succession between Heraclius and Phocas
may have had an unsettling effect on Cyrenaica, since Heraclius' invasion of
strategically vital Egypt was based on the Pentapolis and his army and its barbarian allies spent some time there.[1] Equally unsettling for the entire empire,
and ultimately debilitating for both contestants, was the long-drawn-out series
of wars with the Persian Sassanid monarchy that followed Heraclius' triumph
over Phocas. The possibility that, following their conquest of Egypt, a Persian
invasion of Cyrenaica might have taken place sometime after A.D. 619, thus
explaining the apparent disarray that contributed to the sudden success of the
Arab invaders, has had its proponents.[2] But Stratos has expressed doubts that
the Persians ever advanced far into Libya[3] and this is supported by the absence
of any specific reference to a Persian advance on the Pentapolis in the historical

---

work on the Byzantine Governor's Palace reveal no signs of a siege at the time
of the Arab invasion. Richard G. Goodchild, "Cyrenaica," p. 144.

[1] Joannes, Bishop of Nikiou Chronicle 107. 2-3.

[2] Hyslop and Applebaum, Cyrene, p. 12, believed that the Persians leveled
the walls of Cyrenaica's cities and left them defenseless against the Arabs.
Alfred J. Butler, The Arab Conquest of Egypt and the Last Thirty Years of the
Roman Dominion (Oxford: Clarendon Press, 1902), pp. 10, 91, follows Gibbon
in attributing a conquest of the Pentapolis to the Persians, but his familiarity
with the Arabic source material describing a prosperous Cyrenaica on the eve
of the Arab conquest leads him to question the destructiveness of a Persian
invasion.

[3] Andreas N. Stratos, Byzantium in the Seventh Century, I (trans. by Marc
Ogilvie-Grant; Amsterdam: Adolf M. Hakkert, 1968), p. 114, claims the conviction of many historians that the Persians reached Tripoli and Carthage is
based on an erroneous translation of Theophanes' Chalcedon as Karchedon (Carthage).

records of the Alexandrian Coptic Church.[1] Similarly, Goodchild has found no archaeological evidence at either Cyrene or Apollonia to suggest that the Persians played a major role in seventh century Cyrenaican history.[2] Although clearly contributing factors to a weakening of Byzantine military effectiveness, the full explanation lies elsewhere.

Religious dissent in North Africa would seem to offer a reasonable explanation. The successive reappearance of dissenting doctrines challenging the orthodoxy of the moment is one of the leitmotifs of North African history.[3] Speel has maintained that the rapid collapse and disappearance of Christianity shortly after the Islamic conquest of North Africa is a direct result of affinities between the Arianized population of Vandalic Africa, cultural similarities between tribal Berbers and Muslims, and the destruction of Catholic orthodoxy by Arian Vandal persecution.[4] A diametrically opposite position is taken by Kaegi,[5] who insists that Arianism never spread widely among the population of Africa and that the destruction of the Vandal descendants by the Orthodox Byzantine administration eliminated Arianism as a factor in the following century. Since Cyrenaica was never conquered by the Vandals, this is a theoretical case. But not so the general issue of religious dissent, for there are indications that all was not well in the religious life of the Pentapolis.

Goodchild contends that the unsuccessful Byzantine resistance was due to a combination of the benevolent neutrality (or outright support) displayed by the Berber tribes to the Arab invaders and the religious hostility of the Monophysite peasant population toward the Orthodox supporters of the government. The case for support from the Berber tribes, both nomadic and sedentarized, is a strong

---

[1]B. Evetts, trans., "History of the Patriarchs of the Coptic Church of Alexandria," in R. Graffin and F. Nau (eds.), Patrologia Orientalis, I (Paris: Firmin Didot, 1903), 485-86. Joyce Reynolds kindly has called my attention to this reference.

[2]Goodchild, Cyrene and Apollonia, p. 28.

[3]For example, the parallels between the Arianism of Justinian's reign and the Donatist doctrines of a century and a half earlier recounted by R. A. Markus, "Reflections on Religious Dissent in North Africa in the Byzantine Period," Studies in Church History, III (1966), 140-49.

[4]C. J. Speel, "The Disappearance of Christianity from North Africa in the Wake of the Rise of Islam," Church History, XXIX (1960), 379-97.

[5]Walter E. Kaegi, "Arianism and the Byzantine Army in Africa 533-546," Traditio, XXI (1965), 52-53.

one.  Not only did 'Amr ibn al-'Āṣ make Barqa, the city with the strongest tradition of links with the indigenous Berbers, the first object of his expedition, but also any opposition encountered at Barqa collapsed expeditiously.  This point is forcefully conveyed by use of the verb saliha[1] (he made peace; he reached a compromise settlement) to describe the terms offered to the inhabitants of Barqa; usually terms of this kind were only granted if a non-Islamic group submitted to conquest peacefully.  Although the kharāj (poll-tax levied on non-Muslims) was high, the Berbers were noted for their punctuality in meeting its terms so the price of cooperation must have been worth the cost.

Moreover, evidence exists attesting to Egyptian Coptic support of 'Amr's successful land and sea expedition against Tokra in A.D. 645.[2]  In addition to doctrinal disputes between Monophysites and the Orthodox hierarchy, which presumably were typical of Cyrenaica as well as of Egypt, archaeological finds confirm the existence of two churches in many of the small rural villages.  Limnias is one such; a massively fortified church in the village itself presumably served as a religious and military center for the Orthodox party while an unfortified church at some distance from the village met the religious needs of the Monophysite population.[3]  Knowledge of the political and religious situation in Cyrenaica was undoubtedly in the possession of 'Amr ibn al-'Āṣ and the other Arab commanders in Egypt as a result of their experience in the Delta[4] and from the Byzantine practice of using Arab mercenary cavalry.  Although the settlement of large numbers of Arab tribesmen before the conquest can be discounted, the presence of Arab troops in Cyrenaica around A.D. 400, and presumably thereafter as well, is attested to by Synesius.[5]  The knowledge thus gained,

---

[1]Ibn 'Abd al-Ḥakam, Futūḥ Miṣr wa 'l-Maghrib, p. 229.

[2]The literary and papyric evidence for this support is assembled by Richard G. Goodchild, "Byzantines, Berbers and Arabs in 7th-century Libya," Antiquity, XLI (1967), 116-18.

[3]Ibid., p. 120, points out that several other rural sites, not to mention the major urban centers with numerous Byzantine period basilicas, have more than one known church.

[4]The internal dissension over religious issues as well as the weakness of will of the local Byzantine leadership in Egypt that so successfully was exploited by the Arabs is discussed by H. I. Bell, Egypt from Alexander the Great to the Arab Conquest (Oxford: Clarendon Press, 1966), particularly pp. 130-34.

[5]Synesius Letters 4, mentions a shipwreck on the Cyrenaican coast in which he was involved wherein a number of his fellow passengers were Arab mercenary cavalry. Ibn Khaldūn, Histoire des Berbères, I (trans. by de Slane;

assuming the continued employment of Arab soldiers in Cyrenaica, could have
been transmitted eventually to the Muslim armies and have proved useful in
encouraging a lightning raid into Cyrenaica.

Nevertheless, Goodchild's theory of religious dissent as the prime cause
seems almost too neat. Although such dissent was a contributing factor it may
not have been as overwhelming as it appears. The very large numbers of fortified buildings throughout the jabal evidence a substantial governmental involvement in the area, an investment far greater than would be expected if the governmental party was an isolated and precariously-situated minority. The numerous
officially-sponsored rural fortifications probably reflect not so much an attempt
to hold down a hostile population of Monophysite peasants as it does the defensive
arrangements required to protect settled life in the face of constant nomadic
harassment. Religious dissent, nomadic raiding, government inefficiency, the
debilitating effect of the long conflict with the Sassanid monarchy (regardless of
whether Cyrenaica ever physically was conquered by the Persians or not), and
the political neutrality or hostility of the only slightly Christianized Berber
tribes taken in combination contributed to the rapid disintegration of Byzantine
control in the face of the Arab onslaught.

Results of the Arab Conquest

Considerable changes were instituted by the Arab conquest, but their
immediate effect was not apparent. Since the number of soldiers involved in the
initial Arab invasion was small, their impact on the settled communities of the
jabal was minimal. Extraction of tribute revenue was their main concern and,
since the inhabitants of Barqa[1] were noted for the regularity with which they paid
their assessment, it can be assumed that as long as the funds were forthcoming
they were left undisturbed by their new overlords. Settled life is known to have
continued,[2] and the best measure of this settlement continuity is the difficulty

---

ed. by Paul Casanova; Paris: Paul Geuthner, 1925), 40-41, indicates that analogous precursors in the person of the Banī Corra may have smoothed the progress
of the subsequent invasion of their kinsmen, the Banī Hilāl.

[1] Barqa, derived from the Greek city of western Pentapolis, became the
term used throughout the Arab world for Cyrenaica.

[2] Richard G. Goodchild, "The Decline of Libyan Agriculture," Geographical Magazine, XXV (1952), 155-56. Although archaeological work on this transition era is limited, some instances can be cited: (1) the existence of a tower,
rebuilt in the Early Islamic period, at Cyrene reported by R. G. Goodchild,
"Archaeological News 1963-1964 (Cyrenaica)," LA, II (1965), 137-38; (2) the

experienced by archaeologists in distinguishing between late Byzantine and early Islamic structures. As late as the ninth century A. D. Muslim travelers in North Africa could still find villages and towns where at least part of the population was identifiable as Rumi (Byzantines or Greek Orthodox Christians) and where agricultural traditions from the era preceding the conquest were carried on.[1]

But if the continuity of settled agriculture was to a considerable extent maintained in the immediate post-conquest period, clearly the Islamic conquest saw a shift in the relative importance of the various Cyrenaican cities and a reorientation towards the interior previously encountered only during the halcyon days of Roman agricultural expansion. Both the routes followed and the cities visited and described by Muslim geographers and historians bear witness to this altered orientation. Curiously, nearly all routes mentioned are in western Cyrenaica; few remarks are made about the eastern parts of the jabal. Heavily settled during the Roman empire and possessing at least three metropoli of major importance (Cyrene, Apollonia, and Darnis), the eastern jabal should receive at least some attention. Goodchild has suggested[2] that this reflects a bias present in the accounts of most of the Arab geographers who, he argues, limited their reports solely to places located on the main routes of travel. This explanation is attractive, especially since settled life is known to have continued at Cyrene and elsewhere after the Arab conquest. But it is by no means conclusive for, although most of the Muslim travelers report only the major towns and routes, comments can be found on sites not located on the itineraries of Qudāma and Ibn Khurdādhbih.[3] The lack of comment about eastern Cyrenaica may reflect

repair and secularization of the western church at Apollonia for use as a stable or barracks mentioned by Walter M. Widrig and Richard G. Goodchild, "The West Church at Apollonia in Cyrenaica," PBSR, XXVIII (1960), 71; and (3) the recent discovery at Tokra of walls constructed after A. D. 645 and of a green-glazed Arabic lamp dated to the tenth century by G. D. B. Jones, "British Archaeological Expedition to Tokra and Euhesperides 1969" (unpublished MS; mimeograph), pp. 2 ff.

[1] al-Ya'qūbī, Kitāb al-Buldān (Leiden: E. J. Brill, 1967), 343-44, mentions such communities at Barqa, Barnīq (Berenice), and Ajdābiya (Corniclanum). Qudāma, Kitāb al-Kharāj (Leiden: E. J. Brill, 1967), p. 222, describes the village of Takanist, situated in the jabal east of Barqa as "belonging to the Christians." Ward, "Place-names of Cyrenaica," p. 10, suggests that Takanist should be identified with modern Taknis.

[2] Goodchild, "Roman and Byzantine Limes, " p. 72.

[3] See, for example, al-Idrīsī's comments in Kitāb Nuzhat al-Mushtāq fī

a decline in the importance and population of the area, but it is more likely that
the Christianity of the bulk of the population in the east discouraged visitors and
that it was quite natural for Islamic travelers to visit and describe those areas
where their co-religionists were most numerous and where in consequence
security for travelers was greatest.

Although it is generally impossible positively to identify most of the
individual way-stations listed in the route descriptions of the Arab geographers,
a general outline of the route system and its remarkable similarity to the highways at the height of Roman agricultural development does emerge (Figure 26).
The main postal highway from Egypt followed the coast quite closely before turn-
ing inland to the Wādī Makhīl; a further three days' journey brought the traveler
to Barqa, and from thence to Ajdābiya, Ṭarāblus (Tripoli), and al-Maghrib.
Qudāma[1] mentions an alternative highway through eastern Cyrenaica to Barqa
via the more coastal parts of Jabal al-Akhḍar. This track is more difficult to
follow than the inland highway and the impossibility of locating the villages mentioned, together with indications that there may be gaps in the listing, make its
location obscure. Its course may have been that of the classical highway from
Paliuros to Agabis or it may even have gone as far north as Darna, while the
Wādī Makhīl cut-off proceeded more directly to Barqa.

The ascendancy of Barqa over the historically more important urban
centers of the eastern jabal and the western Byzantine coastal ports is typified
by its position as the terminus of the postal route from Egypt. Situated in the
midst of a fertile plateau, surrounded by mountains, and protected from Byzantine naval raids by its inland location, Barqa rapidly became the garrison center
for Islamic political and military control in Cyrenaica. The majority of the
town's population in the early Islamic period was Berber, although Arab immigrants, largely the descendants of soldiers, formed a prominent part of the
urban community. The Berbers were settled both in Barqa itself and in villages
surrounding the city and they were primarily engaged in agricultural pursuits
using wells and cisterns constructed by the ancient Romans.[2] The conspicuous

---

Ikhtirāq al-Āfāq (Alger: La Maison des livres, 1957), pp. 101-3, on Tukra,
Ṭulmaytha, and other communities on the north coast of Cyrenaica.

[1]Qudāma, Kitāb al-Kharāj, p. 221. The editor (p. 168) suggests that this
route proceeds along the coast whereas the route through the Wādī Makhīl leaves
the coast at Qūṣūr ar-Rum in order to follow a more interior orientation. Qūṣūr
ar-Rum (The Roman Castles) is to be identified with modern Ṭubruq.

[2]al-Istakhrī, Kitāb Masālik al-Mamālik (Leiden: E. J. Brill, 1927), p. 38;
al-Yaʿqūbī, Kitāb al-Buldān, p. 343.

presence of large numbers of sedentary Berber agriculturalists, while only cursory mention is made of nomadic Berber tribes in this part of Barqa, confirms the absence of major change from the settlement pattern of Byzantine Cyrenaica.  In keeping with the subsistence agricultural economy of the Byzantine era, little of real value was exported from the coastal regions of northern Barqa.  Most of the products were consumed locally or sold cheaply to travelers, although a small trade with Spain in woolen garments was carried on[1] and the coastal regions around Ṭulmaytha were marginal suppliers of honey, aloeswood, cooking butter, and the tar or pitch extracted from 'Ar'ar (Juniperus phoenicia).[2]

From Barqa a number of routes carried travelers on to the west.  One such road ran to Barnīq (the Greek Berenice, on the site of modern Banghāzī), the only site with a decent natural harbor in the region, and then continued to Ajdābiya along a slightly inland route.[3]  The most frequently traveled route avoided Barnīq entirely and proceeded directly to Ajdābiya via Sulūq.[4]  At this period Sulūq functioned as a local road junction, since the coastal and postal roads joined here only to separate again and follow different routes to Ajdābiya.[5]  In addition, another track, this one running through the fringes of the steppe south of al-Jabal al-Akhḍar, left the main Barqa to Sulūq route one day's journey from Barqa and rejoined the main road at Sulūq.[6]  Because of its location in a more marginal ecological zone than the other routes, this road was of minor commercial importance, but the identification of one of its most important stopping places with a local tribal chief indicates both that it may have been important for contact with and control over the local nomad population, and that nomadic tribes were now operating in areas that had once been within the settled agricultural zone.

The major beneficiaries from the Arab conquest were the caravan-

---

[1] al-Muqaddasī, Kitāb Ahsan it-Taqāsīm fī ma'rifa 'l-Aqālīm (Leiden: E. J. Brill, 1967), p. 236.

[2] al-Idrīsī, Kitāb Nuzhat al-Mushtāq, pp. 102-4.

[3] al-Ya'qūbī, Kitāb al-Buldān, p. 343.

[4] Ibn Khurdādhbih, Kitāb al-Masālik wa 'l-Mamālik (Leiden: E. J. Brill, 1889), p. 85; al-Muqaddasī, Kitāb Ahsan it-Taqāsīm, p. 245; Qudāma, Kitāb al-Kharāj, p. 222.

[5] The occurrence of two routes along this section of the coast conforms to conditions in the Greco-Roman era. See Goodchild, Tabula Imperii Romani: Cyrene (1:1, 000, 000).

[6] Qudāma, Kitāb al-Kharāj, pp. 222-23.

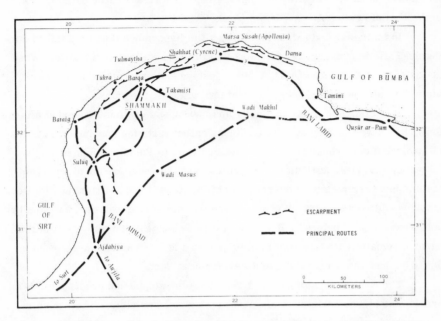

Fig. 26.--Barqa (Cyrenaica) after the Islamic conquest

oriented cities around the Gulf of Sirt, particularly Ajdābiya on the site of Roman
Corniclanum, and Surt further to the west. Located on the fringe between steppe
and the desert, Ajdābiya had little in the way of natural resources to recommend
it as the site of a large urban settlement. Indeed, during the Roman and Byzantine eras it had been simply a frontier post designed to prevent incursions into
the agricultural areas of the jabal by the nomadic tribes of the Sirtic region.
Building upon the system of wells and cisterns originally constructed by the
Romans, the local people were able to cultivate enough wheat, barley, cotton,
dates, and vegetables to supply their own needs and the requirements of the
numerous caravans traveling between North Africa and Egypt.[1] The city population was mixed, being composed of Arabs, Berbers, descendants of the ancient
Romans, Copts, and Jews. The city functioned as an entrepôt for Sudanese
exports and imports, for Awjila dates, and for the exchange of imported goods
for the wool and mediocre quality garments made in the city but undoubtedly

---

[1]al-Idrīsī, Kitāb Nuzhat al-Mushtāq, p. 99; Ibn Hawqal, Kitāb Sūrat al-
Ard (Leiden: E. J. Brill, 1938), p. 67; al-Bakrī, Description de l'Afrique
septentrionale (2nd ed.; ed. by de Slane: Alger: Adolphe Jourdan, 1911), p. 5.

representing the output of animals herded by the area's nomadic Berbers.  The
Islamic remains on this site are impressive, the fortress dating from the reign
of the Fatimid caliph Abū al-Kasīm (A.D. 934-946). [1]

In their size and extent they reflect the importance the site attained during the Fatimid dynasty due to its control of the coastal caravan traffic.  When
al-Idrīsī visited the area (A.D. 1150), Ajdābiya had experienced a severe decline and only one fort remained operational amongst the ruins. [2]

A similar history of continuity and subsequent decline unfolded at a large
town, five days' journey west of Ajdābiya, called Surt, the contemporary ruins
of Madīna Sultān, whose roots can be traced back to Punic and Roman origins. [3]
Its walls, mosques, agricultural activities, and the peculiarities of its inhabitants figure prominently in the accounts of Ibn Hawqal and al-Bakrī and its flourishing condition as a caravan center in the Islamic period exceeded anything that
it had experienced before. [4]  Recent excavations suggest that almost all of the
surface remains date from the Fatimid period and that the tenth and eleventh
centuries saw the height of urban development at Surt. [5]

The final two major routes ran through the steppe and desert regions and
avoided the higher portions of al-Jabal al-Akhḍar completely.  Their position
far south of areas occupied by Greco-Roman agriculturalists and their dependence on the camel for successful large-scale use is symptomatic of the changed
orientation of the country after the Arab conquest.  At no time during the Roman
period is there any indication that lateral movement through the steppe and desert attained any importance; indeed, the approaches to advanced Roman posts
such as Masūs and al-Makīlī were from the upper terrace and resembled ribbons

---

[1] Abdulhamid Abdussaid, "Early Islamic Monuments at Ajdabiyah, " LA, I
(1964), 115-19.

[2] al-Idrīsī, Kitāb Nuzhat al-Mushtāq, p. 98.

[3] For the checkered history of Surt, see Richard G. Goodchild, "Medina
Sultan (Charax - Iscina - Sort) " LA, I (1964), 99-106.

[4] Ibn Hawqal, Kitāb Ṣūrat al-Arḍ, p. 68; al-Bakrī, Description de l'Afrique
septentrionale, p. 6.

[5] Mohamed Mostafa, "Excavations in Medinet Sultan: A Preliminary Report, " LA, III-IV (1966-1967), 145-54, and Abdulhamid Abdussaid, "An Early
Mosque at Medina Sultan, " LA, III-IV (1966-1967), 155-60.  The discovery of
coins issued in A.D. 1023/1024 in the oasis of Zawīla attest the importance of
this region to the Fatimids both during and immediately after their conquest of
Egypt.  Mohamed Mostafa, "Islamic Objects of Art, " LA, II (1965), 123-27.

or tentacles extending southward from the Jabal. Not so the interior routes of the Islamic period. al-Bakrī is the main source for the desert track which figured in the east-west caravan traffic of the period. [1] Made practicable by the camel, it linked the oases of Jālū and Awjila via Santarīya (Siwa) and Bahnasā to upper Egypt; shorter distance, assured year-round water supplies, and security from Byzantine naval interference contributed to its development.

Between the oasis caravan route and the jabal road there was also an intermediate track traversing the arid steppe zone at the foot of the dip-slope and connecting Wādī Makhīl directly with Ajdābiya. At the junction of the jabal road and the arid steppe track, the Wādī Makhīl flourished as an important stopping place whose fort, mosque, markets, wells, and cisterns gave it an appearance "like a city." [2] Its population "rabble," largely composed of the representatives of various Berber tribes, conjures up images of a transitory frontier boom town. The five day journey that al-Bakrī suggested was required from the Wādī Makhīl to Ajdābiya seems of reasonable magnitude to account for the 125 kilometer distance from contemporary al-Makīlī area to Ajdābiya. This road is specifically described by both Qudāma and Ibn Hawqal and, despite some discrepancies in the spelling of certain staging points [3] and differences in the names of others, the route described by both authors is essentially the same. However, the extent of its use is unknown. Unlike the more southerly route through the oases, this section of Cyrenaica does not possess numerous permanent water sources. Indeed, the present nomadic regime in the Cyrenaican steppe is adjusted to this fact; grazing and water resources only allow its use during the winter rainy season, while during the summer months herds and herders withdraw northward to the more reliable water supplies of the jabal. Although the distances between Wādī Makhīl and Wādī Masūs, and from Wādī Masūs to Ajdābiya are not overly long, substantial bodies of men and animals could only negotiate the distance during the rainy season. At other times small, fast-moving parties carrying their own water might have traversed the desert fringe, but commercial caravans would be forced to follow other routes. This explains why the main east-west road used the safer and more reliable route through the jabal via Barqa.

---

[1] al-Bakrī, Description de l'Afrique septentrionale, pp. 14-15.

[2] Ibid., p. 5; Ibn Hawqal, Kitāb Ṣūrat al-Arḍ, p. 62; Qudāma, Kitāb al-Kharāj, p. 223.

[3] Qudāma's Jubb Jarawa and Wādī Masūs, for example as opposed to Ibn Hawqal's Jirawa (or Taym Laylayn) and Wādī Masūsh. Wādī Masūs is probably in the same area as the present Zāwiyat Masūs.

Ajdābiya, Surt, and the Wādī Makhīl[2] flourished in an era of governmental security but their inland location dramatically illustrates the changing orientation of the country. Urban and agricultural values reflecting a sedentary way of life were giving way to a value system that emphasized the importance of animals in life style adjustments. The change was not abrupt, nor was it due to the military triumph of constant nomadic raiding over the settled population. Agricultural activities continued to be an important part even of the nomadic community, settled farming survived side-by-side with pastoral life for several centuries after the Arab invasion, and continuity with the sedentary infrastructure was continued even when the pastoral genre de vie became the dominant livelihood form in Cyrenaica.

Reasons for the decline of settled life in eastern Libya should not be sought solely in factors relating directly to conditions in the Pentapolis, although these may well have had an important effect, but rather in trends outside the region over which its inhabitants had little or no control. In order for the expanded agriculture of the third and fourth centuries to be continued, strong political and military control from outside the region was required. Local resources alone were insufficient to maintain settled life in marginal areas where their continued existence posed a direct menace to the nomadic community. The Arab conquest, relying for its smooth and rapid success on the tacit, if not the overt, support of the nomadic Berber population and its latinized and sedentarized kin, resulted in only a partial triumph of the nomadic value system. A new equilibrium between the two groups was established. Nomads now had greater access to the better-watered higher elevations of the jabal, but farming communities still were able to sustain a viable level of existence. Fatimid interest in the communications network between North Africa and Egypt implicitly encouraged this development, although the new economic and political conditions favored the cities in the country's interior over those along the coast. Their rapid decline once the political control and stability exerted by power centers outside the country slackened points out the precariousness of settled life in these environmentally marginal zones.

## Mass Migration of the Banī Hilāl and Banī Sulaym

Various reasons have been advanced to explain the decline of urban and sedentary society in North Africa during the Middle Ages. The most common

view, drawing its support from Ibn Khaldūn, [1] blames the Hilalian invasion of
A.D. 1050-52 for the disaster.  Purportedly the enemies of all things urban and
civilized, these tribes are supposed to have swept out of Egypt, the blessings of
the Egyptian government sanctifying their punitive expedition, and destroyed
everything in their path.  To Gautier[2] this eleventh century nomadic invasion
was an extraordinarily virulent disease which infected the social and economic
body of North Africa and resulted in its decline.  The belief that nomadic and
agricultural societies are antithetical opposites contributed to acceptance of this
interpretation, and the Hilalian tribes thus became "locusts" who followed a
"scorched earth policy"[3] in which the "goats of the invaders ate lustily in the
gardens and orchards"[4] of the sedentary community and eventually demolished
them.

In exposed and isolated sites such as Ajdābiya and Surt the insecurity
caused by nomadic attacks might well dry up the stream of caravan travel upon
which their economy depended.  But for those parts of Barqa and North Africa
where urban centers were supported by a substantial population of peasant farmers, permanent submersion under a wave of nomadic invaders would be unlikely
unless other intervening factors were present.  Recently Poncet and Cahen have
argued that the Hilalian invasion followed a long-term economic and political
decline in North Africa and that a weakening of the central administrative power
exposed North Africa to the consequences of invasion, not vice versa. [5]  In Pon-

---

[1] Ibn Khaldūn, The Muqaddimah, I (trans. by Franz Rosenthal; New York:
Pantheon, 1958), 304-5.  Although the invasion of North Africa was launched
from Egypt, Ibn Khaldūn, Histoire des Berbères, I, 28 ff., is careful to point
out that the Hilalian tribes did not begin their career in the valley of the Nile.
Originally located in northwest Arabia, the Bani Hilal were nomads who vigorously raided the pilgrimage caravans to Mekka.  So obnoxious did their raids
become that they were driven first to Syria and then to Egypt.  When their turbu-
lence continued unabated, the Fatimid administration decided that unleashing the
Bani Hilal on a recalcitrant North Africa was an expedient mechanism by which
to guarantee the peace of Egypt and punish rebels.

[2] E. F. Gautier, Les siècles obscurs du Maghreb (Paris: Payot, 1927),
pp. 385-89.  Although seldom stated in such flamboyant terms, similar conclu-
sions about the destructiveness of the Hilalian invasion are advanced by Ch.-
André Julien, Histoire de l'Afrique du Nord (Paris: Payot, 1931), pp. 373-402,
Robert Brunschvig, La Berbérie orientale sous les Hafsides, I (Paris: Adrien-
Maisonneuve, 1940), 395, and Hady Roger Idris, La Berbérie orientale sous les
Zīrīdes (Paris: Adrien-Maisonneuve, 1962), pp. 205-47.

[3] Nina Epton, Oasis Kingdom (London: Jarrolds, 1952), p. 94, uses these
terms in expressing a common anti-bedouin bias.

[4] Goodchild, Cyrene and Apollonia, p. 31.

[5] J. Poncet, "Le mythe de la 'catastrophe' hilalienne," AESC, XXII (1967),

cet's view a series of crises, ranging from economic stagnation and internal disunity to naval defeats at the hands of Norman Sicily, came to a head precisely the moment the Banī Hilāl appeared, thus paving the way for their success.

Moreover, nomadism and agriculture certainly are not mutually incompatible livelihood forms. Cyrenaican bedouin practice a mixed pastoral-agricultural regime and many North African farmers maintain small flocks of goats. Even under conditions of greater production specialization, Ibn Hawqal's description[1] of the importance of meat, milk, and wool supplied by nomads to the urban population of Surt and Ajdābiya in return for dates demonstrates that the two ways of life can arrive at a satisfactory modus vivendi. But if Poncet is correct in believing that a decline in the caravan trade and the specialized agriculture adjacent to the urban caravan centers caused farmers to place increased reliance on producing the basic staples of grain and animals, emphasis in the more marginal areas inevitably would shift toward the nomadic end of the agricultural-pastoral continuum. Increased concentration on animals would necessitate an enhanced role for the nomadic way of life as the most effective way of adapting to the changed conditions. The augmented importance of nomadism thus becomes an effect rather than a cause of economic decline[2] and precedes the Hilalian invasion and becomes a precondition for its success.

The problem of assessing the impact of the Hilalian invasions is increased by the difficulty of accurately determining the numbers of people involved in the migration process. The initial conquest of Barqa in A.D. 642 by 'Amr ibn al-'Āṣ was achieved by a few thousand horsemen. Troops that remained after the conquest were quartered in a small number of towns, the most important of which was Barqa. These garrison centers eventually developed into the economic and religious hubs of their hinterland and constituted critical foci for the Arabization of the indigenous population. [3] However, initially the Arab element functioned as a ruling élite with relatively little cultural and linguistic impact on

---

1099-1120, and Claude Cahen, "Quelques mots sur les Hilaliens et le nomadisme," Journal of the Economic and Social History of the Orient, XI (1968), 130-33.

[1] Ibn Hawqal, Kitāb Sūrat al-Arḍ, p. 78. The nomadic seasonal regime described by Ibn Hawqal is remarkably similar to the one found in the region today.

[2] Jean Poncet, "L'évolution des genres de vie en Tunisie," Les Cahiers de Tunisie, II (1954), 321.

[3] A fuller treatment of the acculturation process is presented by William Marçais, "Comment l'Afrique du Nord a été arabisée," Annales de l'Institut d'Etudes Orientales, IV (1938), 10 ff.

the bulk of the population.  Prosperity was maintained, [1] the mass of the Berber
population remained unaltered despite some acculturation near urban centers,
and Christian villages still were found in the jabal by Muslim travelers.

The migration of the Banī Hilāl and Banī Sulaym was a different phenomenon involving not a few thousand soldiers but rather the movement of entire
tribes complete with families, flocks, and material possessions.  Ibn Khaldūn
clearly exaggerated when, 300 years later, he described their numbers as analogous to a swarm of locusts. [2]  Yet the impression of great numbers is suggested
by sources other than Ibn Khaldūn.  Marçais claims that in a census taken in
Egypt well before the Hilāl crossed the Nile, and at a time when many of the
Hilāl were still in Hijaz, a total of 500, 200 (including women and children) were
counted. [3]  At the time of the actual migration an unidentified source quoted by
Marçais escalated the figure to a total of one million. [4]

Clearly such figures are inflated even if the invasion is viewed as a process requiring several hundred years and several migrations waves to complete.
Although the surviving evidence is difficult to assess, it appears that the number
of Arab horsemen present in Tunisia at Ḥaydarān, the decisive battle with the
Zīrīd caliph al-Mu'izz, did not exceed 7, 500 and may have been as low as 3, 000. [5]
Admittedly only a portion of the tribal confederation was actually present at the
decisive conflict, but by no conceivable extrapolation of the existing meagre data
can migrating hordes of apocalyptic proportions be envisioned.  This conclusion
is supported by the observation that a substantial proportion of the nomadic confederation never reached the urban centers of the Maghrib.  Many were diverted
westward along the Saharan fringes toward the Atlantic and never penetrated the
coastal mountain ranges, while the Banī Sulaym never proceeded beyond Cyrenaica and eastern Tripolitania.  Even in Cyrenaica, where the majority of the
Sulaym remained, punitive expeditions conducted against the local population by
the Zīrīds [6] before A.D. 1050 cleared the way for the Hilalian invaders by reduc-

---

[1] Ibn Khaldūn, The Muqaddimah, I, 365, reports that under Abbāsid control
Barqa annually paid 1, 000, 000 dirhams into the treasury in Baghdad.

[2] Ibn Khaldūn, Histoire des Berbères, I, 34.

[3] George Marçais, Les Arabes en Berbérie du XIe au XIVe siècle (Constantine: D. Brahim, 1913), p. 69.

[4] George Marçais, La Bérberie musulmane et l'Orient au Moyen Age (Paris:
Aubier, 1946), p. 194.  Marçais regarded this figure as an overstatement.

[5] Idris, La Berbérie orientale, pp. 214-15.

[6] Ibid., p. 210.

ing the cohesion and effectiveness of the indigenous Berbers. In sum, it seems unlikely that a total population in excess of a quarter million ever crossed the Nile, that deletions en route reduced the confederation's numerical strength still further, and that the factors that facilitated their apparent success were rooted in the nature and condition of North African sedentary society and were antecedent to the eleventh century invasions.

However, the nomadic tribes were able to expand their influence and territorial extent in Cyrenaica in the centuries following the Hilalian invasion. Little literary evidence is available to support this contention. Only a cursory remark by al-Idrīsī[1] indicates that tribally organized Arabs herding sheep and goats were present in the coastal plain near Ṭulmaytha in the twelfth century. Although the entire Jabal al-Akhdar is potential grazing country, large portions of it can be devoted to agriculture. This is particularly true of the two terraces and parts of the coastal plain, and the Greeks and Romans were successful in denying nomadic tribes access to these areas. Thus, the presence of nomads in the extreme northern zone of Cyrenaica would suggest an increasingly powerful nomadic population.

In the absence of a strong centralized opposition, nomadic influence gradually expanded throughout the region forcing the sedentary population to come to terms with their militarily more powerful bedouin neighbors. The relative richness of the Jabal al-Akhdar for a pastoral people, coupled with the mixed agricultural-animal economy of the local bedouin, made them relatively independent of sedentary and urban products. Finding little of profit to be derived from the settled population, the bedouin went their own way, gradually incorporating the rural farmers and the vast majority of the urban population into the nomadic tribal structure either as outright genealogical equals or as marābṭīn client lineages. For the sedentary population the change was not an impossible one; animals always had held an important place in their economic system, now it increasingly superseded agriculture as the focus of attention. By the time Leo Africanus described the area in the sixteenth century, the dominance of a nomadic life style was complete. Moreover, Leo indicates that the urban centers of the Nile already derived a large part of their meat supply from the nomads of Barqa,[2] a marketing pattern that continued to have great importance to the Cyrenaican

---

[1] al-Idrīsī, Kitāb Nuzhat al-Mushtāq, p. 103.

[2] Joannes Leo Africanus, Description de l'Afrique (trans. by A. Epaulard; Paris: Adrien-Maisonneuve, 1956), II, 528-29.

nomads until after the Italian conquest. An alteration of style as much as of substance, this process of gradual acculturation culminated in a nearly complete bedouinization of al-Jabal al-Akhḍar and a return to the same pattern of land use in vogue when Battus led the first party of Greek colonists to Cyrene in 631 B.C.

# CHAPTER VII

# THE ITALIAN CONQUEST AND ITS IMPACT

Following the Hilalian invasion sources for Cyrenaican history are scanty for, with a shift in the political focus to Tripoli, Cyrenaica became a backwater. After a confused period during which a number of local Muslim dynasties exercised varying degrees of control over Tripoli and Cyrenaica, Libya passed under the control of an expanding Ottoman empire.[1]

## The Turkish Era

### Extension of Turkish Control

Using Tripoli as a base, the Turks gradually extended nominal authority throughout Libya. Banghāzī, after nearly having ceased to exist, was reoccupied in A.D. 1635 and a fort built to house the local administration. Darna, which managed to preserve a precarious existence thanks to Andalusian Muslim refugees, was occupied somewhat later. In both instances, however, Ottoman authority, as Rossi points out,[2] was of limited extent, indirect in its application, and seldom extended beyond the immediate environs of the coastal towns. Control from Constantinople was interrupted when the Qaramanli family usurped the pashaship of Tripoli in A.D. 1711 and, under the loosest imaginable Ottoman suzerainty, ruled Tripolitania, eventually extending their control to Cyrenaica in the last decade of the eighteenth century.[3]

Only after the reassertion of Ottoman authority between 1835 and 1858 did Turkish influence and physical presence reach the interior. Forts at al-

---

[1] For a brief interlude (A.D. 1510-1551) Tripoli was controlled first by the Spanish and then by the Knights of St. John at Malta. The best single volume summation of the history of Libya after A.D. 643 is found in Ettore Rossi, Storia di Tripoli e della conquista araba al 1911 (Rome: Istituto per l'Oriente, 1968).

[2] Ibid., p. 186.

[3] N. Slousch, "La Tripolitaine sous la domination des Karamanlis," Revue du Monde Musulman, VI (1908), 62.

Marj (Barka) in the western and at Qayqab in the eastern jabal were completed
about the time that Hamilton made his tour of the antiquities of Cyrenaica.[1]
Both were built on former Greco-Roman centers and were designed to increase
control over the bedouin inhabitants of the interior, which included an attempt to
tax the tribal shaykhs and through them from the tribesmen themselves. Perhaps for this reason bedouin relations with the Turkish administration lacked
warmth and friendliness.

European Impressions of Turkish Libya

European knowledge of Cyrenaica in the nineteenth century was limited.
Imprecise acquaintance with the goals, organization, and influence of the Sanūsīyya religious order, which took root and flourished in Cyrenaica during the
middle and late nineteenth century, bears out this contention. Duveynier's 1883
study[2] of the followers of Muhammid ibn 'Alī as-Sanūsī reflects uncertainty
about the distribution of tribes in Cyrenaica and the location of various Sanūsī
zawāyā, and also misinterprets the political aims of the order, which he sees as
an irreconcilable opponent of French interests everywhere in North Africa and
as a sinister manipulator of Muslim opinion as far away as Senegal and Morocco.
A few reconnaissances were carried out in Cyrenaica, but most of these either
passed through the area rapidly or were devoted to specific objectives.

Archaeological matters were a primary concern of many of the visitors[3]
and both scholarly expeditions and amateur travelers had much to say about the
numerous Greek and Roman ruins that dotted the landscape. In their accounts
only two cities of any size are mentioned, Banghāzī, the Turkish administrative
center, and Darna. All other sites were either of minor administrative importance, such as Susa, al-Marj, or Qayqab, or were ruined Greco-Roman villages
noted for wells and cisterns which were of seasonal importance to the bedouin

---

[1] James Hamilton, Wanderings in North Africa (London: John Murray,
1856), particularly pp. 55 and 134.

[2] H[enri] Duveynier, La confrérie musulmane de Sîdi Mohammed Ben 'Ali
Es-Sanousî et son domaine géographique en l'année 1300 de l'hégire = 1883 de
notre ère (Paris: Société de Géographie, 1886), pp. 14-15.

[3] The most notable of the archaeological expeditions was that of F. W. and
H. W. Beechey, Proceedings of the Expedition to Explore the Northern Coast of
Africa from Tripoly Eastward (London: John Murray, 1828). Although the primary purpose of the Beechey brothers was to map the coast of Libya with particular reference to potential harbors, their maps of the surface remains of major
cities on or near the coast form an important documentary starting point for
most modern archaeological excavations.

population. Nearly all the classical sites in the upper terrace that subsequently developed into minor villages in the Italian and post-independence era are mentioned by the early travelers.[1]

The contrast between the profuse and magnificent Greco-Roman ruins and the bedouin utilization of the same area fascinated the early European observers and led many to contrast " . . . the monumental industry of fallen civilization with the slothful hut of victorious barbarism."[2] To the casual eye, nomadic activity appeared to be a regression from the advanced economic prosperity and urban life of Greco-Roman civilization.

Not only were visitors convinced that the countryside was under-utilized, but also they were certain that it was underpopulated. H. Weld Blundell, in a letter written from the Fountain of Apollo at Cyrene on December 4, 1894, doubted whether, with the exception of al-Marj, he had seen more than fifty people during his entire journey from Banghāzī.[3] However, the validity of this observation is questionable since it was made in winter and thus at a time of year when most nomads had shifted to interior pastures.

Moreover, the conviction developed that this seeming lack of population was not related to the productive potential of the area. Optimists calculated that up to one million inhabitants occupied the Cyrenaican plateau at the height of classical settlement and that proper developmental policies could attain this figure once again.[4] As late as 1912, after the recognition of Italian authority over the northern coastal districts, enthusiasts, while admitting lack of knowledge about the specific territorial extent of Greco-Roman settlement, looked forward to the settlement of 700,000-800,000 Italians in the Jabal al-Akhdar on the basis of projections of a classical population of the same magnitude.[5] As

---

[1]For example, Andrea Pedretti, "Un' escursione in Cirenaica (1901)," BRSGI, series 4, IV, part 2 (1903), pp. 889-929, who mentions the Roman ruins of Cyrene, Ṣafṣaf, al-Abraq, Tīrt, Lamlūda, Zāwiya Bishāra, al-Qubba, Bayt Thamir, and ʿAyn Marra.

[2]Hamilton, Wanderings in North Africa, p. 79.

[3]H. Weld Blundell, "Mr. Weld Blundell in the Cyrenaica," Geographical Journal, V (1895), 168.

[4]Gotthold Hildebrand, Cyrenaika als Gebiet künftiger Besiedelung (Bonn: Carl Georgi, 1904), pp. 317-19. Hildebrand obtained this figure by multiplying an estimated cultivable area of 20,000 $km^2$ by an average population of 50 per $km^2$, both representing excessively optimistic projections of the area's productive potential.

[5]Roberto Almagià, "La Cirenaica: Il paese ed i suoi aspetti nel passato e nel presente," BRSGI, series 5, I (1912), 498.

usual, it was the existence of a small nomadic population and the presumed
under-utilization of the resource base that made developmental prospects seem
so promising. Favorable assessments of the environmental potential also contributed to the euphoria surrounding the prospects for colonial development.
Thus Gribaudi, though cautious about the total population that might be supported
in the jabal, [1] concluded after a lengthy historical summary that climatic change
was an insignificant factor in the area and that the rebirth of Libya under Italian
leadership could attain results worthy of its ancient grandeur.

To all who visited Cyrenaica it was the "Terrible Turk," decadent, venal,
and oppressive, who was responsible for the sorry state of Libya's economic life.
Regarded as being obstinately opposed to progress in any form, the Ottoman
administration was accused of frittering away the bounties of a generous nature.
To Hamilton, Cyrenaica was

> like so many countries belonging to the Turkish Empire, most bountifully
> endowed by nature with every source of wealth. Under former rulers it was
> flourishing and populous, but it has now become a waste; its scanty inhabi-
> tants are sunk in hopeless barbarism, and even their poverty is no defence
> against the grasping avarice of their governor. [2]

Nor were neglect and malfeasance the only charges laid at the door of Libya's
Turkish rulers. In a contemporaneous apologetic for Italy's military intervention in Turkey's North African possessions war correspondent Charles Lapworth
declared that

> the Turks were absolutely unfitted to hold and govern Libya, just as they are
> unfitted for government in other countries. Their presence has been a posi-
> tive blight on the place. Having stolen it, their only method of governing it
> was to plunder it; and it is not too strong to say, even having regard to the
> grave faults of other Colonising Powers, that the continuance of Turkish con-
> trol in Tripoli and Cyrenaica was a crime against civilisation. [3]

The list of wrongs supposedly perpetrated by Turkey was long and covered nearly every item calculated to offend and outrage European exponents of
progress and civilization. The catalogue of Turkish faults is instructive. Opposition to progress was exhibited by the exploitation of the agricultural wealth of

---

[1] Dino Gribaudi, "Sono mutate in epoca storica le condizioni climatiche
della Libia?" BRSGI, series 6, V (1928), 211-12, footnote 4. Despite the inflated estimates of Hildebrand and Rohlfs, Gribaudi doubted that the Graeco-
Roman urban population exceeded 50,000 individuals, although he was more hope-
ful about the potential for agricultural settlement.

[2] Hamilton, Wanderings in North Africa, p. 157.

[3] Charles Lapworth, Tripoli and Young Italy (London: Stephen Swift, 1912),
pp. 42-43.

Libya by ruinous taxes which destroyed the foundations of economic life. Fear of European culture expressed itself in the prevention of scientific study and exploration. The torture and massacre of the Libyan Arabs, and the tacit, if not official, sanction of the murder of Europeans in general and Italians in particular were dredged up to rally nationalistic European consciences behind the Italian program of armed military intervention. If Turkey was the "Sick Man of Europe" during the last decades of the nineteenth and early decades of the twentieth centuries, then Libya, in ethnocentric European eyes, was one of the most infected and dangerously ill of his component parts.

## Italian Intervention:
## Colonization from 1911 to 1923

### Italy's Search for an Empire

Italian failure to carve out a colonial empire when other European powers fulfilled their imperial ambitions was a result of her late development as a unified nation-state.[1] In 1881, as Italian ambitions began to focus on Tunisia, France declared a protectorate over Tunis and Italy was forced to search elsewhere for whatever scraps of African real estate had been overlooked by the other powers in the scramble for colonial possessions. Initially attention was focused in the Red Sea where a colonial enterprise was set up in Eritrea.[2] However, the stunning defeat administered at Adowa curbed Italian plans for expansion into the Ethiopian highlands and reduced Italian zest for colonial adventures.

Blighted hopes elsewhere led by process of elimination to interest in the Turkish-controlled African coast. A number of factors contributed to Italian determination to establish a colonial domain in Libya. Perhaps the most important was the oft-expressed belief that a colonial enterprise was an essential material and moral outlet if Italy was to avoid reduction to a servile status.[3]

---

[1] For a review of events leading up to Italy's declaration of war on Turkey, consult William C. Askew, Europe and Italy's Acquisition of Libya 1911-1912 (Durham, N.C.: Duke University Press, 1942), pp. 3-63.

[2] Maxwell H. H. Macartney and Paul Cremona, Italy's Foreign and Colonial Policy 1914-1937 (London: Oxford University Press, 1938), particularly pp. 275-95, offers a succinct summary of the history of Italian colonial activity.

[3] See Lapworth, Tripoli and Young Italy, pp. 4-5. Georges Guyot, L'Italie devant le problème colonial (Paris: Société d'éditions géographiques, maritimes et coloniales, 1927), pp. 1-18, sounds this theme, particularly as it relates to problems of over-population in the Italian mainland. Similar arguments were used somewhat later by Charles de Peyret-Chappuis, L'Italie: a-t-elle besoin

Haunted by the humiliation of Adowa, Italy's initial penetration in Libya was limited to peaceful attempts to gain commercial privileges and concessions. Although the amount of actual Italian investment in Libya remained small, Italy viewed with utmost suspicion the supposed designs of the other European powers, particularly the French and the Germans, on her private preserve.

For the small scale of investment, the Italian government and nationalist leaders blamed a hostile and uncooperative attitude of the Ottoman government, although how they could have expected a different attitude on the part of the Young Turk regime in the light of blatantly expressed Italian designs is obscure. Tension and hostility between the two states steadily increased. Mutual suspicion of each other's intentions and the Italian conviction that the Turks were perpetually hostile to Italy's commercial interests contributed to a deterioration in diplomatic relations. Finally, after fear that the French occupation of Morocco in 1911 Germany might look to Libya as an outlet for its frustrated colonial ambitions, precipitated an Italian ultimatum to Turkey followed by a declaration of war on September 29, 1911.[1] To many Italians war with Turkey over Libya seemed " . . . dictated by inexorable economic and political necessity."[2]

Early Years of the Colonial Venture

No attempt is made here to review in detail the course of the subsequent fighting.[3] Although Turkey was unprepared for the Italian intervention, a more effective opposition was organized by the few Turkish officers and troops and

---

de colonies? (Paris: Presses de France, 1936), to justify the Fascist colonial adventure in Ethiopia.

[1] Askew, Europe and Italy's Acquisition of Libya, pp. 45 ff.

[2] Carlo Schanzer, "Italian Colonial Policy in Northern Africa," Foreign Affairs, II (March 15, 1924), 446.

[3] A brief, but straight-forward, account stressing the naval aspects of the campaign is given by W. H. Beehler, The History of the Italian-Turkish War, September 29, 1911 to October 18, 1912 (Annapolis, Md.: By the Author, 1913); W. K. McClure's Italy in North Africa (Philadelphia: John C. Winston, 1913), devotes more attention to the land fighting. A more sensational and less flattering account, emphasizing the harshness of the Italian military toward the civilian population and the alleged massacres of innocent noncombatants, is found in Francis McCullagh, Italy's War for a Desert (London: Herbert and Daniel, 1912), particularly pp. 249-381. The official Italian version is found in Italy, Ministero degli affari esteri, L'Italia in Africa (Serie storico-militare), Vol. I: L'Opera dell'esercito; Tomo III Avvenimenti militari e impiego: Africa settentrionale (1911-1943) (Massimo A. Vitale, ed.: Rome: Istituto poligrafio dello stato, 1964).

their local Arab allies than could have been expected. Misled by presumed Arab hostility to the Turkish administration,[1] the Italians instead encountered nearly universal and unified opposition to their presence. While the port towns of Banghāzī, Darna, and Ṭubruq were seized with only limited opposition, all attempts to extend control beyond the coastal plain met with vigorous resistance.

Even after peace was concluded in October, 1912, the Italian position failed to improve dramatically, for after the withdrawal of Official Turkish participation, leadership in the Cyrenaican resistance movement passed to representatives of the Sanūsīyya religious order. Already a power in bedouin religious affairs, the Sanūsīyya began to express national and political aspirations as well.[2] Subsequent Italian involvement in World War I meant a diminution in Italian attention to the Libyan adventure despite the assistance rendered its position when a Sanūsī attempt to invade Egypt in support of the Turkish war effort was crushed by Great Britain.[3] Although at one point Italian troops nominally controlled all of the Cyrenaican jabal, revolts in Tripolitania, the continued hostility of the rural Cyrenaican population, difficulties in supplying isolated garrisons, and the competing demands of the European theater of operations led to a withdrawal of the military forces to the coastal districts and the environs of the major urban centers. In such a state of near continuous combat, insecurity precluded the possibility of agricultural settlement by Italians in the interior of Cyrenaica, just as the initial attempts at agricultural development in Tripolitania ran afoul a widespread revolt in 1915 and collapsed when troops were withdrawn from interior security duties and concentrated in the vicinity of a few coastal towns.[4]

---

[1]N. Slousch, "Le nouveau régime Turc et Tripoli, " Revue du Monde Musulman, VI (1908), 54, is typical of travelers whose reports of anti-Turkish hostility encouraged expectations of Arab neutrality if not outright support.

[2]Evans-Pritchard, The Sanusi of Cyrenaica, pp. 103-6.

[3]Sir Duncan Cumming, "The Sanusiya in the First World War" (unpublished MS from the Libya in History conference; Banghāzī: University of Libya, 1968), and Evans-Pritchard, The Sanusi of Cyrenaica, pp. 125-33. S. C. Rolls, Steel Chariots in the Desert (London: Jonathan Cape, 1937), pp. 20-142, gives a more personalized account of the use of mechanized mobility in these campaigns.

[4]Gary L. Fowler, "Italian Agricultural Colonization in Tripolitania, Libya" (unpublished Ph. D. dissertation, Syracuse University, 1969), pp. 151-66. Fowler's study is an exhaustive examination of the political background to Italian colonization and the agricultural systems introduced with varying degrees of success into the Libyan landscape.

The extent of Italian influence in Libya remained minimal even after the end of the First World War.  Preoccupation with the domestic political scene, where disillusionment over the terms of the Treaty of Versailles and Italy's share of the spoil was fanned by extreme nationalistic elements and where the competition of mutually antagonistic factions served to paralyze the democratic process, made the formulation and vigorous execution of an effective Libyan policy impossible.  Among the many forces contributing to the subversion, corruption, confusion, and disarray of the supporters of Italian parliamentary democracy was the Italian Nationalist Association.  Prime movers in organizing public support for the Libyan adventure, Italy's nationalists were able to utilize the support generated for their Libyan policy to undermine democracy and pave the way for the triumph of Fascism.[1]

Throughout the post-war era Italy's Libyan policy was essentially a holding operation and Italian ineffectiveness in dealing with local Arab opposition to its rule is typified by the so-called modus vivendi of Acroma ('Akrama).[2]  Formally signed on April 17, 1917, the Acroma accords brought an end to hostilities by recognizing the existing spheres of influence of the two parties.  Italy's authority over the coastal areas was confirmed, de facto recognition was extended to Sanūsī control of the interior, and the ultimate question of sovereignty was left ambiguous.  With both sides exhausted and neither in a position to enforce its will on the other a pause in hostilities seemed the only solution.  Thus, from 1912 to 1923 Italy was too weak politically and militarily to assert other than nominal authority; as soon as the situation altered in her favor, she set about rectifying the situation.

## The Italian-Sanūsī War (1923-1932) and Economic Colonization

The Establishment of Full Italian Control

The Fascist assumption of power in Italy in October, 1922 signalled a changed policy toward the Sanūsī.  Once Italian control of northern Tripolitania

---

[1]For detailed treatment of the role played by Libya in the domestic Italian political scene, consult Ronald S. Cunsolo, "Libya, Italian Nationalism, and the Revolt against Giolitti," Journal of Modern History, XXXVII (June, 1965), 186-207.  The reverse aspect of the problem, whereby the colonial situation in Cyrenaica changed according to the vagaries of Italian domestic politics, is described in E. E. Evans-Pritchard, "Arab Status in Cyrenaica under the Italians," The Sociological Review, XXXVI (1944), 1-17.

[2]The best English-language account of the period covered by the uneasy Sanūsī-Italian accords is Evans-Pritchard, The Sanusi of Cyrenaica, pp. 134-56.

was established, the military authorities began to assert their control beyond
Cyrenaica's narrow coastal belt. Pacification proceeded slowly and nine years
of bloody fighting were required before the Arab resistance finally was suppressed (Figure 27). The number of fortified outposts established was considerable and the prominence in the contemporary Cyrenaican landscape of their ruins,
often serving now as dwellings for sedentarized bedouin, bears mute testimony
to the severity and longevity of bedouin resistance. The losses sustained by the
bedouin during this period is another indication of the traumatic impact of the
period and most authorities suggest that one third to one half of the nomadic
population perished during the hostilities.[1]

Attempted Economic Colonization

Two basic, largely antithetical, policies successively dominated plans
for the development and exploitation of the colony. During the initial stages
"economic" colonization was the policy followed, although it was later replaced
by a program of demographic settlement. Briefly stated, economic colonization
represented a belief that maximum benefit could be derived from the colony's
resources by encouraging large-scale farming operations undertaken by those
private individuals or companies who possessed enough capital to develop their
property on a rational and profit-making basis. Once the government was satis-
fied that a potential grantee met its financial requirements, land was deeded to
it from the public domain or from newly confiscated tribal or communal holdings.
Only in the smallest holdings in areas considered suitable for irrigated agriculture was settlement by Italian peasant farmers anticipated. In all large-scale
estate operations, the managerial and technical levels were to be filled by Italians but the labor would be supplied by the native Arab population.

It was in Tripolitania, where Italian control, and consequently security,
was established by 1923, that the largest-scale economic enterprises were established. Yet even in Tripolitania there were considerable problems, the pace of

---

[1]The anonymous author of "La colonisation italienne en Libye," Revue des
deux mondes, 8. période, LI (June 15, 1939), 912-13, bases his calculations on
published Italian estimates of the animal population owned by Libyan Arabs and
the drastic decline that they show for the period 1926-1933. This argument is
based on the seemingly valid assumption that if the herd size declines drastically
a similarly catastrophic reduction in the human population depending on them
also can be expected. Evans-Pritchard, The Sanusi of Cyrenaica, p. 191, while
admitting the difficulty of arriving at more than an impressionistic assessment
of the casualty figures, maintains that losses as high as one half to two thirds of
the bedouin population may have been sustained between 1911 and 1932.

171

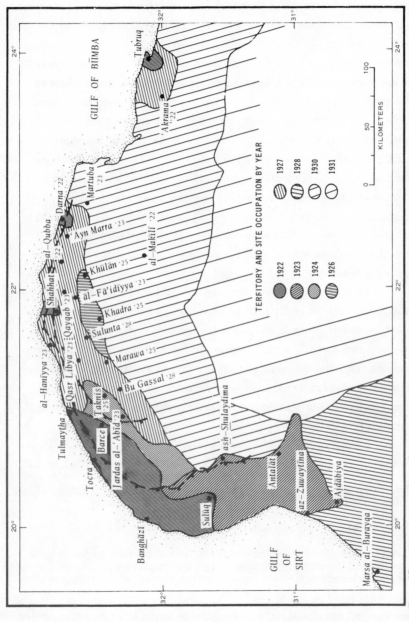

Fig. 27.--The expansion of Italian control in Cyrenaica, 1922-1932 (after Italy, Ministero degli affari esteri, L'Italia in Africa, pp. 112-13).

colonization lagged, and a number of successive plans were developed as the authorities experimented with techniques, cropping systems, and development strategies.[1] In Cyrenaica Italian experience was different and proceeded at a slower pace not only because of differences in the environmental and historical settings of the two provinces,[2] but also because of the delay imposed by the insecurity endemic throughout Cyrenaica until 1932.

Nevertheless some attempts were made during the war years to start economic colonization. These efforts were confined to those areas where at least a modicum of security could be provided, primarily in the coastal zone from Banghāzī to Tocra and the lower terrace from al-Abyar to Barce (al-Marj) in the west, and the Darna oasis in the east. In Darna most of the effort was by small-scale proprietors who attempted to utilize the local variety of banana, introduced from Egypt in the sixteenth century, to organize an export fruit trade.[3] Locally unique environmental conditions of plentiful water, mild winters, rich soil, and abundant shade from the oasis' palms encouraged an increase in the number of banana plants to around 40,000 after 1926, but the limited size of the oasis prevented the development of major economies of scale and the further expansion of the industry.[4]

In western Cyrenaica the granting and occupation of concessions proceeded slowly and with generally indifferent success. Security was the major problem and the unsettled conditions made fortification of the concession centers a practical necessity.[5] In this respect the initial Italian attempts to colonize Cyrenaica resemble the fortified farms of Roman and Byzantine settlement, although they were less numerous, were constructed on a larger scale, and reflected changes in military technology in their provision of semi-circular machine gun turrets in the corners.

---

[1]Fowler, "Italian Agricultural Colonization in Tripolitania," pp. 88-237.

[2]Jean Despois, La colonisation italienne en Libye (Paris: Larose, 1935), is particularly sensitive to these differences.

[3]Ibid., p. 112.

[4]Despois considered the extension of the banana plantations to the even smaller oasis of al-Atrūn (and possibly also to the coastal plain at Susa) a possibility, but its development for subsistence Arab agriculturalists eliminated this option.

[5]See the photographs of fortified concession farms in Angelo Piccioli (ed.), La nuova Italia d'oltremare (2 vols.; Verona: A. Mondadori, 1933), I, 575, 585, 599, 604.

The 1927 Tocra concession of the Colonia Libica del Fascio Milanese, comprising 1, 600 hectares south of the town, was typical of the unsuccessful agricultural enterprises of the era.  In 1931, when failure was obvious, management of the estate was placed under the direction of the Director of Agricultural Services for Cyrenaica.  Graziani, in imitation of the limitanei settlements of Roman frontier experience, then established a militia unit in an old fort four kilometers outside Tocra in an attempt to bring the concession's land into production. [1] In so doing Graziani was simply following an earlier prediction that " . . . the Italian soldier turned civilian will 'make good' where the indigenous, indolent Arab and Bedouin have barely scraped a living. "[2] With a large area to be cultivated and with only limited mechanized equipment available, considerable reliance had to be placed on local Arab labor and partially as a result the future of the concession remained in doubt.  Another group participating in economic colonization was the Unione Coloniale Italo-Arabe which specialized in small-scale, intensive agricultural activities and concentrated its main efforts at al-Qawārisha (Guarscia) near Banghāzī.  By 1932 the Unione had nine colonists and 330 hectares developed at Banghāzī, 2 colonists and 217 hectares at Barce, and 2 colonists and 83 hectares at Darna, [3] not a very impressive achievement for an organization that was one of the earliest in the field.

Despite an occasional imaginative effort to deal with an unsatisfactory situation, the failure of economic colonization to provide the impetus necessary to encourage large-scale settlement and development was clear to all.  By 1931 only 82 agricultural families had been settled on Cyrenaican concessions[4] and a mere 96 farm houses had been constructed in the same period. [5] The total acreage granted was limited with only 12, 276 hectares firmly committed in concessions and a further 2, 017 hectares provisionally assigned. [6] These concessions all had been granted in the immediate vicinity of Banghāzī, Tocra, Barce, al-

---

[1]Mario Pigli, "La colonisation démographique italienne en Libye," Revue Economique Internationale, 26$^e$ Année, IV (October, 1934), 153.

[2]Lapworth, Tripoli and Young Italy, p. 153.

[3]Piccioli, La nuova Italia d'oltremare, I, 588.

[4]Ibid., p. 592.

[5]Some Data on Italian Activity in the Colonies (Florence:  Istituto Agricolo Coloniale, 1945), Plate XXII.

[6]Piccioli, La nuova Italia d'oltremare, I, 556-57.

Abyar, and Sulūq; no concessions in the jabal east of the Wādī al-Kūf had been assigned and all existing plans for development were limited to the western jabal. Here 34,400 hectares at Banghāzī, Tocra, al-Abyar, and Sulūq and 14,000 more at Barce were slated for development.[1]

## Demographic Colonization in Cyrenaica

### Background to Demographic Colonization

Fascist dissatisfaction with the pace of colonization led to attempts to accelerate development and to change the basic purpose and objectives of the colonial endeavor. This changed prospective ushered in the second period of Italian settlement, the era of "demographic colonization." This policy envisaged the mass settlement of large numbers of landless Italian peasants on small subsistence-oriented farms in settlements organized, financed, and directed by the paternalistic foresight of the state.[2] Three main themes can be identified in the literature supporting this shift in objectives.

The first theme harked back to arguments presented earlier in the century[3] and stressed Italy's obligations to advance the cause of civilization in the eastern Mediterranean in general and in Libya in particular. Almost invariably this is the theme emphasized when Italy's actions were justified to foreign audiences,[4] and the role of Italian civilization and progress in more effectively utilizing the Libyan environment commonly was echoed by uncritical foreign commentators. Underlying the civilizing mystique was the quixotic conviction that Fascist Italy was following the footsteps of Caesar, Augustus, and Marcus Aurelius. The remnants of imperial grandeur that impressed nineteenth century travelers in Libya served to inspire the dreams of Fascist functionaries and colonial officials. It was no accident that Graziani entitled his book Libia redenta ("Libya redeemed") or that the first two sections in Piccioli's bibliography refer to the "re-conquest" of Tripolitania and Cyrenaica. What better way to

---

[1]Ibid., p. 548.

[2]An overview of the plans and rationale for Italian colonization is presented by Italo Balbo, "Coloni in Libia," Nuova Antologia, XVII (1938), 3-13.

[3]For example, Paolo De Vecchi's archtypical justification of Italy's Civilizing Mission in Africa (New York: Brentano's, 1912).

[4]An interesting example of this imperialist theme is Count Aldobrandino Malvezzi's "Italian Colonies and Colonial Policy," Journal of the Royal Institute of International Affairs, VI (1927), 233-45.

demonstrate the superiority of the New Rome than to restore to the bosom of the motherland provinces that had been wrenched from her in earlier moments of weakness? How else to exhibit the excellence of Italian civilization than by resurrecting from their present degraded and decadent condition the commercial, agricultural, and urban glories of these lost Roman provinces? That such an undertaking was a monumental one, requiring massive infusions of state aid, large numbers of agricultural colonists, and a high level of technical skill in coping with a difficult environment, merely increased the transcendent significance of the undertaking.

If the colonial settlement of Libya could be justified by the psychological necessity to prove Italy's worth by recapturing past imperial glories, more mundane justifications and arguments were also put forward. Perhaps the most compelling argument advanced was the need to alleviate Italy's overpopulation problem. Southern Italy in particular was replete with landless peasant farmers and traditionally this population had found opportunities for economic improvement by permanent emigration overseas. Although encouraged under previous regimes, the Fascist government regarded permanent, as opposed to temporary labor, migration as a positive evil robbing the state of its most valuable resource. [1] It was the desire of Mussolini's government to discourage permanent emigration except when it could be directed to colonies firmly under Fascist political control.

Economic colonization was clearly incompatible with this goal for without massive state assistance it was impossible to offer enough incentives to encourage the emigration of large numbers of Italians to Libya. The change in the policy was signaled by June, 1928 decree which projected the parallel development of "economic" and "demographic" colonization. [2] Hopes for massive demographic settlement continued to be colored by optimistic assessments of the potential capacity of the Cyrenaican jabal. Enthusiasts anticipated settling between 1,000,000 [3] and 2,000,000 [4] Italian peasants in Cyrenaica and the official statement on the total size of the area ultimately considered suitable for agricul-

---

[1] For a full treatment of the subject see Attilio Oblath, "Italian Emigration and Colonisation Policy," International Labour Review, XXIII (1931), 805-34.

[2] Ibid., p. 831.

[3] "La colonisation italienne en Libye," p. 923.

[4] Oblath, "Italian Emigration and Colonisation Policy," p. 834.

tural production was 900, 000 hectares. [1] Overly sanguine though they were, such ambitions are a measure of the magnitude of the program the Italian government anticipated initiating.

Far more than an expanding population governed the rationale for demographic settlement. The central Mediterranean and its control was of vital significance to Italy's strategic security. [2] Control of Italy's Libyan "fourth shore" would not only give Italy a strangle-hold on ocean traffic through the Mediterranean, but also would permit Italy to develop sources of supply under her own control for those vital commodities such as olive oil and grain of which she was a net importer. Simultaneously, the vulnerability of the North African territories to attack by hostile powers was great, so the settlement of large numbers of Italian peasants in Libya would serve a fourfold purpose. Labor supply would become available to develop the unproductive colonial territories, a military reserve of loyal Fascists would be created to defend the newly won territories, overpopulation on the metropolitan homeland could be reduced by settling landless individuals on state-owned land in the colonies, and the population so settled would remain under the control of the Italian state, rather than serving to strengthen potentially hostile nations. None of these objectives was necessarily compatible with an economic solution to the colonial question, for while the state hoped to be reimbursed ultimately for part of the cost invested in each individual settled, there was no guarantee that such would be the case. Concern for the economic feasibility of the various demographic settlement schemes did not weigh heavily with Fascist planners. In its devotion to strategic, social, and political ends, Italian colonization in the 1930's thus differed markedly from the more free-wheeling, economically-oriented colonial development of other European powers. [3]

Although governmental moral and financial commitments guaranteed the level of support needed to implement successfully a demographic settlement policy, one major problem still awaited solution. The implementation of potential settlement schemes was delayed because the colonial government was not in undisputed possession of enough arable land to develop fully a rational and effi-

[1] Piccioli, La nuova Italia d'oltremare, I, 552.

[2] Delfino Deambrosis, "Importanza del Mediterraneo centrale nell' espansione coloniale italiana," BRSGI, series 7, I (1936), 226-32, sets out the strategic case for Italian control of the central Mediterranean.

[3] Sir E. J. Russell, "Agricultural Colonization in the Pontine Marshes and Libya," Geographical Journal, XCIV (1939), 273.

cient settlement program. Until October, 1932 the state had acquired by a variety of means some 120, 790 hectares.[1] Of this amount, 9, 124 hectares had come into the public domain by "natural" right,[2] 43, 441 by expropriation and revocation, 68, 225 from Sanūsī zawāyā and "rebels, " while a further 6, 000 hectares to complete the total were apparently confiscated from or revoked by individual rebels.[3]

Not wishing to expropriate the remaining land required in a completely arbitrary fashion, the seizures were cloaked in a quasi-legal guise. One method utilized before the era of outright confiscation was to acquire land from Sanūsīyya lodges without payment. This method guaranteed to the zāwiya perpetual rights to the land, but vested the use of the land totally within the state's prerogative provided a small annual rent was paid.[4] Since the land controlled by the Sanūsī zawāyā was usually the richest available in the jabal, the very large expenses associated with purchase at full value could be avoided and costs could be further reduced by keeping the annual rent nominal.

But for the purposes of massive demographic settlement, the land acquired in this way hardly was sufficient. Associated, as much of it was, with the zawāyā lands of the Sanūsīyya, it occupied scattered, discontinuous blocks of territory. Much of this confiscated land was located in areas outside the planned economic concession zones of 1932, or in areas too marginal to be considered conducive to demographic settlement. The inadequacy of the public domain for demographic colonization demanded a new approach to the problem.

This new departure involved the wholesale confiscation of land held as collective property by the tribes. The method chosen was to require the tribes to register their ownership of the land before a certain date, after which time all land not registered was considered to be property of the state. In a sense this procedure formalized earlier Turkish claims to absolute sovereignty over public land (miri) not having buildings or agricultural improvements. However, Turkish law never was applied outside the immediate vicinity of the main towns

---

[1]Piccioli, La nuova Italia d'oltremare, I, 548.

[2]Roads, woods, barren or unexploited wasteland were considered to be incontestably part of the public domain.

[3]Piccioli, La nuova Italia d'oltremare, I, 556-57.

[4]E. E. Evans-Pritchard, "Italy and the Sanusiya Order in Cyrenaica, " Bulletin of the School of Oriental and African Studies (University of London), XI (1943-1946), 850.

and, although tax collection was founded ultimately upon presumed state ownership of all land, in practice the bedouin were neither required to register their
holdings nor challenged in their perpetual utilization of them. But failure to
register in compliance with the new Italian regulations carried fatal consequences,
since the colonial government claimed the right to dispose of such "derelict"
property as it saw fit and had plans in progress to fill up the unoccupied space
with Italian settlers.

The procedure followed in confiscating the tribal lands was particularly
unscrupulous.[1] Notification of the land registration requirement was published
in Italian in government offices where none of the interested parties were likely
to see it. Small wonder that a nearly clean sweep was made and most of the
tribal land officially reverted to the state. Even when, perhaps as a sop to international opinion, compensation was offered to the dispossessed, no opportunity
for impartial assessment of the value of the property was made available and
only paltry and inadequate compensatory sums were furnished. With the advantage of hindsight Malvezzi's claim that "from the outset of her colonial expansion
Italy has recognized the native right to property [and] wherever it has been expedient to make native reserves, such reserves have been rendered inalienable"[2]
assumes a special irony.

Although the amount of land actually allocated in 1932 for colonization
schemes was limited, the developing Italian agricultural frontier consciously
excluded the native population from meaningful participation. In this respect
the Italian colonial enterprise was similar to the "frontiers of exclusion" that
characterized in varying degrees the European settlement experience in the
United States, Canada, Australia, and South Africa.[3] Denied access to the best
agricultural land (some 400,000-500,000 hectares of which were confiscated[4]),
the bedouin were relegated to the southern slopes of the jabal. Here they were

---

[1] For the entire process see Evans-Pritchard, The Sanusi of Cyrenaica,
pp. 221-25.

[2] Malvezzi, "Italian Colonies and Colonial Policy," p. 236.

[3] A review of the frontier experiences of these areas and their significance
is presented by Marvin W. Mikesell, "Comparative Studies in Frontier History,"
AAAG, L (March, 1960), 62-74.

[4] The exact amount of land expropriated is unclear. Oscar Schmieder and
Herbert Wilhelmy, Die faschistische Kolonisation in Nordafrica (Leipzig: Quelle
and Meyer, 1939), p. 98, favor the low figure, while Russell, "Agricultural
Colonization in the Pontine Marshes and Libya," p. 282, suggests a figure of
492,000. Evans-Pritchard, The Sanusi of Cyrenaica, p. 223, opts for a median
total of 450,000 hectares.

expected to eke out a precarious existence based on animal herding and catch-as-catch-can cereal cultivation. As conceived by the Italian planner, the bedouin role was to contribute animal products to the colonial economy while serving as a seasonally available labor pool that would make unnecessary the formation of a metropolitan proletariat. [1] Such agricultural labor would, it was hoped, yield additional benefits by encouraging nomadic sedentarization and a more "rational" method of stockraising.

The zone of Italian colonization in the upper terrace depicted in Figure 28 neatly bisects the northern and southern zones reserved for native exploitation. Since access to the water supplies of the lower terrace and Ṣāhil were recognized as necessary if the bedouin and their flocks were to survive the drought condition of summer, some provision had to be made to permit passage of bedouin flocks through the agricultural colonies to the coastal zone. Demarkation of a number of corridors within which seasonal movements could be undertaken under the control and with the authorization of colonial officials was the solution adopted. As part of the policy of separate development for the Italian and Arab communities, emphasis was placed on improving the material conditions of the bedouin principally by making provision for improved stock-breeding. Breeding stock and a veterinary service was provided by a pastoral village built at Jardas al-'Abīd (Nahiba/Risorta) in western Cyrenaica to assist in re-establishing the decimated bedouin flocks and an additional center was planned (though never built) for eastern Cyrenaica at Khadra (Verde). [1] The success of these activities in maintaining the bedouin life style is difficult to assess, although the suspicion and passivity with which they were received by the bedouin and the small-scale and limited resources devoted to them undoubtedly reduced their effectiveness. Since much of the Italian effort was directed toward breaking down bedouin social and kinship structures and remaking them in a Fascist mold, [3] the dim view taken by Arabs of most Italian efforts was justified.

---

[1] Piccioli, La nuova Italia d'oltremare, I, 622; Pigli, "La colonisation démographique italienne en Libye," pp. 155-56.

[2] Evans-Pritchard, The Sanusi of Cyrenaica, p. 226.

[3] Lack of time, rather than absence of desire, prevented the achievement of this result. For a review of Italian policy toward the bedouin from 1932 to 1940 see E. E. Evans-Pritchard, "Italy and the Bedouin in Cyrenaica," African Affairs, XLV (1946), 12-21. Fascist attempts to use the educational system to achieve this Italianization of the Muslim population are recounted by Roland R. De Marco, The Italianization of African Natives (New York: Teachers College, Columbia University, 1943), pp. 17-21.

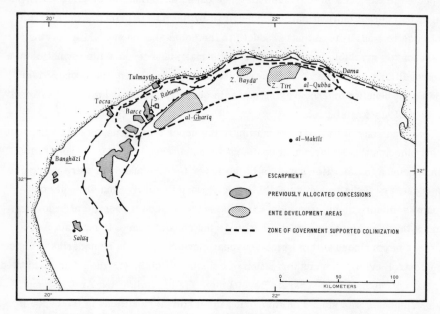

Fig. 28.--Status of economic colonization and planned Ente development areas in 1932. Sources: Piccioli, La nuova Italia d'oltremare, I, 531-625, and Istituto Agricolo Coloniale, Firenze, La colonizzazione della Cirenaica, map 1.

The Ente per la colonizzazione della Cirenaica

The break with the economic colonization policies of the twenties was symbolized by the creation of a parastatial organization to organize, promote, and carry out the demographic settlement of Cyrenaica. Although possessing autonomous status, the organization was responsible to the government and was dependent upon it for grants of public land and money. Created in June, 1932, the Ente per la colonizzazione della Cirenaica actually began its work in March of the following year. Of the more than 400,000 hectares then in the public domain slightly less than 100,000 were initially assigned to the Ente for developmental projects (see Figure 28). These fell into four discontinuous tracts with two small, nearly congruous blocks of property totalling roughly 3,000 hectares being located on the lower terrace near the earlier economic concessions at Barce. A further 4,000 hectare segment was centered on Zāwiya al-Bayḍā', while nearly 30,000 between Ṣafṣaf, Tīrt (Primavera), Lamlūda, Qayqab (Acqua-viva), and al-Fā'idīyya (De Martino) combined former zāwiya land and the newly confiscated tribal holdings. Subsequent surveys from Cirene to Massa (Luigi Razza) and al-Qubba to 'Ayn Marra added 20,000 more hectares to the Ente's eastern jabal holdings for a total of 55, 000. [1] Development plans in these areas represented a significant extension of the field of colonial exploitation to areas formerly blocked by hostile guerrilla operations. The final segment (al-Gharīq), some 45, 000 hectares on the upper terrace between the terrace crest and Taknis, was the largest single tract assigned to the Ente but it was not slated for immediate development.

Plans, based on the experience of several years of agricultural activity in the Barce plain and with appropriate modifications to fit the cooler climatic conditions of the upper terrace, were drawn up rapidly and the work of farm construction began early in 1933 (Figure 29). Initial plans called for the clearing of about 5, 000 hectares and the construction of 150 farmhouses at Luigi di Savoia (al-Abraq) and Beda Littoria (al-Baydā'). [2] The first seven families arrived in April, 1933 at Beda and the remaining families were installed in 1934. Further surveys in the Lamlūda to 'Ayn Marra zone and from Beda to the Wādī al-Kūf resulted in the addition of about 20, 000 hectares to the former tract and doubling in size of the latter. A few months later these areas were delimited into two more villages, Luigi Razza (Massa), named in honor of the president of the Ente, and Giovanni Berta (al-Qubba). Since the object of the Ente was to create a total community environment each colonization area was provided with a village center equipped with church, school, stores, coffee shop, Fascist clubhouse, and governmental and Ente administrative offices designed to provide all the goods and services peasants on the surrounding farms might desire.

Construction during this period involved the use of a distinctive house-type. [3] Built of rough-hewn fieldstone, the houses were flat-roofed, single-story structures designed to accommodate two families. Their unplastered stone exterior makes the several varieties of these houses a striking feature in the Cyrenaican landscape. A few two-story houses in this style also were constructed, although considerations of privacy made them unpopular; most of those built are confined to Luigi Razza (Massa) or to the Marzotta agricultural-pastoral concession land on the road to Jardas al-'Abīd where twenty-four families were settled

---

[1] Piccioli, La nuova Italia d'oltremare, I, 552.

[2] Schmieder and Wilhelmy, Die faschistische Kolonisation, pp. 160-62; Despois, La colonisation italienne, pp. 121-22.

[3] For an introduction to the colonial developmental plans and the major house types utilized see Enrico Bartolozzi, "Gli sviluppi della colonizzazione demografica intensiva in Libia, " L'Agricoltura Coloniale, XXXIII (1939), 3-11.

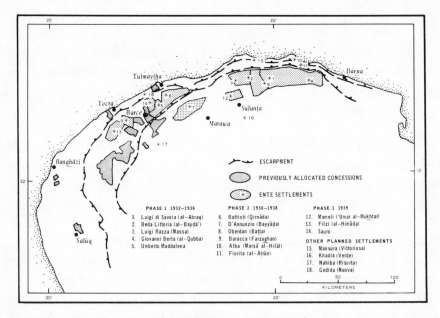

Fig. 29.--Demographic settlement, 1932-1939 (after Istituto Agricolo Coloniale, La colonizzazione della Cirenaica, map 1).

on the last private concession granted.[1]  Each house was provided with a cistern in an attempt to establish an assured water supply and, although some conceptual mistakes did occur (the most notable being the failure to provide a roof for the animal shed in the erroneous assumption that such cover was unnecessary in an African climate),[2] every attempt was made to provide for the comfort and success of the initial colonizers.  The development of a settlement can be dated approximately by the type of house constructed, since the earliest settlements, for reasons of security, avoided isolated farmsteads and instead concentrated houses in groups of two as a minimum and preferably into larger hamlet clusters.  Some 157 two-family houses were constructed in the eastern jabal between 1933 and 1938[3] and most are found close to the four village centers in the eastern jabal.

The Ente also had visions of engaging in pastoral activities.  Zāwiya Tīrt (Primavera) was one area considered suitable for this type of enterprise

---

[1]Schmieder and Wilhelmy, Die faschistische Kolonisation, p. 153.

[2]Ibid., p. 167.          [3]Ibid., p. 166.

and some Italian shepherds were brought in to supervise the work of local labor in the pastoral operation.[1] More ambitious plans for the al-Gharīq tract were projected. Here a concessionaire, the Colonizzazione agricola pastorale, was allocated a significant portion of the block to be developed into 300 to 350 hectare plots utilized by Italian shepherd families.[2] Ultimately much of the al-Gharīq tract was destined for subsistence agricultural settlement but for the moment pastoral exploitation seemed to offer a prospect for a small profit on animal products that could be used to subsidize the Ente's agricultural operations. Although a few agricultural-pastoral plots were developed north of Jardas al-ʿAbīd and some of the Ente's breeding herds were kept in the area, the project appears never to have caught on. Certainly direct large-scale competition of the Ente with the pastoral activities of the indigenous population would have been a serious irritant in Italo-Arab relations (as if there were not problems enough) and an inefficient duplication of effort if an attempt was to be made to utilize local labor and pastoral expertise on a rational basis.

The Ente per la colonizzazione della Libia

Planning for Massive Demographic Colonization

As part of a policy to improve the efficiency of colonial development the Ente was authorized in 1934 to supervise settlement projects in Tripolitania.[3] In recognition of this expansion in scope the organization's name was changed to the Ente per la colonizzazione della Libia. Work continued in Cyrenaica and concentrated on the Barce Plain. Here the Sīdī Rahuma tract was combined with surrounding land, subdivided, a village center constructed, and the community of Umberto Maddalena created and settled in 1936. Activity was less intense at the four upper terrace villages, although by March, 1938, 294 families totalling 2,157 people had been established on completed farmsteads.[4]

However, the government remained dissatisfied with the slow pace of the demographic settlement program. In consequence, a policy of massive demo-

[1] Pigli, "La colonisation démographique italienne en Libye," pp. 160-61.

[2] Schmieder and Wilhelmy, Die faschistische Kolonisation, p. 90.

[3] Fowler, "Italian Agricultural Colonization in Tripolitania," p. 316.

[4] Schmieder and Wilhelmy, Die faschistische Kolonisation, p. 172. Most of these families were located on farms and Schmieder and Wilhelmy estimate that no more than 100-150 support personnel were actually living in the 4 village centers.

graphic colonization with an accelerated rate of settlement was proclaimed.
This envisaged the transfer en masse of large groups of settlers to previously
prepared farms and villages. The only criteria used in selecting settlers for
the program were that they have some connection with the Fascist party or its
auxiliary organizations, that the family unit be in good health, and that it be
large enough to provide all of the labor required for the family's agricultural
activities. With requirements so modest there was no dearth of applicants.
Yearly allotments of 20,000 settlers for a minimum of five years was the goal
and to support the program increased state financial support was made available.

The Royal Legislative Decree of May 17, 1938 defined the terms under
which the first group of 1,800 families were to be settled in Libya.[1] The Ente
was made responsible for the preparation and division of the agricultural land
and the provision of the necessary infrastructure of roads, villages, farmhouses,
water supply, and tree plantings. Technical assistance on a continuing basis
was provided by Ente experts on such matters as the proper crops to plant, the
appropriate mix of tree and cereal crops, the timing of planting and harvesting
and so on until the farm had demonstrated its ability to attain self-sufficiency.
In addition, the Ente undertook the marketing at assured prices of all surplus
crops produced by the farmers.[2] A grant of 100 million lire was made available by the state to the Ente for five years beginning in 1937-1938.

Direct monetary grants were not the only form of assistance contributed
by the Italian government. Further indirect support for agricultural settlement
was provided by such development projects as the provision of harbor facilities
at Darna and Banghāzī, the construction of a railroad from Banghāzī via al-
Abyar to Barce with a branch line to Salūq, and the completion of the Via Balba
(the coastal autostrade). Schools, hospitals, churches, clinics, theaters, and a
variety of other facilities were constructed in the major cities and towns. All
of these public works contributed to the agricultural sector by increasing the
level of available amenities and by providing the means by which surplus crops
could reach the mainland market, but their financing was not part of the Ente
budget.

---

[1]International Labour Office, "Italian Colonization of Libya," Industrial
and Labour Information, LXVIII (1938), 406-8.

[2]For a study of the wine industry planned for the province of Darna and
the large central grape-processing plant established at al-Bayḍā' to produce an
export product consult Antonio Ferrara, "La cantina sociale di Beda Littoria,"
L'Agricoltura Coloniale, XXXII (1938), 3-15.

The object ultimately was to achieve a network of self-sufficient, independent farmers who owned their own land. Both to encourage candidates for the mass migration and to make the achievement of self-sufficiency a reality, easy credit terms were offered to the new settlers. For the first five years of occupancy the farmer paid nothing and, in fact, was a paid employee of the Ente. Decreasing salary payments, inversely proportional to projected increases in farm income, were made to the farmer for each of the first five years in order to free him from financial cares. For the next three years repayment at the rate of 2 per cent of the mortgage loan on each property was to be made and only in the ninth year did repayment of the Ente's original capital investment begin. Twenty-seven equal annual installments (plus a further one per cent of the total value of the property for the Ente's administrative expenses) would result ultimately in full ownership.

The emphasis in the 1938 settlement plan was to combine the greatest possible number of colonists settled in the minimum amount of time with the most scientific and thorough planning conceivable. To achieve these ends large numbers of workers were organized to complete the clearing of land and its preparation for planting, the construction of houses, the provision of water supply, and the grading of roads before the arrival of the first settlers. All of the agricultural equipment, furniture, utensils, seed, and animals needed to begin successful operation were provided by the Ente. Great attention was paid to details, complete to having animals in the stable, seed for the autumn wheat crop already in the ground, and a hot meal on the table when the farmer first stepped across his threshold.

Eighteen hundred families totaling 20,000 individuals left Italy in October, 1938 with 800 of them destined for Cyrenaica; their installation in their new homes was completed by the end of the month.[1] All of the work from preparation of the land and houses to installation of the settlers was completed in seven months. The combination of speed, scale, and social engineering fascinated foreign observers who in varying degrees echoed Lowdermilk's observation that

> never before have pioneers in a new land found colonization so de luxe as in Italian controlled North Africa, now called Italian Libya. It seems as though a fairy wand has been waved across desert or neglected areas and suddenly they were transformed into completely established agricultural regions, with beautiful new model towns to serve them.[2]

---

[1] "Come si svolgera la colonizzazione demografica in Libia," BRSGI, series 7, IV (1939), 86-88.

[2] W. C. Lowdermilk, "Colonization de luxe in Italian North Africa," American Forests, XLVI (July, 1940), 315.

Settlement of the Green Mountain

Four new settlement centers were planned for Cyrenaica for the period
1936-1938. Only one of these, Battisti, was located in the eastern jabal (Figure 29) where it filled in the gap between the Beda-Razza zone to the west and
the Savoia-Berta segment to the east. One hundred seventy-eight families were
settled here in newly prepared dwellings.[1] West of the Wādī al-Kūf in the al-
Gharīq - Tāknis (Borgo Torelli) tract, the southern portion of which had previously been developed as an agriculture-pasture concession, the settlement center of D'Annunzio with 54 farms was established. Additions to the previously
settled jabal villages were also made and 23 families moved to Razza, 36 to
Beda, 51 to Savoia, and 31 to Berta. A further 50 families were scattered along
the "south" road through the jabal outside the existing structure of village centers, some in farmhouses along the road from al-Fā'idīyya to Sulunṭa and the
remainder in the old fort centers of al-Fā'idīyya (which was renamed De Martino), Sulunṭa, and Marawa. In all a total of 394 families were brought to the
eastern jabal, more than doubling the previous Italian agricultural population.
The remaining families in Cyrenaica's allotment moved to the new settlements
of Oberdan (Baṭṭa) and Baracca (Farzūgha) and was almost equally divided between the two sites.[2]

The success of the 1938 operation encouraged plans for further massive
migration in 1939. On this occasion 11,000 settlers[3] moved to five sites in
Tripolitania and to the third phase of planned communities at Mameli, Sauro,
and Filzi in Cyrenaica. Original expectations that a full complement of 20,000
settlers[4] would arrive were not realized. The outbreak of World War II effectively stopped further Italian settlement although there was an attempt to maintain momentum by continuing a token settlement program. Just how many settlers actually came to Cyrenaica in 1939 is uncertain, but it seems clear that
the planned villages were not ready to receive very many. Only Filzi seems to
have been completed. At Mameli little more than the village center and a few

---

[1] All of the figures for and locations of the new settlers in the upper terrace are derived from Schmieder and Wilhelmy, Die faschistische Kolonisation,
pp. 172-73.

[2] Ibid., pp. 155-57.

[3] "I nuovi centri rurali della Libia," BRSGI, series 7, V (1940), 143.

[4] Jean Leyder, "Voyage en Libye: Remarques sur le colonat italien,"
Bulletin de la Société Royale Belge de Géographie, LXIII (1939), 222.

farmhouses were finished and work at Sauro appears never to have been initiated. By late 1939 the momentum generated by the first years of massive demographic settlement had dissipated and the colonization scheme thereafter was a holding operation as Italian attention and effort was diverted into military channels.

Stages in Italian Settlement at al-Qubba

The progress of settlement can be illustrated by consideration of the area around al-Qubba (Giovanni Berta). Here three stages in the settlement of the district can be observed and some evaluation of the effectiveness and achievements of the program made.

Housetypes provide a key to the emerging settlement pattern. During the period of economic settlement and the early years of demographic colonization a one-story fieldstone house was most common. These were usually grouped in pairs in small hamlet clusters (Figure 30) at varying distance from, but always within support of, the village center. Once conditions of security had improved, this housestyle together with the hamlet cluster was abandoned and single-family dwellings were dispersed along the line of the autostrada. Characterized by their use of concrete material, a smooth exterior finish, and an entrance porch with two arches, they typify a sharp break from the settlement pattern of the past. Symbolically attesting to total Italian control over the jabal and to the Fascist ideal of independent peasant settlement supported by the bounty of the state, their location along the major highways connecting the earliest village centers represents the first stage in an anticipated total occupation of the agriculturally productive parts of the Jabal al-Akhdar.

Built just prior to the 1938 mass migration, these second period properties were only partially developed. Frequently only the house itself was finished and the work of clearing maquis from field allotments and setting out orchard plantings had barely begun when the first of the mass-migrants arrived. This is in sharp contrast to the development on the earlier progressive demographic holdings where the planting of olives, almonds, and figs and the initial attempts at reforestation with eucalyptus, pine, and cypress had made some headway. Even here the achievements, while impressive when related to the amount of time available for development, failed to attain the figures set out by the Ente's plans. At Berta farm units of 24-26 hectares were originally planned, but these were never cleared completely and most settlers made do with only 10-12 hectares.[1] Not only were grain and pasture fields frequently smaller than

_____

[1] Schmieder and Wilhelmy, Die faschistische Kolonisation, p. 162.

188

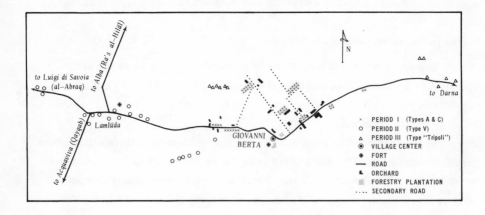

Fig. 30.--Stages in the Ente settlement of Giovanni Berta (al-Qubba) compensorio. Sources: NASA, Compensorio Gubba (1:25,000), Bartolozzi, "Gli sviluppi della colonizzazione demografica intensiva in Libia," pp. 3-11, United States Army Map Service, Marsā al-Hilāl (1:50,000), and field observations.

the minimum required for self-sufficient operation, but also the amount of tree crops planted was far less than the Ente regarded as an essential minimum. According to Ente requirements 25 per cent of the farm unit had to be planted in olives, almonds, or similar tree crops after the first eight years of occupation, and 50 per cent was expected to be planted in wheat after only five years. When the first ten years of occupancy were completed only one quarter of the farm could remain undeveloped if the farmer were to remain in the good graces of the Ente. By these standards most settlements fell far short of their goals and at al-Qubba only a tiny fraction of the land was in orchards (Figure 30) with most of the remainder lying idle or planted in wheat.[1]

For these delays in achieving the announced goals of the settlement program the outbreak of the Second World War and the consequent diversion of resources from the colonizing venture to military and strategic priorities is to blame. The lack of progress in establishing the demographic settlements on a

[1]Ibid., p. 92.

firm footing is apparent particularly in the last areas settled. The "Tripoli" housetype[1] is the dominant dwelling of the third settlement phase and some 100 were built in the eastern jabal during the spring and summer of 1938. Invariably they reflect the absence of opportunity to do more than build the house for they seldom have fields cleared or orchards planted. In eastern Cyrenaica the newly settled Italian peasants had possessed their new properties for only two years and barely had begun to reduce their total dependence on Ente support when the Italian army was first driven from the jabal by the British Eighth Army.

The departure of Italian military forces resulted in an immediate decline in security. The British military government noted numerous breaches of law and order as elements of the bedouin tribes originally displaced by the Italian agricultural settlements attempted to return and reclaim their land.[2] The Italian-German counteroffensive in April, 1941, drove out the British and reestablished a modicum of security, but when the Eighth Army returned in December, 1941 it found nearly all of the Italian administrators and police had withdrawn leaving the farmers behind. This time security problems were so great that outlying farms had to be abandoned and the agricultural population concentrated in the village centers.[3] When the Axis forces recaptured the jabal during 1942 in an offensive that eventually came to grief at al-Alamayn, it was decided to evacuate the entire agricultural population in Cyrenaica. Thus, when the Eighth Army returned in 1943 it found the demographic settlements derelict.

Planned Arab Settlements

Parallel to the development of demographic settlements for Italians was a program for the settlement of Libyan Arabs in agricultural villages. Unlike the policies of compensation for confiscated property, of restriction to unskilled agricultural labor, and of relegation to the interior steppe that characterized Italian treatment of the native population, these agricultural villages aimed at

---

[1]The term is used by Schmieder and Wilhelmy, Die faschistische Kolonisation, pp. 166-67, to describe the most modern and advanced of the colonial housetypes. The name apparently derives from its widespread use in Tripolitania, particularly at the Crispi and Gioda colonies near Misarata. Its use in Cyrenaica is much more limited.

[2]Rennell of Rodd, Lord [Rennell, Francis J. Rennell Rodd, baron], British Military Administration of Occupied Territories in Africa During the Years 1941-1947 (London: His Majesty's Stationery Office, 1948), pp. 37-38.

[3]Ibid., p. 245.

the complete assimilation of elements of Arab population into an italianized sedentary community. In Cyrenaica two such villages, Alba (Marsā al-Hilāl) and Fiorita (al-Aṭrūn) were constructed on the coastal plain west of Darna. A third village, Mansura (Vittoriosa), near Susa was planned but never built, while a fourth, Gedida (Nuova), on the coastal plain between Tulmaytha and Tocra was constructed in 1939[1] but does not appear to have functioned fully.

The object of the program was two-fold. On the one hand the coastal plain at both Ra's al-Hilāl and al-Aṭrūn had relatively abundant perennial water supplies which were sufficient to develop small-scale, labor-intensive irrigation agriculture but were not abundant enough to support large numbers of Italian settlers. Simultaneously, with the sāḥil not viewed as suitable for Italian exploitation, its development for the Arab tribes could be used both to indicate that Italian development schemes did not exclude the native and to further the goal of civilizing and italianizing the bedouin. These purely political motives were aimed at creating model settlements complete with village center, mosque, coffee shop, irrigation aqueducts, and all of the trappings of sedentary civilization.

By 1939 a village center and twenty-two farmhouses had been built at Fiorita and supplied with an irrigation system drawing water from springs in the Wādī al-Aṭrūn. Dry farming of wheat and the irrigated production of vegetables and fruit were the main agricultural products, while all of the land developed around the village center of Alba was irrigated. The terms of mortgage payment, eventual ownership, and Ente control over the crops produced were the same as those applying to Italian settlers. Yet the Italians had difficulty recruiting Arab families to settle the new plots and the overall contribution of the two settlements to the total economy hardly could have been more than nominal. In all only 32 farm units, totaling a mere 43 hectares, were ever developed.[2] The projects were little more than showcase efforts, similar to the minimal amounts of compensation offered for confiscated tribal lands, and they were treated as such by the bedouin.[3]

---

[1] Guglielmo Narducci, Storia della colonizzazione della Cirenaica (Milan: Editoriale arte e storia, 1942), pp. 130-31.

[2] Some Data on Italian Activity in the Colonies, Plate XXIX.

[3] Evans-Pritchard, The Sanusi of Cyrenaica, p. 226.

## Assessment of the Italian Impact

The era of Italian demographic settlement was not long enough to reorder totally the material organization of, and human relationships in, the Jabal al-Akhḍar. It was one, rather, of grandiose, often unrealistic, scheming, of imperfectly executed designs, of unfulfilled promise. For the bedouin it was not a happy era and the history of the period can be viewed as the story of the cultural and economic conflict of two mutually suspicious and hostile life styles for control of the same set of resources in the upper terrace. In the limited amount of time available to the Ente from the end of bedouin guerrilla resistance to the beginning of the Second World War an impressive start was made. Two thousand seventy-seven farmhouses were constructed, 2206 farm families settled, a total of 143,580 hectares ceded to the Ente from the public domain, and 79,831 hectares cultivated.[1] An equally impressive infrastructure of roads, airports, village centers, water systems, roadside cantonieri, schools, hospitals, railroads, and harbors were developed by the Ente and the colonial government throughout the province.[2] The cost was considerable. Some 718,764,315.40 lire were expended on both private and public agricultural schemes with the public projects being significantly more expensive than their private counterparts,[3] not to mention funds allocated to other public works. Italy realized little economic return on this prodigious investment. Although a large amount of land had been colonized by 1939 (Figure 29), considerable potentially exploitable land, both within the earlier demographic settlements and in the gaps between them, was still available. With this in mind, the desire of Air Marshal Balbo, the governor of Libya, eventually to settle 5,000 Italian families in the highlands between Banghāzī and Darna[4] does not seem unreasonably optimistic provided subsistence was the standard of living desired for the peasant colonizers. In pursuit of these settlement goals as many as 140,000 Italian citizens may have migrated to both Tripolitania and Cyrenaica by 1940, with the greatest concentration of metropolitans in relation to the native population being in the Jabal

---

[1] Some Data on Italian Activity in the Colonies, Plates XXI-XXIII.

[2] For a full statement of the public works projects of Italy in Libya and the other African colonies see volume II of Piccioli, La nuova Italia d'oltremare.

[3] Istituto Agricolo Coloniale, Firenze, La colonizzazione della Cirenaica (Rome: Tipografia del Senato, 1947), p. 29.

[4] Reported by Leyder, "Voyage en Libye," p. 222.

al-Akhḍar of Cyrenaica.[1]

But as Pan points out,[2] it is questionable how great an asset this migration was to the total productivity of the country.  Not only were the farms unable to attain a self-sufficient economic status in the time available, but also they withdrew resources that formerly had been utilized by, and were essential to, the native population.  The net result of the Italian occupation and colonization was to reduce the viability of traditional pastoral livelihood forms by pushing the bedouin into the most marginal areas of Cyrenaica.  The agricultural frontier was one that consciously excluded the bedouin from equal participation in the colonization process except for a few small showcase projects.  The separate development of the two cultural and economic systems, bedouin and farmer, with the best land being reserved for the Italian peasant immigrant, was the goal of massive demographic colonization.  The long-range prospects for the success of the project will never be known, for the intervention of outside forces arrested its development in its initial stages.

As for the bedouin, the period was one of frustration and trauma.  Constriction of movement, confiscation of tribal land, reduced agricultural holdings, decimated herds, loss of freedom, power, and prestige, and enforced concentration on the resources of more marginal areas served to place their genre de vie in grave jeopardy.  For the survival of their life style and of indigenous traditions, it is well that the Italian venture was so brief.

---

[1]Chia-Lin Pan, "The Population of Libya," Population Studies, III (June, 1949), 113-17.

[2]Ibid., p. 115.

# CHAPTER VIII

## CONTINUITY AND CHANGE AFTER WORLD WAR II

Throughout Cyrenaican history nomadic pastoralists and sedentary agriculturalists alternately have dominated the fertile plateau areas of the Jabal al-Akhḍar. Although the same basic resources were used by both, nomads always practising some agriculture and farmers keeping some animals, the life styles of each livelihood form were remarkably different. Each successive period saw the reuse of the previous era's resource base and landscape, but found them reconstituted and regrouped to express the life style and culture of the dominant group. Periodic oscillation between pastoral and agricultural dominance is a constant feature in Cyrenaican settlement history and the massive contemporary changes instituted by oil development simply reflect the latest installment of an ancient theme.

### Continuity and Change in the Cyrenaican Landscape

When the first Greek settlers arrived, they found a mixed agricultural-pastoral economy throughout the jabal. The same springs and agricultural areas that were important to the Berber nomads became foci for Greek settlement. But the life style created was totally different and involved an urban orientation, the surviving ruins of which rival in size and splendor the monuments preserved today in the heartland of Greco-Roman civilization. An urban civilization broadly based on sedentary subsistence farmers survived, despite periodic vicissitudes and occasional hostilities with the nomadic population, until first the Arab conquest and then the Hilalian invasion tipped the balance away from a concentration on farming and toward greater reliance on pastoral values.

Yet reversion to pre-Greek conditions was not complete and the post-Hilalian Arab bedouin, albeit with considerable adaptation, built upon the structure left by the Greeks and Romans. One of the major changes in the post-Hilalian period relates to the vegetation of the jabal. At no time in the Roman era, even at the height of agricultural expansion, was the jabal cleared completely of its natural vegetation. The most striking feature to Muslim travelers

193

in the area was its greenness. To travelers from the Marmarican desert the contrast between the largely barren coastal route and the lushness of Barqa must have been overwhelming and it is not surprising that their name for the Cyrenaican hills was al-Jabal al-Akhḍar, the Green Mountain. Rather than becoming contributors to further destruction of the arboreal vegetation of al-Jabal al-Akhḍar, the Cyrenaican bedouin are responsible for its preservation. One of the interesting implications of the bedouin animal orientation was de-emphasis of the role of agriculture. Rather than forming a central focus of interest, cereal farming played a secondary, though vital, role. As insecurity increased following the Hilalian invasion, land that formerly had been cultivated by the sedentary population began to go out of production. Seasonal movements of people and animals to pastures south of the jabal made it impossible to use all the land that had once been farmed. Marginal farmland ceased production first as the more mobile proclivities of the population reduced the long-term labor supply available to clear and improve potential fields. The best agricultural land, now owned by the nomads, remained in production as a complement to the animal component of the pastoral economy. But in derelict fields the maquis reoccupied land from which it had been removed at the cost of centuries of toil.

Continued use of the jabal's best agricultural land is not the only example of continuity between Greco-Roman civilization and the increasingly bedouinized society that replaced it after the twelfth century. Elements of the settled population were incorporated into the nomadic social structure, began to emphasize animal husbandry, and become nomads themselves. Also much of the framework of the former agricultural community survived to give shape and substance to the bedouin milieu. The bedouin settlement pattern, while a nomadic and shifting one, retained regularities that were related intimately to the pre-existing settlement scheme and these fixed points remain important today.

Cemeteries are one example of this. Almost without exception within the zone of Greco-Roman settlement, the siting of Muslim cemeteries is determined by access to loose, easily worked stones. Ruined farm sites are replete with this valuable commodity. Because burial is invariably on the surface, the body being covered with a cairn of stones, gravitation toward former agricultural centers for burial purposes is natural. Although it is possible to find numerous farmhouses without a nearby cemetery, it is the exceptional jabbana that is not in close proximity to a classical farmhouse. Until recently the same also could be said for the domed murābiṭ tombs, the burial places of local saintly figures,

that dot the landscape, for they were dependent on building supplies from classical ruins. Only since the introduction of cement blocks as a construction material has this absolute dependence been reduced.

Trails and paths followed by the bedouin are another tie to a bygone era.
In the higher jabal elevations pathways through the dense maquis are difficult to
keep open. Because both main and secondary Greco-Roman roads usually were
laid out with an eye to terrain, their gradient is often a relatively easy one. For
this reason it was natural for the bedouin to utilize them when moving flocks
from place to place, on the daily trips to the well, during seasonal migration,
or for journeys to market. Constant movement, although reduced in volume
from the high point of agricultural prosperity, has kept open the classical routes
of communication. Often roads have been reduced to the width of footpaths, but
the evidence of wheel-ruts and of shallow roadbed cuttings in outcrops is there
for the cross-country wanderer to see. The eye-for-country of the ancient
engineers has been confirmed in the contemporary era, for both the Italian
routes through the jabal and the recently constructed Tunisia-to-Egypt coastal
highway follow the third-century Roman roadway. Between Tīrt and Lamlūda
classical wheel-ruts and modern tarmac are seldom more than one hundred
yards apart, while the course of the Lamlūda to Ra's al-Hilāl road, constructed
by the Italians, in sections obliterates the ancient roadbed as it crosses the
lower terrace. Even in the southern slopes of the jabal as far south as Khūlān
the correspondence between ancient and modern tracks often is striking.

Tombs and cisterns also figured prominently, as they still do today, in
the bedouin landscape. In northern Cyrenaica the Greek practice of inhumation
in rock-cut tombs has found a place in the bedouin milieu. No respecters of the
spirits of the long-departed dead and unmoved by idle superstition, the less
mobile of the Cyrenaican bedouin have long followed a troglodytic existence.
Natural caves are also put to use as dwellings, but the abundance of classical
tombs in itself has eased the transition. Especially frequented during the summer months when the tribes are near the coast, tombs and caves slowly are
losing place as dwellings to the tin shacks of contemporary technology. Where
tombs are unused for human habitation, they frequently function as storage facilities for grain or straw. Indeed, in contrast to the southern jabal slopes and
desert fringes, where hand-dug pits are the common storage facilities, dampness
in the ground makes storage of more than a few years' grain supply impossible
and so the small, handy, pre-existing tomb is ideal for its changed functions.
The larger tombs, as well as cisterns that survive total collapse, also make

convenient stables for sheep and goats as the unwary explorer is apt to discover
to his chagrin. Both in the upper terrace and in the southern jabal slopes stab-
ling is not restricted to funeral or aqueous relics. Often elaborate corral complexes fashioned from the rubble remains of farmhouses or villages present the
uninitiated with an intricate maze, a veritable labyrinth of crumbling stone, that
still has functional significance to the bedouin shepherd.

Cisterns, well, and springs, however, form for the bedouin, as they did
for the ancient agriculturalist, the crucial central focus of livelihood activities.
A cistern does not have to survive as a viable water-storing device to remain
important. Even a collapsed cistern, provided only that the fallen roof can be
cleared away without too much trouble or that the original structure is deep
enough to absorb the fallen stone, can have inestimable value. Forming an
enclosed pocket, the cistern normally has a deep soil deposit on its floor either
from siltation in the original water catchment or from erosion of the surrounding soil subsequent to collapse. Sited with the idea of maximizing run-off collection from the surrounding catchment area, even ruined cisterns periodically
are subjected to substantial flooding. A combination of rich soils and concentrated local run-off make these cisterns a valuable garden spot when planted in
prickly pear or olives, not to mention their importance as an aid to navigation
in a landscape that is often devoid of other vegetation.

Cisterns and wells that are still capable of storing water are even more
valuable. Many of the classical structures retain enough plaster to be operational, and their ownership is highly prized. Cracked cisterns or those otherwise inoperational because of neglected repairs still have limited importance as
water-storage facilities after heavy local downpours. Their renovation by either
governmental or private initiative has been one of the beneficial results of the
post-1960 oil boom. In the seasonal north-south oscillations undertaken by the
bedouin between summer and winter pastures, it is the cisterns and springs of
the upper terrace and southern dip-slope that form the most important summer
consideration. Their ownership in the more arid southern zones is essential to
survival of men and animals and they form the most prized possession of a cor-
porate lineage group. In the north, where ownership is more commonly expressed in terms of land, they are no less crucial, for possession of or access
to them is part and parcel of controlling an area's agricultural resources. Summertime each year finds the pastoralist back in his tribal group's home territory
harvesting his grain and watering his animals and drawing his supplies for domestic water from a well, cistern, or spring that may well bear his own name
as the ultimate expression of ownership.

Thus, the classical settlement pattern, while reduced to its bare bones, continued to function after the influx of the Banī Sulaym in the Hilalian invasion. These same points formed a focus for the abortive Italian agricultural settlements. Continuity with the past was inescapable, but found its expression through the medium of a different culture. Shaped and adapted to fit the predilections of a pastoral mystique, firm ties to the area's classical heritage were nonetheless maintained. The best agricultural land, ruined farmhouses, tombs, roads, collapsed as well as still functioning cisterns, wells, and springs remained not simply as mute monuments to departed agricultural glory but as functioning ingredients in a different culture's way of life. This nomadic life style itself is experiencing rapid change as altered economic conditions encourage a re-emergence of sedentary values and a reintegration of nomadic culture into agrarian society.

The Impact of the Oil Economy

The pastoral nomadic regime analyzed in chapters two and three has undergone massive change in the last decade as a direct result of the discovery of oil. Although the oil fields south of the Gulf of Sirt are far removed from the main centers of urban, rural, and bedouin population, the impact of oil development and the far-reaching train of events instituted by it extend to every level of Libyan society. Contrary to the pessimistic assessments of development experts who inundated Libya following independence in the early fifties, [1] the abrupt discovery of extensive oil reserves has provided the Libyan government with the revenue to institute a variety of development projects.

As the pace of oil exploration accelerated government revenues increased dramatically, and the impact of changes introduced as a consequence of oil development soon was felt throughout Libyan society. Whereas in 1957 there was little

---

[1] The forecasts were universally gloomy. Benjamin Higgins, The Economic and Social Development of Libya (New York: United Nations, 1953), maintained that the challenge was to prevent further decay rather than initiate development, while John Lindberg, General Economic Appraisal of Libya (New York: United Nations, 1951), decried the lack of natural and human resources suitable to modernization. Even O. J. Wheatley, Draft Report on Agriculture in Libya (New York: United Nations, 1952), who was more sympathetic than most to the rationale of indigenous agricultural and animal husbandry methods, saw little prospect of achieving higher living standards if the population were to grow. As late as 1960, the International Bank for Reconstruction and Development, The Economic Development of Libya (Baltimore: Johns Hopkins Press, 1960), despite reports of possible major oil discoveries near the Gulf of Sirt, only indicated guarded optimism.

more to report than considerable exploration activity and optimistic expectations based on discoveries in Algeria,[1] by 1964 a total of 423 successful wells, both exploratory and developmental, had been drilled,[2] and in 1965 governmental revenue derived from the petroleum industry exceeded £L81.5 million (Table 4). Steadily expanding petroleum revenues continued to accrue to the government and the effect of this income on traditional Libyan society through inflation, increased employment opportunities outside the traditional livelihood modes, greater personal income, government development projects, accelerated imports, and increased exposure to alien customs and values was tremendous. From a position as a solicitor of foreign aid assistance, Libya was converted in the space of a decade to an independently wealthy benefactor with more funds to spend than eligible domestic projects.

TABLE 4

OIL PRODUCTION AND OIL REVENUE

| Year | Production (U.S. Barrels) | Petroleum Revenue (Libyan Pounds)[a] |
|------|---------------------------|--------------------------------------|
| 1961 | 6,642,000 | ... |
| 1962 | 66,543,000 | ... |
| 1963 | 161,272,000 | ... |
| 1964 | 313,796,000 | ... |
| 1965 | 445,253,000 | 81,565,000 |
| 1966 | 550,504,000 | 141,630,000 |
| 1967 | 631,705,000 | 184,954,000 |
| 1968 | 948,203,000 | 277,227,000 |

[a]At the official rate £L1 = $2.80.

Sources: Libyan Arab Republic, Ministry of Planning, Statistical Abstract 1968 (Tripoli: Census & Statistical Dept., 1969), p. 140; Kingdom of Libya, Ministry of Planing [sic] and Development, Report of the Annual Survey of Petroleum Mining Industry 1969: Ref. Year - 1968 (Tripoli: Census and Statistical Dept. [1969]), p. 20.

[1]Johnson Bennett, "Libya," in Hollis D. Hedberg, "Petroleum Developments in Africa in 1956," BAAPG, XLI (1957), 1568-73.

[2]Donald E. Barrett, "Libya," in J. D. Moody, "Petroleum Developments in Africa in 1963," BAAPG, XLVIII (1964), 1645.

Many of the traditional life styles of Libya have undergone modification, if not outright change, as a result of these oil-generated pressures. Whereas in the past travel outside Cyrenaica and contact with alien cultures and ideologies were rare, today large numbers of Libyan males have been outside the country and at any one point in time several hundred students are enrolled in foreign universities. Another example of increased contact with the outside is illustrated by the bedouin. In the past bedouin were so noted for their lack of religiosity that Evans-Pritchard could maintain that he had never met an ordinary bedouin who had been to Mekka or had contemplated going there.[1] Such is hardly the case today. Inexpensive airfares to Mekka are offered by the government airline. Although statistical evidence is lacking, the visual evidence of small white flags adorning rural dwellings during Ramadan, placed to invoke Allah's blessing on the hajji (pilgrim), indicates that the observance of pilgrimage is more widespread than two decades ago.

Imported consumer items have become commonplace in Libya. Electronic equipment is very popular,[2] with television sets, phonographs, tape recorders, and stereo systems particularly being widespread in the cities. Even in the countryside few tents or barakahs are without a transistor radio or cassette tape recorder. At less technologically sophisticated levels, a bewildering array of foreign products have deluged Libya. Rural markets are the catalysts for the introduction of imported goods to the bedouin and the diligent shopper is hard-pressed to find items of local manufacture. The bedouin is apt to depart the weekly market with plastic sandals from Hong Kong, baggy trousers from China, a porcelain teapot from Rumania, a pair of sheep-shears from Italy, Panamanian bananas, and Lebanese apples, all carried in an American surplus wheat sack. Local craft industries are losing ground rapidly as imported products are substituted for them.

Mechanized vehicles are acquired with particular élan. Today nearly every bedouin or rural family owns or has access to a Toyota, a Land Rover, or a similarly rugged vehicle, while Fiats, Peugeots, and Mercedes Benzes crowd the streets of the major cities. One consequence is a decline in the importance

---

[1]Evans-Pritchard, The Sanusi of Cyrenaica, p. 63.

[2]There is approximately one piece of electrical equipment for every Libyan, a statistic assisted by the Libyan penchant for purchasing new rather than repairing old equipment. For an analysis consult Aly R. Ansary and Abdallah El Abboud, "A Market Study of Consumer Electric Equipment in Libya," Dirassat (The Libyan Economic and Business Review), V (1969), 1-32.

of the camel. This is reflected in a steady decrease in the number of camels
recorded for Cyrenaica. Between 1965 and 1968 the camel population dropped
from 58,163 to 47,807[1] mirroring the camel's reduced importance as a ploughing and baggage animal. Indeed, bedouin and farmers are quite opportunistic in
their perception of the potential utility of both the four-wheel drive vehicle and
the tractor. Only the smallest and rockiest plots in the jabal are still ploughed
by camel and in recent years the tractor has become a common sight in the balta
zone in early winter where it is used to plough speculative barley plots.

The selective adoption of products of non-Libyan technology is not surprising nor is it necessarily unsettling. Exposure to western culture and attitudes through direct personal contacts with foreigners or by virtue of employment in various aspects of the "modern" economy[2] can be more so. The major
factors affecting the bedouin tend to be generated by forces outside their control.
These pressures have resulted in massive alterations in rural settlement and
livelihood patterns as the bedouin population increasingly has become sedentarized.

Factors in Nomadic Sedentarization

Perhaps the most striking change occurring in the Cyrenaican countryside is an alteration in the residence patterns of the rural population. Whereas
in the past the majority of the Cyrenaican population was composed of tent-
dwelling bedouin of varying degrees of mobility, today they are becoming increasingly "fixed" and stationary. Although the de Agostini figures do not make clear
the distinction between a semi and a full nomad, that element clearly identifiable
as nomadic in the 1920's was numerically the dominant component of the population.[3] By the 1964 census only 6,073 out of a total of 16,520 family households
in the Darna muhafadhat indicated that they were nomadic by virtue of their type
of settlement.[4] Despite the absence of more recent statistical measures, it is

---

[1] Libyan Arab Republic, Statistical Abstract 1968, p. 91.

[2] For a thoughtful discussion of the problems associated with such culture
conflict as it relates to work attitudes, see Frederic C. Thomas, Jr., "The
Libyan Oil Worker," Middle East Journal, XV (1961), 264-76.

[3] de Agostini, Le popolazione della Cirenaica, p. 444. See also the discussion of the difficulties of enumerating a nomadic population in Y. T. Toni,
"The Population of Cyrenaica," Tijdschrift voor Economische en Sociale Geo-
grafie, XLIX (1958), 1-11.

[4] Kingdom of Libya, Ministry of Economy and Trade, General Population
Census 1964 (Tripoli: Census and Statistical Department, 1964), p. 82.

certain that the number of nomadic households, particularly when defined as those living in a tent, has declined still further.

It is important to point out that in eastern Libya the process of sedentarization cannot be characterized by, or analyzed by means of, alterations in the genealogical and sociological relationships of the parties involved.[1] Unlike other parts of the Middle East, where sedentarizing pressures have a longer heritage and a correspondingly greater impact,[2] large-scale nomadic settlement in Libya is a recent phenomenon. Thus, changes in social relationships are difficult to distinguish given an extremely brief time horizon and they offer little insight into the processes at work. Moreover, the bedouin are not being absorbed into a larger peasant population with a resulting diminution of tribal and kin relationships. Instead, the tribal social structure is transferred to a new and evolving residence pattern with little breakdown in traditional arrangements. Tribal life retains its vitality and family affiliation continues to exercise a controlling influence among most migrants to urban centers; traditional social pressures are correspondingly greater in rural districts.

The sedentarization process is ubiquitous throughout Libya and has four basic configurations: spontaneous settlement, utilization of former Italian farmhouses, planned governmental housing projects, and rural to urban migration. The processes motivating sedentarization and the morphological features of the resulting settlement patterns produce distinctive patterns.

Spontaneous Settlement

Sedentarization of a spontaneous nature occurs when a nomadic family living in the countryside decides to abandon the tent and replace it with a barakah, or "zinco." As the latter name implies, the primary construction material for this type of dwelling is corregated zinc or tin. The barakah is symbolic of the transition taking place in the nomadic value system.[3] Even though many families

---

[1] Mohamed Awad, "The Assimilation of Nomads in Egypt," Geographical Review, XLIV (1954), 240-52, is an incisive account emphasizing the loss of tribal and genealogical identity through intermarriage with settled fellahin as one of the primary means of distinguishing a five-stage sedentarization process.

[2] For example, the combination of first pressure by the Ottoman government followed by alienation of pasture to an expanding agricultural community described by Wolfram Eberhard, "Nomads and Farmers in Southeastern Turkey," Oriens, VI (1953), 32-49, that resulted in near total nomadic sedentarization.

[3] For the symbolic role of the tent in social relations as well as its characteristics as a house type consult Stella M. Peters, "A Study of the Bedouin (Cyrenaican) Bait" (unpublished B. Litt. thesis, St. Hilda's College, Oxford, 1952).

abandoning the tent for the barakah seldom migrated over great distances in their seasonal cycle, the construction of the tin shed is symbolic of the partial abandonment of one set of values and the adoption of another.

The tin hut (barakah) is distributed widely in a dispersed pattern throughout the jabal. The distribution is not random and it is not solely the product of bedouin desire to ensure privacy and seclusion.[1] Rather it is correlated closely with patterns of tribal land ownership. Each of the tribal tertiary sections is intimately associated with a particular tract of land. Thus, land on the upper terrace (Figure 31) east of the Lamlūda - Ra's al-Hilāl road belongs to Ait Khādim, while land west of the same road is held by Ait Madī (both subdivisions of Ait Ghayth). Similarly, Ait Khādim territory extends as far north as the crest of the upper scarp, but the lower terrace is in the possession of the marāb-ṭīn Shuwayr.

Within each tertiary section, the tribal land is divided among the component families and, although theoretically subject to periodic redistribution, certain families are associated with specific tracts of land for long periods of time. When the shift from tent to tin hut takes place it is common for the barakah to be located either in isolation or in small genealogical clusters close to the lands that serve as the site for subsistence agricultural operations. Clusters of barakahs are most common in those areas where important water resources complement agricultural land. This explains the concentration of barakahs south of the Darna road two kilometers east of Lamlūda, for they are near an important summer watering point. Even in those instances where barakahs are more widely dispersed as an expression of reduced agricultural possibilities, territorially contiguous settlers tend to be genealogically related.

The tin house represents an intermediate stage in the sedentarization process. It is transitional between the tent and the stone hoosh (house). It is not a poor man's structure and for this reason is built by families who have a fair amount of capital. Because it is constructed entirely of imported materials, the cost is high. The investment in a fixed capital resource, a sharp break from the movable wealth in animals and carpets characteristic of the nomadic life style, is of fundamental significance. Neither the corrugated tin sheets nor the 2" x 4" and 3" x 6" wooden frames are cheap. The cost of a large two-room barakah can run as high as £L80 while even a relatively modest one is difficult

---

[1]See the comments of David K. Amiran and Y. Ben-Arieh, "Sedentarization of Bedouin in Israel," Israel Exploration Journal, XIII (1963), 161-81, in describing the sedentarization process in the Negev.

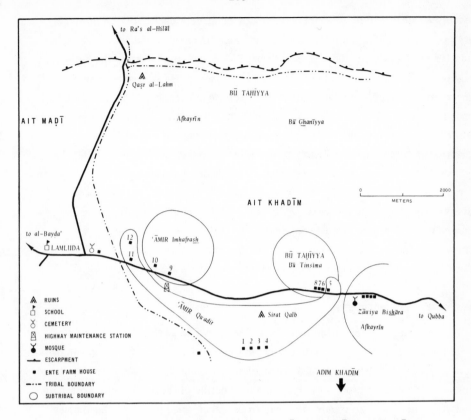

Fig. 31.--Ente farmhouses between Lamlūda and Zāwiya Bishāra.

to assemble for less than £L50. By comparison, the tent costs the nomadic family very little, since the potentially most expensive item, the hair and wool woven to form the tent roof strips, is produced by the nomad's own flocks. With female labor available within the family, the only expense is for the squares of cotton cloth frequently used to line the inside of the tent walls and for the cotton thread now increasingly employed to replace homespun wool in the weft. The transition from tent to stone house takes place gradually and mixed settlement clusters of tents and barakahs are frequently seen. Use of locally abundant field stone to replace worn-out tent walls while retaining the woven tent roof is often a first step, followed by the construction of a tin shed. As more resources are invested in the fixed dwelling, a concrete floor frequently is poured. Eventually, as funds permit, the tin walls are replaced by unshaped local stone or by newly quarried limestone blocks and the forecourt is surrounded by a stone wall.

In many respects the tin house is unsuited to the conditions of life still being pursued. For if the house type has changed, the traditional pattern of goat herding and subsistence wheat and barley farming that has characterized the maquis shrub areas for centuries continues relatively unchanged. Unbearably hot in summer and frightfully chilly in winter, the barakah makes a poor substitute for the high-ceilinged Cyrenaican bayt (tent) which possesses the diametrically opposite characteristics of shadiness, airiness, and coolness in summer and relative warmth in winter. The very stationary aspect of the tin house that prompts its adoption conspires to make it a health hazard. The relatively heavy winter-spring rains and the tramping of men and beasts focused in one area frequently turns the environs of the barakah into a sticky, oozing quagmire. The daily return of the animals to the immediate locale of the barakah contributes to a rapid fouling of the site. The heavy financial investment represented by a barakah precludes the possibility of moving easily into a new site, as does the labor involved in dismantling the structure. None of these problems were present when the tent was the common house type and a move of a hundred feet sufficed to escape from human and animal contamination and parasites.

The ex-Ente Farmhouses

Another feature of the sedentarization process is the use to which the Italian agricultural infrastructure created for demographic settlement was utilized following the departure of their original occupants. Because the Ente farmhouses were constructed on tribal land the question of their ultimate ownership and disposition was an important issue to the jabal nomads. Both the British Military Administration and, following independence, the Libyan government claimed that title to all property belonging to the Italian colonial government reverted to the state. However, political pressure brought to bear by the tribes plus the desire to maintain in, or bring into, production the Ente farms resulted in rental of the farms at nominal rates to individuals interested in productively utilizing the property.

Although numerous disputes, occasionally resulting in violence, characterized the distribution process, conflict was reduced by operating within the context of the tribal genealogies. The basic principle followed was that Italian farmhouses built within the recognized territory of a tribal segment should be rented only to members of the tribal segment concerned. The twelve farmhouses in the Ait Khādim territory between Lamlūda and al-Qubba (Figure 31) are an instructive illustration of the process. Located on both sides of the main east-west highway between the Italian cantonieri (now reused as a school) one kilometer east of Lamlūda and the Sanūsīyya zāwiya at Bishāra, the houses involved were acknowledged to belong the Khādim subsection of Ait Ghayth.

However, not all sections of Ait Khādim shared equally in the distribution
of the available property. A glance at the tribal genealogy (Figure 32) reveals
that only three of the six subsections received a share. The basic principle operating was the identification of the two major bifurcations of the Ait Khādim with
different parts of the tribal area; Ait 'Amir traditionally held the southern and
western portions of the region while Ait Bū Tahīyya occupied the northern and
eastern zones. Those subdivisions of 'Amir and Bū Tahīyya holding land outside
the areas in which the Ente houses had been built were excluded from the distribution. Thus, 'Adim Khādim of 'Amir, whose agricultural areas were further
south and whose life style required more substantial southward seasonal migrations, lacked a valid claim to the former Italian property. Similarly, the Bū
Tahīyya sections of Afkayrīn and Bū Ghanīyya, whose holdings were closer to
the upper escarpment in areas undeveloped by the Italians, also were excluded.
The Afkayrīn are something of a special case, in that part of their ancestral
land once included the Zāwiya at Bishāra. Four large farmhouses were built at
Bishāra by the Ente but, because the Afkayrīn had deeded this land to the Sanūsīyya, thus making it available to all the tribes equally, they were considered to
have alienated their property rights irretrievably. Instead, these farmhouses
were assigned to Misamir marābtīn who worked as shepherds and agriculturalists for the Bishāra lodge.

Within those sections recognized as having rights in the former Italian
property the distribution mechanism was different. Here the principle was that
each family, regardless of its numerical strength, should share in the property.
Each of the three families of Qwadir (Kirhawhā, Mahjūb, and Bū Brayq) as well
as the two families of Imhafrash (Aghzayl and Bū't-Tay'a) have houses and wherever possible lower level bifurcations in the genealogy are represented as well.
Thus, both 'Aqūb and Yadim of Kirhawhā and Mūsa and Dhayfalla of Bū Brayq
are represented in roughly equal proportions. Only Mahjūb of Qwadir failed to
have one of its three families represented, a direct consequence of the limited
housing supply. The same observation can be made with reference to Bū Tin-
sīma of Bū Tahīyya, only two of whose six families actually are represented in
the distribution. The other sections either possessed land elsewhere in the tribal territory or had shifted their location permanently to the city of Tubruq.

Although the guiding rule at the family level was an equal right to share
in the abandoned Ente property, within each family, a distribution based on
egalitarian principles was impossible. Too many individuals existed to make
total participation and satisfaction possible. Indeed, no firm rules can be de-

duced from the data available. Elder brothers did not necessarily possess first claim on the property. The absence of many family members, either as a result of a disruption in residence patterns during the war or of developing postwar employment opportunities in Darna, Ṭubruq, or Banghāzī, helped to reduce the number of claimants. Thus, within the constraints imposed by the need to represent fully each branch of the Ait Khādim having a claim on Ente property, the choice of actual homeowners appears to have been somewhat random, fortuitous, and determined by what eligible individuals happened to be in the vicinity when the distribution was made. While the agricultural agencies of the Libyan government retained veto power over property users and although removal for failure to farm was possible, little alteration in the original list of renters took place and where it did replacement by kinsmen was standard.

Settlement of the former Italian holdings within a tribal framework was typical throughout the jabal. [1] Notwithstanding the recognition on the part of most tribesmen that the government owned the Ente buildings, tribal ownership of the land on which the buildings stood was equally incontestable. In such circumstances any solution other than a tribal one was fraught with the danger of potential hostility. Moreover, the Ente properties were of potentially great value to the tribes. Located on the best pre-war tribal agricultural land, their repossession was essential if the nomadic economy was to resume viable operation. Although the houses themselves were of little value to people accustomed by preference and way of life to dwelling in tents, the cisterns attached to each farm represented a significant addition to tribal and family water supplies. Similarly in recent years government plans to complete the clearing of shrub from the Ente farms at low cost to the occupier has enhanced the value of their possession.

In this way the ex-Ente properties functioned as a magnet attracting substantial elements of the nomadic population to settle in them. This has been a gradual process and initially the farmhouses were used to stable the animals rather than to serve as human habitations. Where full occupation occurred, it has usually involved a substantial modification in the structure of the Italian farmstead. Whereas the Ente designed considerable open space between the farmhouse and the animal and tractor shed to the rear, sedentarized bedouin close in both ends of the courtyard with additional tin sheds and fences to increase privacy. Although it is still possible to see tents pitched beside houses,

---

[1] For an additional example from the Barā'asa tribal area between Massa and al-Baydā' see Tillson, Community Development Studies, pp. 111-14.

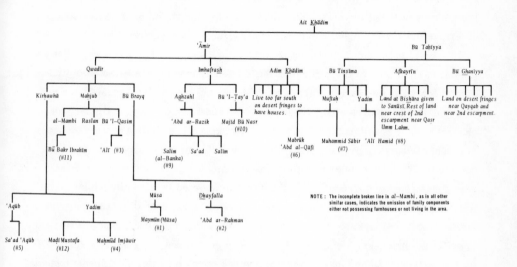

Fig. 32.--Genealogy of the Ait Khādim

increasingly this relic survival of the nomadic era is being abandoned and total occupation of the Ente farmhouses, often in conjunction with the house repair and land clearance activities of N.A.S.A.,[1] is proceeding at an accelerating pace.

## Government Programs: Social Welfare Policies and Planned Housing Projects

Government-sponsored social welfare programs have played a large role in encouraging bedouin sedentarization. Part of the policy of the former royal government was to create conditions favorable to a retention of population in rural areas.[2] To this end, considerable investment was made in providing the amenities of settled life for people living in the countryside. Scarcely a Cyre-

---

[1] The National Agricultural Settlement Authority. For an account of the agricultural projects proposed for the jabal see "New Farms for the Green Mountains," Libyan Review, II (August, 1967), 18-21.

[2] The need to direct development funds into rural growth in order to retard rural-urban migration and to prevent excessive concentration of wealth in a small privileged class is stressed by John I. Clarke, "Oil in Libya: Some Implications," Economic Geography, XXXIX (1963), 40-59.

naican village is without electricity and a modern schoolhouse, while the visually most striking feature of each village is its mushroom-shaped water tower. Nor were the religious aspects of life neglected for, as might be expected given the former king's leadership of the Sanūsīyya, new mosques were provided in even the most remote settlements. The provision of these social services, among others, all served to make life in the rural villages more attractive.

Policies of the Department of Agriculture and N.A.S.A. also contribute to sedentarization. In their planning these agencies envision a three-fold division of the jabal into forest, farmland, and grazing land. Forest tracts, as yet poorly defined and protected, are to be preserved from cutting for timber and charcoal and if possible extended. At present control is limited to a licensing of potential charcoal producers and the confiscation of the charcoal of violators, neither of which have deterred violations completely. The delimitation of farmland zones roughly corresponds to the areas restricted to agricultural use during the Italian era, many of the Ente plans having been adopted for this purpose. Within tracts so classified nomads are to be excluded and all nomads encouraged to settle in permanent locations. Spontaneous settlement is partially a response to this, although other, less direct, pressures operate as well. Although nomads are now permitted to graze on harvest stubble during the summer, the expectation is that the provision of adequate resources elsewhere plus continued shrub-clearing operations on over 700 hectares of ex-Ente properties between al-Abraq and al-Qubba ultimately will make even this limited concession undesirable. Nomads will be expected to use only the sub-humid and semi-arid steppe regions in future. Although an expansion of water resources through well-drilling and cistern clearance programs is planned for the nomadic areas, only limited progress has been made during the last few years. The fourteen Roman cisterns and twenty-two new cisterns of 200 cubic meter capacity constructed in al-Qubba region have been for use by farmers and only a few wells in the vicinity of al-Makīlī have been provided for nomadic sections. Clearly regarded as marginal contributors to the national economy, the nomadic life style is declining in vitality partly as a result of the benign neglect of its fellow countrymen in planning positions rather than from the type of active hostility characteristic of Italian administrators.

The single greatest contributor to bedouin settlement due to the government's social action program was its housing schemes. Some eight hundred and fifty family units have been constructed in the Darna mutasarrifiyya alone and the provision of standardized houses in other provinces is on an equally large scale. Begun in 1965 as the Popular Housing Scheme, the object was to concentrate the bedouin population so that services could be provided conveniently and efficiently. Houses were of a standardized one-story, three-room design and were linked in five-unit rows. No fence walls were provided and, although internal plumbing was complete, many of the sites selected lacked local water supplies. In part this was a product of the absence of firm site-selection criteria, for the location of individual housing clusters was determined on the basis of tribal influence, personal status, political loyalties, and perceived or imagined housing needs as mediated by the provincial governor. Solidly built of concrete blocks with a reinforced concrete roof, many of these housing units never were occupied since they failed to meet the cultural needs of their prospective occupants. The absence of any provision for animals, the closeness of units to each other, the failure to provide for occupation of contiguous units by neighbors from former herding groups, and the lack of privacy reduced their acceptability. Instead, it was a common practice for renters of the Popular Houses to store grain and other perishables therein, while either continuing to live in a tent or constructing a tin barakah. This practice has been prevalent in isolated villages such as Khūlān and Karsa where the provision of electricity and other amenities is more difficult.

In 1967, a new housing project, the Idris Housing Scheme (now simply called the Housing Scheme), was instituted. By providing more fence walls and court yards in both front and rear an attempt was made to deal with some of the cultural objections to the earlier housing projects. In theory these houses were available to all strata of Libyan society. But in practice middle income individuals, particularly government employees with housing allowances, prefer to build their own homes with low-interest government loans. Houses assigned to them or blocks of houses procured by wealthy tribesmen are rented in turn to fellow tribesmen, usually from the lowest income strata. Although empirical evidence is lacking to support this generalization, occupants of the governmental housing schemes tend to be derived primarily from the poorest strata of nomadic society. Since their resources are the most limited, the standardized housing unit offers a realistic prospect for improved living conditions.

Rural-Urban Migration

Massive drift of population from rural areas to urban centers has been typical of post-war Libya. The discovery of oil, with associated increases in the attractiveness of employment opportunities in the cities, has accelerated the

trend during the last decade. Indeed, it is the differential in attractiveness between city and countryside and the massive shift in population in the direction of
the urban opportunities, rather than the old regional political dichotomies, that
is the salient characteristic of contemporary Libya.[1] Although Banghāzī has
been the focus of urban migration in Cyrenaica, other urban centers have experienced appreciable, if less spectacular, growth. Darna, comprising 15,974
inhabitants in 1954,[2] has increased to 30,870 as of August, 1970,[3] and the
growth of such towns as al-Bayḍā', Ṭubruq, and Ajdābiya has been equally substantial. The latter two towns have benefited from their proximity to oil fields
and terminal facilities respectively while al-Bayḍā' was the recipient of a massive construction program stemming from the former royal government's decision to make it the site of a new federal capital.[4]

One of the results of rural to urban migration has been the development
of shanty towns on the outskirts of the major urban centers. Tripoli and Banghāzī have received the brunt of the incoming migrants.[5] Overwhelmed by the
number of people involved, crowded, dirty, squalid conditions have been the
result notwithstanding the best efforts of the authorities concerned to rectify the
situation. In the smaller urban centers such as Darna shanty slums have not
developed to a great extent as housing construction has been adequate to absorb
most of the in-migrants. Such construction, however, has had its unfortunate
aspects, since Darna's constricted coastal site reduces the amount of available
land suitable for building purposes. Much of the new housing is erected in the
oasis gardens, alienating them permanently from agricultural production.

Many of the migrants to the cities come from the lower strata of rural
and bedouin society, from those segments without a share in the ex-Ente properties or with insufficient animals to make construction of a barakah near their

---

[1] R. G. Hartley and J. M. Norris, "Demographic Regions in Libya: A
Principal Components Analysis of Economic and Demographic Variables," TESG,
LX (1969), 227.

[2] United Kingdom of Libya, Ministry of Economy and Trade, Preliminary
Result of the General Population Census, 1954 (Tripoli: Department of Census
and Statistics, May 1955), p. 5.

[3] Unpublished Official Provincial figures.

[4] Johannes Obst, "Die Erdölexploration in Libyen-Erfolge and Auswirkungen," Die Erde, XCIX (1968), 265 ff.

[5] The best available analysis of the phenomenon for the Libyan Arab Republic is Robert S. Harrison's study of "Migrants in the City of Tripoli, Libya,"
Geographical Review, LVII (1967), 397-423.

agricultural areas and short-distance herding of goats and sheep viable.  For
these people menial jobs in building construction and roadwork, employment as
domestic help in the households of resident expatriates, work as drivers of government vehicles, or jobs as ghafir (guards) of property or apartment buildings
are the major sources of employment.  Anyone able to buy a horse or bring one
from the countryside usually is able to use scavenged axles and wheels from
derelict trucks to construct a cart and earn a living hauling goods from the Banghāzī port, thus adapting skills learned in the nomadic environment to a new life
style.  Although inflation has been a hardship to the poorer classes even a ghafir
can make as much as £L40 per month and thus a single man, living with frugal-
ity, can hope to amass a substantial amount of money, much of which finds its
way back to the rural family members either as cash remissions or as gifts of
food and gadgetry whenever the migrant returns to visit.

    Accompanying this shift in population to the cities has been a relative
decrease, measured in terms of per capita income, in the prosperity of those
people, generally the older and less well educated, who remain in the countryside.  A 1966 survey indicated an annual per capita income of £L143.4 in the
city of Darna and of only £L35 in al-Makīlī.[1]  These figures are deceptive, however, because they obscure one of the most important characteristics of contemporary Libyan life, that of joint family income.  The crucial factor is not the
amount of money accruing to one individual, but rather how much money is present in each family unit.  Despite the massive changes impacting Libyan cultural
and social organization, family ties remain strong.  Migrants retain close con-
nections with their country relatives.  Even when a segment of the family moves
permanently to the city, tribal and family ties retain their hold, for the process
of change, for all its rapidity and unsettling impact, has thus far failed to disrupt the continuity of Libyan society.

    In many respects younger family members who migrate to the city for
educational or labor purposes (or for both) represent an expansion of the family
economy to exploit locally abundant resources.  Just as families living in the
steppe formerly herded camels, as well as sheep and goats, in order to utilize
grazing areas on the desert fringe inaccessible to more fragile animal species,
so now they send younger sons to the university to acquire an education that will
enable them to find jobs in governmental offices and tap some of the revenue
accruing to the country from oil.  For most nomads in the steppe the camel was

[1]Doxiadis Associates, Eastern Muhafadat Inventory (Tripoli and Beida, 1966), p. 5.

an insurance policy, an animal certain to survive drought conditions that might wipe out other species. Employment in the "modern" and urban sectors of the economy serves the same function, tapping new sources of revenue while protecting the family unit from potential environmental disaster in the "traditional" segment of the joint family economy. A decline in the camel population over the last decade is related directly to this phenomenon, because younger sons previously assigned to the arduous task of camel-herding are no longer available and hired help is both too expensive and too unfamiliar with the grazing resources to make camels a productive investment. Only those sections living in areas too marginal for sheep and goats continue to herd camels. It is interesting to note that much of the money earned in urban employment is returned to the pastoral community, not merely in the form of consumer items, but also as an investment in animals, particularly in sheep. Traditionally a source of capital investment and formation in the nomadic economy, sheep continue today as the primary symbol of continuity and stability in a society undergoing massive change.

Retrospective

Notwithstanding the belief of some archaeologists with experience in Tripolitania[1] that a small decline in rainfall in historic times accounts for the fluctuating fortunes of settled life, a similar opinion seems untenable for Cyrenaica. In the absence of adequate long-range climatological data and in the face of evidence indicating a considerable degree of long-term climatic stability in North Africa, use of climatic change as a primary causal factor explaining the alternating expansion and contraction of sedentary and nomadic life is impossible. However, the fact that Cyrenaica's climate is marginal in most areas for dry-farm agriculture must be kept firmly in mind. Thus, it is conceivable that short term precipitation failures might lead to temporary agricultural regression as well as to stimulation of physical conflicts between herders and farmers. Indeed, it is quite likely that pastoralists, particularly when many of their best lands have been alienated to agricultural use, would increase their raiding activities (which are apt to form a normal component of the nomadic economy under all conditions) in drought years and in so doing bring increased pressure to bear on the sedentary community. Nevertheless, this must be viewed as only one of a complex of factors.

---

[1] Goodchild, "Roman Tripolitania: Reconnaissance in the Desert Frontier Zone," p. 174, and Goodchild and Ward-Perkins, "The Limes Tripolitanus in the Light of Recent Discoveries," p. 95.

The stability, both political and military, of the sedentary community is a major factor in its relationship with a nomadic population. Whenever internal quarrels disrupt governmental cohesiveness, conditions are favorable for increased pressure by a strong pastoral society. Thus, disputes among the ruling Battiad family culminating in the foundation of Barka and civil strife in Cyrene ca. 414 B.C. resulted in associated hostilities with the native Libyan nomadic tribes. Similarly, adequate troops were apparently available in Synesius' day to repulse nomadic attacks, but the disorganization of these military forces and the incompetence of many of their political and military leaders led to a collapse of the defense effort from A.D. 395 to 410. Religious dissension played a crucial role in the weakening of Byzantine resistance to the Arab forces of ʿAmr ibn al-ʿĀṣ, while incipient anarchy in and the economic decline of the Zīrīd possessions in North Africa paved the way for the successes of the Banī Hilāl.

When internal disorganization in the agricultural community and political solidification of the nomadic tribes occur simultaneously, the balance of power is decisively tipped in favor of the pastoralists. The political structure of nomadic society, built around ties of kinship, can only be effectively activated by the emergence of a strong individual leader whose qualities of personality and leadership serve to unite normally contentious and competitive kin organizations. Strong leaders appear periodically and the power base that a political amalgamation of the tribes represents poses a fluctuating, rather than a constant, threat to the sedentary community. When joined to the superior mobility that possession of substantial numbers of horses and camels confers upon nomadic raiders, the disruptive potential of pastoral confederations is multiplied.

In regions of intermediate environmental richness such as al-Jabal al-Akhḍar, where varying ecological zones exist in close proximity, nomadic tribes can avoid long distance movements and achieve within a limited area the balance of agricultural and faunal resources necessary for a largely self-sufficient existence. But where rich resources exist in widely dispersed locations or environmental conditions are excessively marginal, specialization offers the only route to survival. Here reliance on other social groups to provide the products unavailable to specialists results in patterns of mutual interdependence. However, these patterns may be extremely complex and subtle and the temptation to seize essential resources by force is often the result. Where a rough balance between agriculturalists and nomads has been established, raiding is unlikely to be a major activity but when the distribution of power is unequal or one group feels threatened, violence is often the outcome. All of these factors operate together.

Agricultural expansion denies resources to the practitioners of a nomadic lifestyle and forces them to rely on increasingly meager, marginal, fluctuating,
and precarious resources. The periodic appearance of strong leaders leads to
the building of powerful political confederations in the steppe and subsequently to
the channelling of normal raiding activities in an organized way toward the attractive opportunities offered by the neighboring farms and villages; when internal dissension saps the vitality of the settled population and drought adds an
additional disruptive factor the result can be the state of chaos, confusion, and
insecurity described by Synesius.

The pressure situation described above is not a one-way process, since
the military potential available in the large population that can be supported by
agriculture, and agricultural expansion itself, are able to exert great pressure
on the nomadic tribes. In Cyrenaica the pressures generated by an expanding
agriculture have a long history and result from important ecological factors.
The resources of climate, soil, and vegetation found in Cyrenaica are such that,
while pastoral activities can be profitably undertaken throughout the region,
agriculture is restricted in territorial scope. Only on the northern slopes and
the plains of the plateau and on the better watered southern slopes is farming
possible. Thus, once the initial Greek settlement at Cyrene began to expand it
rapidly came into conflict with the native pastoral tribes occupying the upper
reaches of the jabal. Subsequent hostilities generated by this expansion proved
insufficient to impede permanently the expansion of agricultural settlement.
Ultimately a rough equilibrium was established between the agriculturalists on
the north slopes and the crest of the jabal and the pastoralists in the steppe
zones on the southern slopes. However, the humid steppe and the unusually
favored area in the semi-arid steppe still remained potentially usable for agricultural purposes. With the steady expansion of agriculture in the Imperial
period, the settlement of limitanei in the better-watered steppe, the filling-in of
settlement on the plateau, and the extension of dry farming techniques and military settlements into the steppe, conditions became critical for the tribes. As
land was pre-empted for agriculture and as the herds maintained by farmers
reduced the amount of summer pasture and water available for nomadic stock,
the situation of the pastoral tribes was rendered precarious. An increasingly
violent series of nomadic raids, aided by the large-scale adoption of the camel,
was the result. In Cyrenaica these raids were combined with a break-down in
the cohesion and effectiveness of the local government. This in part reflected an
empire-wide malfunctioning of local and imperial organization over which the

indigenous population had little control, and made the nomadic incursions doubly effective.

In short, the very success of agricultural expansion in Cyrenaica, when viewed in its historical context and in combination with other factors, carried with it the possibility of violent opposition on the part of the Libyan nomads, an opposition which proved partially to be responsible for its decline. After the Hilalian invasion the wheel turned full circle and a nomadic life style eventually dominated all of Cyrenaica until the next cycle of agricultural expansion was initiated by the Italian government in the early twentieth century.

Today pastoral nomadism in Libya is experiencing a spectacularly rapid demise. Originally disrupted by the impact of Italian colonialism, nomadic livelihood has experienced even more severe strains since independence. While the Italian conquest challenged the physical survival of indigenous nomadic adaptations, it never succeeded in undercutting the value systems supporting the pastoral genre de vie. The impetus toward modernization made possible by the discovery of oil, the economic power conveyed by huge new sources of revenue, the sudden ability to purchase a wide range of the produce of modern technology, the existence of alternative attractive sources of employment, and the challenge posed by contact with alien cultures and beliefs all have sparked a singularly rapid transformation in traditional patterns of livelihood, the full ramifications of which can be perceived only imperfectly. Adjusted to the utilization at a subsistence level of resources unexploitable by any other livelihood form, pastoral nomadism has lost its appeal in the face of competition from less arduous and more productive alternatives. Originating as a specialized offshoot of agricultural society, the nomadic life style of eastern Libya is in the process of being reintegrated, perhaps permanently, into the sedentary community.

## MATERIAL INVENTORY OF A RECENTLY

## SEDENTARIZED BEDOUIN FAMILY

| Item | Homemade | Always Suq-Bought | Now Suq-Bought |
|---|---|---|---|
| chair | | | x |
| bed | | | x |
| blanket | | | x |
| hidma (hand-woven rug) | x | | |
| pillows[1] | x[1] | x | x |
| suitcase | | | x |
| dowry box[2] | | x | x |
| storage cabinets | | | x |
| wooden storage boxes[3] | | x | |
| farsh (machine-made rug) | | | x |
| straw mat (small) | | x | x |
| spoons | | | x |
| plates | | | x |
| glasses | | | x |
| tea pot | | x | x |
| bottled-gas stove[4] | | | x |
| glass water pitcher | | | x |
| plastic water pitcher | | | x |
| shoes | | | x |
| trousers | | | x |
| shirts | | | x |
| jard (woolen cloak) | x? | x | x |
| barakan (women's cotton garment) | | x | x |
| watch | | | x |
| metal storage cans[5] | | | x |
| jewelry | | x | x |
| tarahiyya (quilt mat) | x | | |
| serving bowl (aluminum) | | | x |
| qas a (wooden serving bowl) | x | x? | |
| straw mat (large)[6] | | x | x |
| knife | | x | x |
| plastic sandals | | | x |
| cotton tent cloth[7] | | x | x |
| gasoline stove | | | x |
| mihgin (wooden funnel) | x | | |
| raha (grinding stones) | x? | x | |
| mabram (spindle) | x | | |
| maghzal (large spindle) | x | | |
| maghraf (wooden spoon) | x | | x |
| minshaz | x | | |

| Item | Homemade | Always Suq-Bought | Now Suq-Bought |
|---|---|---|---|
| jilam (wool shears) | | X | X |
| manjal (sickle)[8] | X | X | X |
| massa (hammer)[8] | X | X | X |
| mishfa (awl)[8] | X | X | X |
| bala (shovel) | | | X |
| mishan (mortar and pestle)[9] | X | X | |
| bumba (mortar)[10] | X | X | |
| mismar (pestle)[11] | X | X | |
| layyan (iron/aluminum basin)[12] | | X | X |
| birmil (jerry can) | | | X |
| qirba (goatskin water bag) | X | | |
| shakwa (goatskin bag)[13] | X | | |
| ghirbal (flour sifter) | | X | X |
| fanar (lantern) | | | X |
| mithra (small metal hook)[14] | X | X | |
| tent poles[15] | X | X | X |
| hawiyya (camel saddle bag)[16] | X | | |
| masda (tent top)[17] | X | | |
| hubal (goat hair rope) | X | | |
| hemp rope | | | X |
| mizra (pitchfork)[18] | X | | |
| shataka (large woven storage bag) | | | |
| hamaddiyya (large woven bag)[19] | X | | |
| transistor radio | | | X |
| bulghar (leather slippers) | | X | |

[1] Cotton pillow-cover cloth purchased in the suq; straw stuffing gathered locally; material gathered at home.

[2] Fancy embroidered cloth exterior; made in Derna.

[3] Used to store and transport household possessions during migrations.

[4] Increasingly used in place of charcoal fire when preparing tea.

[5] Frequently reused coffee or cookie tins.

[6] Always an urban product; now imported almost exclusively from Egypt.

[7] Dyed cotton cloth purchased in bulk at the local suq. Cut into geometric patterns, it is used to decorate the inside of the tent's roof and side walls.

[8] The wooden handles of these implements are often homemade; the metal, however, nearly always is purchased in the suq. Since World War II the mishfa, which has only a small metal component, has been made from scrap metal.

[9] Used by the women to prepare henna.

[10] In this case, made from an expended artillery shell casing.

[11] An iron Italian tent peg is used as a substitute.

[12] Deep, straight-sided vessel used to wash clothes.

[13] Used to process laban (buttermilk).

[14] Used to pull threads tight in weaving.

[15] Large central tent poles apparently always were purchased in the suq.

[16] Traditionally made from goat's hair and sheep's wool. Now rapidly being replaced by burlap flour sacks and canvas bags.

[17] Composed of twelve separate strips. When worn, they are replaced and used as the walls of the tent. Today burlap sacks are taking over this function.

[18] Slowly being replaced by metal pitchforks bought in the suq.

[19] Used to store the straw chaff after winnowing. Now losing out to manila rope nets and most recently to military surplus canvas bags.

# BIBLIOGRAPHY

Abdussaid, Abdulhamid. "Early Islamic Monuments at Ajdabiyah." LA, I (1964), 115-19.

_____. "An Early Mosque at Medina Sultan." LA, III-IV (1966-1967), 155-60.

Abu Sharr, I. Report to the Government of Libya on Crop Agronomy and Improvement in Cyrenaica. Rome: FAO, 1962.

Aeneas Tacticus. On the Defense of Fortified Positions. Ed. by W. A. Oldfather. London: William Heinemann; New York: G. P. Putnam's Sons, 1923.

Agostini, Enrico de. Le popolazione della Cirenaica. Bengasi: Governo della Cirenaica, 1922-23.

Ahlmann, Hans W. "La Libye septentrionale: études de géographie physique et humaine." Geografiska Annaler, X (1928), 1-118.

Alfoldi, A. "The Crisis of the Empire (A. D. 249-270)." Cambridge Ancient History. Cambridge: University Press, 1939. Vol. XII, pp. 165-231.

Almagià, Roberto. "La Cirenaica: Il paese ed i suoi aspetti nel passato e nel presente." BRSGI, series 5, I (1912), 479-504.

Amiran, D. H. K., and Ben-Arieh, Y. "Sedentarization of Bedouin in Israel." Israel Exploration Journal, XIII (1963), 161-81.

Ammianus Marcellinus. The Surviving Books of the History of Ammianus Marcellinus. Trans. by John C. Rolfe. Cambridge, Mass.: Harvard University Press; London: William Heinemann, 1956.

Anderson, J. G. C. "Augustan Edicts from Cyrene." JRS, XVII (1927), 33-48.

Anderson, J. K. "Homeric, British and Cyrenaic Chariots." AJA, LXIX (1965), 349-52.

Ansary, Aly R., and El Abboud, Abdallah. "A Market Study of Consumer Electronic Equipment in Libya." Dirassat (The Libyan Economic and Business Review), V (1969), 1-32.

Appianus. Appian's Roman History. Trans. by Horace White. 4 vols. London: William Heinemann; New York: Macmillan, 1912.

Applebaum, S. "A Note on the Work of Hadrian at Cyrene." JRS, XL (1950), 87-90.

Applebaum, S. "Notes on the Jewish Revolt under Trajan." JJS, II, No. 1 (1950), pp. 26-30.

_____. "The Jewish Revolt in Cyrene in 115-117, and the Subsequent Recolonisation." JJS, II, No. 3 (1951), pp. 177-86.

_____. "Cyrenensia Ivdaica: Some Notes on Recent Research Relating to the Jews of Cyrenaica in the Hellenistic and Roman Periods." JJS, XIII (1962), 31-43.

Arnott, N. M. H. Report to the Government of Libya on the Improvement of the Sheep Industry. Rome: FAO, 1959.

Asad, Talal. The Kababish Arabs: Power, Authority and Consent in a Nomadic Tribe. London: C. Hurst, 1970.

Askew, William C. Europe and Italy's Acquisition of Libya 1911-1912. Durham, N. C.: Duke University Press, 1942.

Atkinson, Kenneth. "The Dynamics of Terra Rossa Soils." BFA, III (1969), 15-35.

Awad, Mohamed. "The Assimilation of Nomads in Egypt." Geographical Review, XLIV (1954), 240-52.

al-Bakrī. Description de l'Afrique septentrionale. 2nd ed. Ed. by de Slane. Alger: Adolphe Jourdan, 1911.

Balbo, Italo. "Coloni in Libia." Nuova Antologia, XVII (1938), 3-13.

Ballu, Abdel Kareem. "Libyan Food Habits." Community Development Studies in Cyrenaica. Ed. by David S. Tillson. [Benghazi?]: Area Development Office, USOM, 1959. Pp. 69-72. (Mimeographed.)

Baradez, Jean L. Vue-aérienne de l'organisation romaine dans le sud-algérien: Fossatum Africae. Paris: Arts et métiers graphiques, 1949.

Barr, F. T. "Upper Cretaceous Stratigraphy of Jabal al Akhdar, Northern Cyrenaica." Geology and Archaeology of Northern Cyrenaica, Libya. Ed. by F. T. Barr. Tripoli: Petroleum Exploration Society of Libya, 1968. Pp. 131-47.

Barrett, Donald E. "Libya." In "Petroleum Developments in Africa in 1963," by J. D. Moody. BAAPG, XLVIII (1964), 1645-53.

Barth, Fredrik. Nomads of South Persia: The Basseri Tribe of the Khamseh Confederacy. New York: Humanities Press, 1964.

Bartolozzi, Enrico. "Gli sviluppi della colonizzazione demografica intensiva in Libia." L'Agricoltura Coloniale, XXXIII (1939), 3-11.

Bates, Daniel G. "The Role of the State in Peasant-Nomad Mutualism." Anthropological Quarterly, XLIV (1971), 109-31.

Bates, Oric. The Eastern Libyans: An Essay. London: Macmillan, 1914.

Beechey, F. W., and Beechey, H. W.  Proceedings of the Expedition to Explore the Northern Coast of Africa from Tripoly Eastward; in MDCCCXXI and MDCCCXXII. Comprehending an Account of the Greater Syrtis and Cyrenaica; and of the Ancient Cities comprising the Pentapolis. London: John Murray, 1828.

Beehler, Commodore W. H.  The History of the Italian-Turkish War, September 29, 1911 to October 18, 1912. Annapolis, Md.: By the Author, 1913.

Bell, H. I.  Egypt from Alexander the Great to the Arab Conquest: A Study in the Diffusion and Decay of Hellenism. Oxford: Clarendon Press, 1966.

Bennett, Johnson. "Libya." In "Petroleum Developments in Africa in 1956," by Hollis D. Hedberg. BAAPG, XLI (1957), 1568-73.

Blundell, H. Weld. "Mr. Weld Blundell in the Cyrenaica." Geographical Journal, V (1895), 168.

Boardman, John. "Evidence for the Dating of Greek Settlements in Cyrenaica." ABSA, LXI (1966), 149-56.

_____. "Bronze Age Greece and Libya." ABSA, LXIII (1968), 41-44.

Boardman, John, and Hayes, John.  Excavations at Tocra 1963-1965: The Archaic Deposits I. Oxford: Thames & Hudson; British School of Archaeology at Athens, 1966.

Bond, R. C., and Swales, J. M. "Surface Finds of Coins from the City of Euesperides." LA, II (1965), 91-101.

Bovill, E. W. "The Camel and the Garamantes." Antiquity, XXX (1956), 19-21.

Bradford, John.  Ancient Landscapes: Studies in Field Archaeology. London: G. Bell, 1957.

Brogan, Lady Olwen. "First and Second Century Settlement in the Tripolitanian Pre-Desert." Paper presented at the Libya in History conference. Banghāzī: University of Libya, 1968.

Brogan, Olwen. "The Camel in Tripolitania." PBSR, XXII (1954), 126-31.

_____. "Henscir el-Ausaf by Tigi (Tripolitania) and some Related Tombs in the Tunisian Gefara." LA, II (1965), 47-56.

Brogan, Olwen, and Smith, David. "The Roman Frontier Settlement at Ghiza: An Interim Report." JRS, XLVII (1957), 173-84.

Brunschvig, Robert.  La Berbérie orientale sous les Hafsides des origines à la fin du XV siècle. 2 vols. Paris: Adrien-Maisonneuve, 1940-47.

Būlis, Lutfī. "az-Zuhūr al-Barrīya fī Lībyā." al-Hisād, August, 1968, pp. 6-14.

Buru, Mukhtar. "Soil Analysis and its Relation to Land Use in el-Marj Plain, Cyrenaica." BFA, II (1968), 41-70.

Butler, Alfred J. The Arab Conquest of Egypt and the Last Thirty Years of the Roman Dominion. Oxford: Clarendon Press, 1902.

Butler, H. C. "Desert Syria, the Land of a Lost Civilization." Geographical Review, IX (1920), 77-108.

Butzer, Karl W. Studien zum vor- und frühgeschichtlichen Landschaftswandel der Sahara. Wiesbaden: Akademie der Wissenschaften und der Literatur in Mainz, 1958.

_____. "Environment and Human Ecology in Egypt during Pre-dynastic and Early Dynastic Times." BSGE, XXII (1959), 43-87.

Cahen, Claude. "Quelques mots sur les Hilaliens et le nomadisme." Journal of the Economic and Social History of the Orient, XI (1968), 130-33.

Capot-Rey, Robert. Le Sahara français. Vol. II of L'Afrique blanche française. Paris: Presses Universitaires de France, 1953.

_____. "Le nomadisme des Toubous." Nomades et nomadisme au Sahara. UNESCO, Recherches sur la zone aride, no. 19. Paris: UNESCO, 1963. Pp. 81-92.

Carter, Theresa H. "Reconnaissance in Cyrenaica." Expedition, V (1963), 18-27.

Cassels, John. "The Cemeteries of Cyrene." PBSR, XXIII (1955), 1-43.

Cassius Dio Cocceianus. Dio's Roman History. Trans. by E. Cary. 9 vols. London: William Heinemann; New York: G. P. Putnam's Sons, 1925.

Cauneille, André. "Le nomadisme des Megarha (Fezzân)." TIRS, XII (1954), 41-67.

Chadwick, Henry. "Faith and Order at the Council of Nicaea: A Note on the Background of the Sixth Canon." Harvard Theological Review, LIII (1960), 171-95.

Chamoux, François. Cyrène sous la monarchie des Battiades. Paris: E. de Boccard, 1953.

Chapelle, Jean. Nomades noirs du Sahara. Paris: Plon, 1958.

Charles-Pichard, Gilbert. La civilization de l'Afrique romaine. Paris: Plon, 1959.

Clarke, John I. "Oil in Libya: Some Implications." Economic Geography, XXXIX (1963), 40-59.

"Come si svolgera la colonizzazione demografica in Libia." BRSGI, series 7, IV (1939), 86-88.

Conant, Louis D., and Goudarzi, Gus H. "Stratigraphic and Tectonic Framework of Libya." BAAPG, LI (1967), 719-30.

Coque, Roger. "Morphogenèse quaternaire du piémont méditerranéen du djebel Akhdar (Cyrénaïque)." Annales de Géographie, No. 433 (1970), pp. 375-85.

Coster, Charles H. "Christianity and the Invasions: Synesius of Cyrene." Late Roman Studies. Cambridge, Mass.: Harvard University Press, 1968. Pp. 218-68.

Courtois, Christian. Les Vandales et l'Afrique. Paris: Arts et métiers graphiques, 1955.

Cumming, Sir Duncan. "The Sanusiya in the First World War." Paper presented at the Libya in History conference. Banghāzī: University of Libya, 1968.

Cunsolo, Ronald S. "Libya, Italian Nationalism, and the Revolt against Giolitti." Journal of Modern History, XXXVII (1965), 186-207.

Deambrosis, Delfino. "Importanza del Mediterraneo centrale nell' espansione coloniale italiana." BRSGI, series 7, I (1936), 226-32.

De Marco, Roland R. The Italianization of African Natives: Government Native Education in the Italian Colonies 1890-1937. New York: Bureau of Publications, Teachers College, Columbia University, 1943.

Demougeot, Émilienne. "Le chameau et l'Afrique du Nord romaine." AESC, XV (1960), 209-47.

Dermenghem, Émile. Le pays d'Abel: Le Sahara des Ouled Naïls, des Larbâa et des Amour. Paris: Gallimard, 1960.

Desio, Ardito. "Brève synthèse de l'évolution morphologique du territoire de la Libye." BSGE, XXV (1953), 9-21.

Despois, Jean. La colonisation italienne en Libye: Problèmes et méthodes. Paris: Larose, 1935.

De Vecchi, Paolo. Italy's Civilizing Mission in Africa. New York: Brentano's, 1912.

Diodorus Siculus. Library of History. Trans. by O. H. Oldfather. London: William Heinemann; New York: G. P. Putnam's Sons, 1933.

Doxiadis Associates. Eastern Muhafadat Inventory: Muhafadah Dernah; Mutassarrifiyah Dernah. Tripoli and Beida: Doxiadis Associates, for the Government of the Kingdom of Libya, Ministry of Planning and Development, 1966.

Dupire, Marguerite. "Trade and Markets in the Economy of the Nomadic Fulani of Niger (Bororo)." Markets in Africa. Ed. by Paul Bohannan and George Dalton. Evanston: Northwestern University Press, 1962. Pp. 335-62.

Duveyrier, H. La confrérie musulmane de Sîdi Mohammed Ben 'Alî Es-Senoûsî et son domaine géographique en l'année 1300 de l'hégire = 1883 de notre ère. Paris: Société de Géographie, 1886.

Eberhard, Wolfram. "Nomads and Farmers in Southeastern Turkey." Oriens, VI (1953), 32-49.

Ente per la Colonizzazione della Libia. Compensorio Luigi di Savoia. Foglio No. 9. 1:25,000. N.p., n.d.

Epton, Nina. Oasis Kingdom: The Libyan Story. London: Jarrolds, 1952.

Eusebius. The Ecclesiastical History. Trans. by Kirsopp Lake. 2 vols. London: William Heinemann; New York: G. P. Putnam's Sons, 1926.

Evans, Arthur. "The Early Nilotic, Libyan, and Egyptian Relations with Minoan Crete." JRAI, LV (1925), 199-228.

Evans-Pritchard, E. E. "Arab Status in Cyrenaica under the Italians." Sociological Review, XXXVI (1944), 1-17.

_____. "Italy and the Sanusiya Order in Cyrenaica." Bulletin of the School of Oriental and African Studies (University of London), XI (1943-1946), 843-53.

_____. "Italy and the Bedouin in Cyrenaica." African Affairs, XLV (1946), 12-21.

_____. "Topographical Terms in Common Use Among the Bedouin of Cyrenaica." JRAI, LXXVI (1946), 177-88.

_____. The Sanusi of Cyrenaica. Oxford: Clarendon Press, 1963.

Evetts, B., trans. "History of the Patriarchs of the Coptic Church of Alexandria." Patrologia Orientalis. Ed. by R. Graffin and F. Nau. Paris: Firmin Didot, 1903. Vol. I, pp. 103-214, 383-518.

Fàntoli, Amilcare. Le pioggie della Libia: con particolare riguardo alle zone di avvaloramento. Rome: Ministero Africa Italiana, 1952.

_____. "Le isole del golfo di Bomba e le prime basi della colonizzazione greca in Cirenaica." L'Universo, XXXVII (1957), 1051-66.

_____. "Le isole della Tripolitania e dello Cirenaica." L'Universo, XXXVII (1957), 923-30.

Faulkner, D. E. Report to the Government of Libya on the Improvement of Cattle. Rome: FAO, 1956.

Ferrand-Eynard, Pierre. "Enquête sur le revenu de quatre tribus nomades de la confédération des Ouled Naïl." TIRS, XX (1961), 91-134.

Ferrara, Antonio. "La cantina sociale di Beda Littoria." L'Agricoltura Coloniale, XXXII (1938), 3-15.

Fisher, W. B.; Fraser, I. R.; and Ross, D. W. "The Aberdeen University Expedition to Cyrenaica, 1951. Part III." Scottish Geographical Magazine, LXIX (1953), 22-32.

Fogg, Walter. "The Suq: A Study in the Human Geography of Morocco." Geography, XVII (1932), 257-67.

_____. "Changes in the Lay-Out, Characteristics, and Functions of a Moroccan Tribal Market, Consequent on European Control." Man, XLI (1941), 104-8.

Fowler, Gary L. "Italian Agricultural Colonization in Tripolitania, Libya." Unpublished Ph.D. dissertation, Syracuse University, 1969.

Fraser, P. M. "Hadrian and Cyrene." JRS, XL (1950), 77-87.

Fuks, Alexander. "Aspects of the Jewish Revolt in A.D. 115-117." JRS, LI (1961), 98-104.

Gautier, E. F. L'islamisation de l'Afrique du Nord: Les siècles obscurs du Maghreb. Paris: Payot, 1927.

Gimingham, C. H. "A Note on Water-table, Sand Movement and Plant Distribution in a North African Oasis." Journal of Ecology, XLIII (1955), 22-25.

Gimingham, C. H., and Walton, K. "Environment and the Structure of Scrub Communities on the Limestone Plateau of Northern Cyrenaica." Journal of Ecology, XLII (1954), 505-20.

Good, Charles M. Rural Markets and Trade in East Africa: A Study of the Functions and Development of Exchange Institutions in Ankole, Uganda. Research Paper No. 128. Chicago: University of Chicago, Department of Geography, 1970.

Goodchild, Richard G. The Roman Roads and Milestones of Tripolitania (Discoveries and Researches in 1947). [Tripoli]: Department of Antiquities, British Military Administration, Tripolitania, 1948.

_____. "Roman Milestones in Cyrenaica." PBSR, XVIII (1950), 83-91.

_____. "Roman Tripolitania: Reconnaissance in the Desert Frontier Zone." Geographical Journal, CXV (1950), 161-71.

_____. "The Limes Tripolitanus II." JRS, XL (1950), 30-38.

_____. "Boreum of Cyrenaica." JRS, XLI (1951), 11-16.

_____. "'Libyan' Forts in South-west Cyrenaica." Antiquity, XXV (1951), 131-44.

_____. "Roman Sites on the Tarhuna Plateau of Tripolitania." PBSR, XIX (1951), 43-77.

_____. "Arae Philaenorum and Automalax." PBSR, XX (1952), 94-110.

_____. "Euesperides: A Devastated City Site." Antiquity, XXVI (1952), 208-12.

_____. "Mapping Roman Libya." Geographical Journal, CXVIII (1952), 142-52.

Goodchild, Richard G. "Farming in Roman Libya." Geographical Magazine, XXV (1952), 70-80.

_____. "The Decline of Libyan Agriculture." Geographical Magazine, XXV (1952), 147-56.

_____. "The Roman and Byzantine Limes in Cyrenaica." JRS, XLIII (1953), 65-76.

_____. "Oasis Forts of Legio III Augusta on the Routes to the Fezzan." PBSR, XXII (1954), 56-68.

_____. Tabula Imperii Romani: Cyrene. Sheet HI 34. 1:1,000,000. Oxford: Society of Antiquaries of London, 1954.

_____. "A Byzantine Palace at Apollonia (Cyrenaica)." Antiquity, XXXIV (1960), 246-58.

_____. "The Decline of Cyrene and Rise of Ptolemais: Two New Inscriptions." QAL, IV (1961), 83-95.

_____. Benghazi (Euesperides - Berenice - Marsa Ibn Ghazi): The Story of a City. 2nd ed. Cyrene (Shahat): Department of Antiquities, 1962.

_____. Cyrene and Apollonia: An Historical Guide. 2nd ed. [Shahat?]: Department of Antiquities (Eastern Region), United Kingdom of Libya, 1963.

_____. "Medina Sultan (Charax - Iscina - Sort)." LA, I (1964), 99-106.

_____. "Cyrenaica." LA, I (1964), 143-45.

_____. "Archaeological News 1963-1964 (Cyrenaica)." LA, II (1965), 137-39.

_____. "A Coin-hoard from 'Balagrae' (El-Beida), and the Earthquake of A.D. 365." LA, III-IV (1966-1967), 203-11.

_____. "Byzantines, Berbers and Arabs in 7th-Century Libya." Antiquity, XLI (1967), 115-24.

_____. "Earthquakes in Ancient Cyrenaica." Geology and Archaeology of Northern Cyrenaica, Libya. Ed. by F. T. Barr. Tripoli: Petroleum Exploration Society of Libya, 1968. Pp. 41-44.

_____. "Graeco-Roman Cyrenaica." Geology and Archaeology of Northern Cyrenaica, Libya. Ed. by F. T. Barr. Tripoli: Petroleum Exploration Society of Libya, 1968. Pp. 23-40.

_____. "The Roman Roads of Libya and their Milestones." Paper presented at the Libya in History conference. Banghazī: University of Libya, 1968.

Goodchild, Richard G.; Pedley, J. G.; and White, D. "Recent Discoveries of Archaic Sculpture at Cyrene: A Preliminary Report." LA, III-IV (1966-1967), 179-98.

Goodchild, Richard G., and Reynolds, J. M. "Some Military Inscriptions from Cyrenaica." PBSR, XXX (1962), 37-46.

Goodchild, Richard G.; Reynolds, J. M.; and Herington, C. J. "The Temple of Zeus at Cyrene." PBSR, XXVI (1958), 30-62.

Goodchild, Richard G., and Ward-Perkins, J. B. "The Limes Tripolitanus in the Light of Recent Discoveries." JRS, XXXIX (1949), 81-95.

Goudarzi, Gus H. Geology and Mineral Resources of Libya - A Reconnaissance. Washington: U.S. Government Printing Office, 1970.

Governo della Cirenaica. Confraternite mussulmane e templi delle diverse religioni in Cirenaica. 1:800,000. N.p., 1922.

Graham, Alexander J. Colony and Mother City in Ancient Greece. Manchester: University Press, 1964.

Graziani, Rodolfo. Libia redenta: Storia di trent' anni di passione italiana in Africa. Naples: Torella, 1948.

Great Britain. Admiralty. A Handbook of Arabia. London: H. M. Stationery Office, 1916.

Gribaudi, Dino. "Sono mutate in epoca storica le condizioni climatiche della Libia?" BRSGI, series 6, V (1928), 171-213.

Guyot, Georges. L'Italie devant le probleme colonial. Paris: Société d'Editions Géographiques, Maritimes et Coloniales, 1927.

Hamdani, Abbas. "Some Aspects of the History of Libya during the Fatimid Period." Paper presented at the Libya in History conference. Banghāzī: University of Libya, 1968.

Hamilton, James. Wanderings in North Africa. London: John Murray, 1856.

Harrison, R. M. "A Sixth Century Church at Ras el-Hilal in Cyrenaica." PBSR, XXXII (1964), 1-20.

Harrison, Robert S. "Migrants in the City of Tripoli, Libya." Geographical Review, LVII (1967), 397-423.

Hartley, Robert G., and Norris, J. M. "Demographic Regions in Libya: A Principal Components Analysis of Economic and Demographic Variables." TESG, LX (1969), 221-27.

Haywood, Richard M. "The African Policy of Septimius Severus." Transactions of the American Philological Association, LXXI (1940), 175-85.

Hellstrom, Bo. "The Subterranean Water in the Libyan Desert." Geografiska Annaler, XXII (1940), 206-39.

Herodotus. The Histories. Trans. by Aubrey de Selincourt. Baltimore, Md.: Penguin Books, 1954.

Hey, R. W. "The Geomorphology and Tectonics of the Gebel Akhdar (Cyrenaica)." Geological Magazine, XCIII (1956), 1-14.

_____. "The Pleistocene Shorelines of Cyrenaica." Quaternaria, III (1956), 139-44.

Hey, R. W. "The Geomorphology of the Jabal al Akhdar and Adjoining Areas." Geology and Archaeology of Northern Cyrenaica, Libya. Ed. by F. T. Barr. Tripoli: Petroleum Exploration Society of Libya, 1968. Pp. 167-71.

Higgins, Benjamin. The Economic and Social Development of Libya. New York: United Nations, Technical Assistance Programme, 1953.

Hildebrand, Gotthold. Cyrenaika als Gebiet künftiger Besiedelung: Eine Landeskunde mit besonderer Berücksichtigung der wirtschaftlichen Verhältnisse. Bonn: Carl Georgi, 1904.

Hodder, B. W. "Rural Periodic Day Markets in Part of Yorubaland." Transactions and Papers, Institute of British Geographers, No. 29 (1961), pp. 149-59.

_____. "Some Comments on the Origins of Traditional Markets in Africa South of the Sahara." Transactions, Institute of British Geographers, No. 36 (1965), pp. 97-105.

Holz, Robert. "Sandstone as a Building Material in Libya." Pennsylvania Geographer, VIII (September, 1970), 1-10.

Hubert, P. Report on the Soil Conditions of the Ente Farm Settlement Area of Farzūghah. Benghazi: FAO, Libya Mission, 1964.

Hyslop, G. S. C., and Applebaum, S. Cyrene and Ancient Cyrenaica: A Guide Book. Tripoli: Government Press, 1945.

Ibn 'Abd al-Ḥakam. Futuḥ Miṣr wa'l-Maghrib. Ed. by 'Abd al-Mun'im 'Āmir. [Cairo, 1961].

Ibn Hawqal. Kitāb Ṣūrat al-'Ard. Bibliotheca Geographorum Arabicorum, Vol. II, Part 1. Ed. by M. J. de Goeje. Leiden: E. J. Brill, 1938.

Ibn Khaldoun. Histoire des Berbères et des dynasties musulmanes de l'Afrique septentrionale. Trans. by Baron de Slane. Ed. by Paul Casanova. 4 vols. Paris: Paul Geuthner, 1925.

_____. The Muqaddimah: An Introduction to History. Trans. by Franz Rosenthal. 3 vols. New York: Pantheon Books, 1958.

Ibn Khurdādhbih. Kitāb al-Masālik wa 'l-Mamālik. Bibliotheca Geographorum Arabicorum, Vol. VI. Ed. by M. J. de Goeje. Leiden: E. J. Brill, 1889.

Idris, Hady R. La Berbérie orientale sous les Zirides: $X^e$-$XII^e$ siècles. 2 vols. Paris: Adrien-Maisonneuve, 1962.

al-Idrīsī. Kitāb Nuzhat al-Mushtāq fī Ikhtirāq al-Āfāq. ("Description de l'Afrique septentrionale et saharienne.") Bibliothèque de l'Institut d'études supérieures islamiques d'Alger, Vol. X. Algiers: La Maison des livres, 1957.

International Bank for Reconstruction and Development. The Economic Development of Libya. Baltimore: Johns Hopkins Press, 1960.

"I nuovi centri rurali della Libia." BRSGI, series 7, V (1940), 143.

International Labour Office. "Italian Colonization of Libya." Industrial and Labour Information, LXVIII (1938), 406-8.

al-Iṣṭakhrī. Kitāb Masālik al-Mamālik. Bibliotheca Geographorum Arabicorum, Vol. I. Ed. by M. J. de Goeje. Leiden: E. J. Brill, 1927.

Istituto Agricolo Coloniale, Firenze. La colonizzazione della Cirenaica. Rome: Tipografia del Senato, 1947.

Italy. Ministero degli affari esteri. L'Italia in Africa. Serie storico-militare, Vol. I; L'Opera dell'esercito; No. III: Avvenimenti militari e impiego: Africa settentrionale (1911-1943). Ed. by Massimo A. Vitale. Rome: Istituto poligrafico dello stato, 1964.

Joannes, bishop of Nikiou. The Chronicle of John, Bishop of Nikiu. Trans. by R. H. Charles. Oxford: Williams & Norgate, 1916.

Jones, Arnold H. M. Cities of the Eastern Roman Provinces. London: Clarendon Press, 1937.

Jones, G. D. B. "British Archaeological Expedition to Tocra and Euhesperides 1969." (Mimeographed.)

Jones, H. Stuart. "Claudius and the Jewish Question at Alexandria." JRS, XVI (1926), 17-35.

Josephus, Flavius. Against Apion. Trans. by H. St. J. Thackeray. London: William Heinemann; New York: G. P. Putnam's Sons, 1926.

_____. Jewish Antiquities. Trans. by Ralph Marcus. Cambridge, Mass.: Harvard University Press; London: William Heinemann, 1956.

_____. The Jewish War. Trans. by H. St. J. Thackeray. Cambridge, Mass.: Harvard University Press; London: William Heinemann, 1926.

Julien, Ch.-André. Histoire de l'Afrique du Nord: Tunisie-Algérie-Maroc. Paris: Payot, 1931.

Kaegi, Walter E. "Arianism and the Byzantine Army in Africa 533-546." Traditio, XXI (1965), 23-53.

Kikhia, Mansour M. Le nomadisme pastoral en Cyrenaïque septentrionale. Aix-en-Provence: La Pensée Universitaire, 1968.

Kleinsmeide, W. F. J., and Berg, N. J. van den. "Surface Geology of the Jabal al Akhdar, Northern Cyrenaica, Libya." Geology and Archaeology of Northern Cyrenaica, Libya. Ed. by F. T. Barr. Tripoli: Petroleum Exploration Society of Libya, 1968. Pp. 115-23.

Klitzsch, Eberhard. "Die Strukturgeschichte der Zentralsahara: Neue Erkenntnisse zum Bau und zur Palaogeographie eines Tafellandes." Geologische Rundschau, LIX (1969), 459-527.

Kraeling, Carl H. Ptolemais: City of the Libyan Pentapolis. Chicago: University of Chicago Press, 1962.

Kwapong, A. A. "Citizenship and Democracy in Fourth-Century Cyrene."
Africa in Classical Antiquity: Nine Studies. Ed. by L. A. Thompson
and J. Ferguson. Ibadan: University Press, 1969. Pp. 99-109.

"La colonisation italienne en Libye." Revue des deux mondes, series 8, LI
(June 15, 1939), 908-28.

Lador, J. Marc. "Libya." In "Petroleum Development in North Africa in 1965, "
by J. N. Bowerman. BAAPG, L (1966), 1681-1703.

Lapworth, Charles. Tripoli and Young Italy. London: Stephen Swift, 1912.

Larsen, J. A. O. "Cyrene and the Panhellenion." Classical Philology, XLVII
(1952), 7-16.

Le Houérou, H. N. Report to the Government of Libya on Natural Pastures and
Fodder Resources of Libya and Problems of their Improvement. Rome:
FAO, 1965.

Leo Africanus, Joannes. Description de l'Afrique. Trans. by A. Epaulard.
2 vols. Paris: Adrien-Maisonneuve, 1956.

Leriche, A. "De l'origine du thé au Maroc et au Sahara." Bulletin de l'Institut
Français de l'Afrique Noire, XV (1952), 731-36.

Leschi, Louis. "Rome et les nomades du Sahara central." TIRS, I (1942),
47-62.

Lewis, I. M. A Pastoral Democracy: A Study of Pastoralism and Politics
among the Northern Somali of the Horn of Africa. London: Oxford University Press, 1961.

Lewis, Naphtali, and Reinhold, Meyer. Roman Civilization. 2 vols. New York:
Columbia University Press, 1955.

Leyder, Jean. "Voyage en Libye: Remarques sur le colonat italien." Bulletin
de la Société Royale Belge de Géographie, LXIII (1939), 217-29.

Libya, Kingdom of. Ministry of Planning & Development. Census and Statistical
Department. Statistical Abstract 1964. Tripoli: Census and Statistical
Department, 1969.

_____. Report of the Annual Survey of Petroleum Mining Industry 1969: Ref
Year-1968. Tripoli: Census and Statistical Department, 1969.

Libya, United Kingdom of. Ministry of Communications. Meteorological Service. Bullettino Meteorologico. Nos. 1-7. Tripoli: Meteorological
Service, June-December, 1954. (Mimeographed.)

_____. Weather Bulletin. Nos. 1 (June, 1954)-24 (May, 1956). [Tripoli:
Meteorological Service, 1954-1956].

_____. Weather Bulletin/Bullettino Meteorologico. Nos. 25 (June, 1956)-
73 (June, 1960). [Tripoli: Meteorological Service, 1956-1960].

_____. Climatological Summary. Nos. 74 (July, 1960)-91 (December, 1961).
[Tripoli: Meteorological Service, 1960-1961].

231

Libya, United Kingdom of. Ministry of Communications. Meteorological Service. Climatological Summary. Nos. 92 (January, 1962)-147 (August, 1966). [Tripoli: Meteorological Department, 1962-1966].

Lindberg, John. General Economic Appraisal of Libya. New York: United Nations-FAO Mission to Libya, 1951.

Livius, Titus. Summaries. Cambridge: Harvard University Press; London: William Heinemann, 1959.

Lowdermilk, W. C. "Colonization de luxe in Italian North Africa." American Forests, XLVI (1940), 315-17.

Lunson, E. A. Sandstorms on the Northern Coasts of Libya and Egypt. Meteorological Office, Professional Notes No. 102. London: His Majesty's Stationery Office, 1950.

Macartney, Maxwell H. H., and Cremona, Paul. Italy's Foreign and Colonial Policy 1914-1937. London; New York; Toronto: Oxford University Press, 1938.

Machu, Jean. "Cyrène: La cité et le souverain à l'époque hellénistique." Revue Historique, CCV (1951), 41-55.

Malvezzi, Count Aldobrandino. "Italian Colonies and Colonial Policy." Journal of the Royal Institute of International Affairs, VI (1927), 233-45.

Marçais, Georges. La Berbérie musulmane et l'Orient au Moyen Age. Paris: Aubier, 1946.

_____. Les Arabes en Berbérie du XI$^e$ au XIV$^e$ siècle. Constantine: D. Braham; Paris: Ernest Leroux, 1913.

Marçais, William. "Comment l'Afrique du Nord a été arabisée." Annales de l'Institut d'Etudes Orientales, IV (1938), 1-22.

Markus, R. A. "Reflections on Religious Dissent in North Africa in the Byzantine Period." Studies in Church History, III (1966), 140-49.

McBurney, C. B. M. "Libya's Role in Prehistory." Paper presented at the Libya in History conference. Banghāzī: University of Libya, 1968.

McBurney, C. B. M., and Hey, R. W. Prehistory and Pleistocene Geology in Cyrenaican Libya: A Record of Two Seasons' Geological and Archaeological Fieldwork in the Gebel Akhdar Hills, with a Summary of Prehistoric Finds from Neighbouring Territories. Cambridge: University Press, 1955.

McClure, W. K. Italy in North Africa: An Account of the Tripoli Enterprise. Philadelphia: John C. Winston, 1913.

McCullagh, Francis. Italy's War for a Desert: Being some Experiences of a War-Correspondent with the Italians in Tripoli. London: Herbert and Daniel, 1912.

Mikesell, Marvin W. "Notes on the Dispersal of the Dromedary." Southwestern Journal of Anthropology, XI (1955), 231-45.

Mikesell, Marvin W. "The Role of Tribal Markets in Morocco: Examples from the 'Northern Zone.'" Geographical Review, XLVIII (1958), 494-511.

_____. "Comparative Studies in Frontier History." AAAG, L (1960), 62-74.

Miller, Konrad. Die Peutingersche Tafel. Stuttgart: F. A. Brockhaus, 1962.

Miller, S. N. "The Army and the Imperial House." Cambridge Ancient History. Cambridge: University Press, 1939. Vol. XII, pp. 1-56.

Milne, J. G. "Trade between Greece and Egypt before Alexander the Great." Journal of Egyptian Archaeology, XXV (1939), 177-83.

Mitchell, B. M. "Cyrene and Persia." Journal of Hellenic Studies, LXXXVI (1966), 99-113.

Monod, Théodore. L'Adrar Ahnet. Paris: Institut d'ethnologie, 1932.

Montel, Anta. "Les terrasses marines de la côte nord de Cyrenaïque." Compte-rendu sommaire des séances de la Société géologique de France, Nos. 13-14 (1955), pp. 256-58.

Mostafa, Mohamed. "Islamic Objects of Art." LA, II (1965), 123-27.

_____. "Excavations in Medinet Sultan: A Preliminary Report." LA, III-IV (1966-1967), 145-54.

Mouterde, R., and Poidebard, A. Le limes de Chalcis: Organisation de la steppe en Haute Syrie romaine; documents aériens et épigraphiques. Paris: Paul Geuthner, 1945.

Mukorji, S.; Yamani, A.; and Hawaiw, Abdelssalem. "Seasonal Movement in the Consumption of Meat in Benghazi." Dirassat (The Libyan Economic and Business Review), V (1969), 81-92.

Müller, K. Fragmenta Historicorum Graecorum. Vol. IV. Paris: Ambrosio Firmin Didot, 1868.

al-Muqaddasī. Kitāb Aḥsan it-Taqāsīm fī maʿrifa 'l-Aqālīm. Bibliotheca Geographorum Arabicorum, Vol. III. Ed. by M. J. de Goeje. Leiden: E. J. Brill, 1967.

Murphey, Rhoads. "The Decline of North Africa since the Roman Occupation: Climatic or Human?" AAAG, XLI (1951), 116-32.

Murray, G. W. "The Artesian Water beneath the Libyan Desert." BSGE, XXV (1953), 81-92.

Narducci, Guglielmo. Storia della colonizzazione della Cirenaica. Milan: Editoriale arte e storia, 1942.

NASA (National Agricultural Settlement Authority). Compensorio Gubba. Folio No. 10. 1:25,000. N.p., n.d.

_____. "New Farms for the Green Mountains." Libyan Review, II, no. 8 (August, 1967), pp. 18-21.

233

Nicolaisen, Johannes. "Some Aspects of the Problem of Nomadic Cattle Breeding among the Tuareg of the Central Sahara." Geografisk Tidsskrift, LIII (1954), 62-105.

Noshy, I. "Arkesilaus III." Paper presented at the Libya in History conference. Banghāzī: University of Libya, 1968.

Oates, David. "The Tripolitanian Gebel: Settlement of the Roman Period around Gasr ed-Dauun." PBSR, XXI (1953), 81-117.

Oblath, Attilio. "Italian Emigration and Colonisation Policy." International Labour Review, XXIII (1931), 805-34.

Obst, Johannes. "Die Erdölexploration in Libyen-Erfolge und Auswirkungen." Die Erde, XCIX (1968), 265-77.

Oliver, James H. "On Edict III from Cyrene." Hesperia, XXIX (1960), 324-25.

Olivero, Gaspare. Il decreto di Anastasio 1° su l'ordinamento politico-militareo della Cirenaica. Documenti Antichi dell' Africa Italiana, Vol. II, No. 2. Rome: Istituto Italiano d'Arti Grafiche, 1933.

Oost, Stewart I. "Cyrene, 96-74 B.C." Classical Philology, LVIII (1963), 11-25.

Orosius, Paulus. Seven Books of History against the Pagans. Trans. by Irving W. Raymond. New York: Columbia University Press, 1936.

Pan, Chia-Lin. "The Population of Libya." Population Studies, III (1949), 100-125.

Patel, Ahmed M. "The Rural Markets of Rajshahi District." Oriental Geographer, VII (1963), 140-51.

Pausanias. Description of Greece. Trans. by W. H. S. Jones. 4 vols. Cambridge, Mass.: Harvard University Press; London: William Heinemann, 1926.

Peck, Harry T., ed. Harper's Dictionary of Classical Literature and Antiquities. New York: Cooper Square, 1962.

Pedley, John G. "Excavations at Apollonia, Cyrenaica: Second Preliminary Report." AJA, LXXI (1967), 141-47.

_____. "Apollonia Excavations, 1966." Archaeology, XX (1967), 219-20.

Pedretti, Andrea. "Un' escursione in Cirenaica (1901)." BRSGI, series 4, IV, part 2 (1903), pp. 889-929.

Peters, Emrys L. "The Sociology of the Bedouin of Cyrenaica." Unpublished Ph.D. dissertation, Lincoln College, Oxford University, 1951.

_____. "The Proliferation of Segments in the Lineage of the Bedouin of Cyrenaica." JRAI, XC (1960), 29-53.

_____. "Aspects of the Family among the Bedouin of Cyrenaica." Comparative Family Systems. Ed. by M. F. Nimkoff. Boston: Houghton Mifflin, 1965. Pp. 121-46.

234

Peters, Emrys L. "Some Structural Aspects of the Feud among the Camel-Herding Bedouin of Cyrenaica." Africa, XXXVII (1967), 261-82.

_____. "The Tied and the Free: An Account of a Type of Patron-Client Relationship among the Bedouin Pastoralists of Cyrenaica." Contributions to Mediterranean Sociology: Mediterranean Rural Communities and Social Change. Ed. by J.-G. Peristiany. Paris; The Hague: Mouton, 1968. Pp. 167-88.

Peters, Stella M. "A Study of the Bedouin (Cyrenaican) Bait." Unpublished B. Litt. thesis, St. Hilda's College, Oxford, 1952.

Peyret-Chappuis, Charles de. L'Italie: a-t-elle besoin de colonies? Paris: Presses de France, 1936.

Pharr, Clyde, trans. The Theodosian Code and Novels and the Sirmondian Constitutions: A Translation with Commentary, Glossary, and Bibliography. Princeton: Princeton University Press, 1952.

Piccioli, Angelo, ed. La nuova Italia d'oltremare: l'opera del fascismo nelle colonie italiane. 2 vols. Verona: A. Mondadori, 1933.

Pietersz, Constans R. "Proposed Nomenclature for Rock Units in Northern Cyrenaica." Geology and Archaeology of Northern Cyrenaica, Libya. Ed. by F. T. Barr. Tripoli: Petroleum Exploration Society of Libya, 1968. Pp. 125-30.

Pigli, Mario. "La colonisation démographique italienne en Libye." Revue Economique Internationale, 26$^e$ année, IV (1934), 133-63.

de Planhol, Xavier. "Small-scale Industry and Crafts in Arid Regions." Arid Lands. Ed. by E. S. Hills. London: Methuen; Paris: UNESCO, 1966. Pp. 273-85.

Pliny. Natural History. Trans. by John Bostock and H. T. Riley. 6 vols. London: George Bell, 1887.

Plutarchus. Plutarch's Lives. Trans. by Bernadotte Perrin. 11 vols. Cambridge: Harvard University Press; London: William Heinemann, 1968.

_____. Moralia. Trans. by Frank C. Babbitt. 15 vols. Cambridge: Harvard University Press; London: William Heinemann, 1968.

Poidebard, A. La trace de Rome dans le désert de Syrie: Le limes de Trajan à la conquête arabe; recherches aériennes (1925-1932). Paris: Paul Geuthner, 1934.

Polybius. The Histories. Trans. by W. R. Paton. 6 vols. London: William Heinemann; New York: G. P. Putnam's Sons, 1923.

Poncet, Jean. "L'évolution des genres de vie en Tunisie." Les Cahiers de Tunisie, II (1954), 315-23.

_____. "Le mythe de la 'catastrophe' hilalienne." AESC, XXII (1967), 1099-1120.

Précheur-Canonge, Thérèse.  La vie rurale en Afrique romaine d'après les mosaïques.  Paris:  Presses Universitaires de France, n. d.

Price, R. W.  Report on the Soil Survey of the Proposed Bu Traba Settlement Area.  Benghazi, n. d.

_____ .  General Appraisal of the Omar Mukhtar Area as a Possible Center for Tribal Lands Settlement.  Tripoli:  Project for the Development of Tribal Lands and Settlements, 1966.

_____ .  The Soils and Agricultural Potential of the El Useta Area for Tribal Land Settlement.  Benghazi:  Development of the Tribal Lands and Settlements Project; FAO, Libya Mission, 1966.

Procopius.  De aedeficiis.  Trans. by H. B. Dewing.  8 vols.  London:  William Heinemann; New York:  G. P. Putnam's Sons, 1914.

Qudāma ibn Ja'far.  Kitāb al-Kharāj.  Bibliotheca Geographorum Arabicorum, Vol. VI.  Ed. by M. J. de Goeje.  Leiden:  E. J. Brill, 1967.

Rebuffat, R.; Deneauve, J.; and Hallier, G.  "Bu Njem 1967."  LA, III-IV (1966-1967), 49-137.

Rennell of Rodd, Lord.  British Military Administration of Occupied Territories in Africa during the Years 1941-1947.  London:  His Majesty's Stationery Office, 1948.

Reynolds, J. M.  "Three Inscriptions from Ghadames in Tripolitania."  PBSR, XXVI (1958), 135-36.

_____ .  "Four Inscriptions from Roman Cyrene."  JRS, XLIX (1959), 95-101.

_____ .  "The Christian Inscriptions of Cyrenaica."  Journal of Theological Studies, new series, XI (1960), 284-94.

_____ .  "Cyrenaica, Pompey and Cn. Cornelius Lentulus Marcellinus."  JRS, LII (1962), 97-103.

_____ .  "Vota pro Salute Principis."  PBSR, XXX (1962), 33-36.

_____ .  "Notes on Cyrenaican Inscriptions."  PBSR, XXXIII (1965), 52-54.

Reynolds, J. M., and Goodchild, R. G.  "The City Lands of Apollonia in Cyrenaica."  LA, II (1965), 103-7.

Reynolds, J. M., and Simpson, W. G.  "Some Inscriptions from el-Auenia near Yefren in Tripolitania."  LA, III-IV (1966-1967), 45-47.

Rikli, M[artin A.]  Das Pflanzenkleid der Mittelmeerländer.  3 vols.  Bern:  Hans Humer, 1943-1948.

Ritterling, E.  "Military Forces in the Senatorial Provinces."  JRS, XVII (1927), 28-32.

Rolls, S. C.  Steel Chariots in the Desert:  The Story of an Armoured-Car Driver with the Duke of Westminister in Libya and in Arabia with T. E. Lawrence.  London:  Jonathan Cape, 1937.

Romanelli, Pietro. "The Province of Crete and Cyrenaica." Cambridge Ancient History. New York: Macmillan; Cambridge: University Press, 1936. Vol. XI, pp. 659-75.

_____. Il limes romano in Africa. Il Limes Romano, Vol. X. Rome: Istituto di studi romani, 1939.

_____. La Cirenaica romana (96 a. C. -642 d. C. ). Verbania: A. Airoldi, 1943.

Rommel, Erwin. The Rommel Papers. Ed. by B. H. Liddell Hart. Trans. by Paul Findlay. London: Collins, 1953.

Rostovtzeff, Mikhail I. The Social and Economic History of the Roman Empire. 2nd ed. 2 vols. Oxford: Clarendon Press, 1926.

Rovere, P. Francesco. "Il christianesimo in Cirenaica: origini-vicende storiche-monumenti." Libia, III (1955), 43-52.

Rowe, Alan. A History of Ancient Cyrenaica: New Light on Aegypto-Cyrenaean Relations; Two Ptolemaic Statues Found in Tolmeita. Supplément aux Annales du Service des Antiquités de l'Egypte, Cahier No. 12. Cairo: Imprimerie de l'Institut Français d'Archéologie Orientale, 1948.

Rowe, Alan; Buttle, Derek; and Gray, John. Cyrenaican Expedition of the University of Manchester, 1952. Manchester: University Press, 1956.

Russell, Sir E. J. "Agricultural Colonization in the Pontine Marshes and Libya." Geographical Journal, XCIV (1939), 273-89.

Salama, Pierre. Les voies romaines de l'Afrique du Nord. Algiers: Imprimerie Officielle du Gouvernement Générale de l'Algérie, 1951.

Salzman, Philip C. "Movement and Resource Extraction among Pastoral Nomads: The Case of the Shah Nawazi Baluch." Anthropological Quarterly, XLIV (1971), 185-97.

Schanzer, Carlo. "Italian Colonial Policy in Northern Africa." Foreign Affairs, II, no. 3 (March 15, 1924), pp. 446-56.

Schmieder, Oskar, and Wilhelmy, Herbert. Die faschistische Kolonisation in Nordafrica. Leipzig: Quelle and Meyer, 1939.

Schönberger, H. "The Roman Frontier in Germany: An Archaeological Survey." JRS, LIX (1969), 144-97.

Shata, A. "Geological Problems Related to the Ground Water Supply of some Desert Area of Egypt." BSGE, XXXII (1959), 247-62.

Sharaf, A. Torayah. "The Hydrological Divisions of the Northern Belt of Libya." Flussregime und Wasserhaushalt. Ed. by Reiner Keller. Freiburger Geographische Hefte, No. 6. Freiburg, 1968. Pp. 33-50.

Sherwin-White, A. N. "Geographical Factors in Roman Algeria." JRS, XXXIV (1944), 1-10.

Sichtermann, Helmut. "Archäologische Funde und Forschungen in Libyen: Kyrenaika, 1959-1961; Tripolitanien, 1942-1961." Archäologischer Anzeiger, 1962, No. 3, pp. 417-535.

Skinner, G. William. "Marketing and Social Structure in Rural China." Journal of Asian Studies, XXIV (1964), 3-43; XXV (1965), 195-228, 363-99.

Slousch, N. "Le nouveau régime Turc et Tripoli." Revue du Monde Musulman, VI (1908), 52-57.

_____. "La Tripolitaine sous la domination des Karamanlis." Revue du Monde Musulman, VI (1908), 58-84, 211-32, 433-54.

Smallwood, E. Mary. "The Hadrianic Inscription from the Caesareum at Cyrene." JRS, XLII (1952), 37-38.

_____. "The Jews in Egypt and Cyrenaica during the Ptolemic and Roman Periods." Africa in Classical Antiquity: Nine Studies. Ed. by L. A. Thompson and J. Ferguson. Ibadan: University Press, 1969. Pp. 110-31.

Some Data on Italian Activity in the Colonies. Florence: Istituto Agricolo Coloniale, 1945.

Speel, C. J. "The Disappearance of Christianity from North Africa in the Wake of the Rise of Islam." Church History, XXIX (1960), 379-97.

Steer, K. A. "The Antonine Wall, 1934-1959." JRS, L (1960), 84-93.

Steier. "Silphion." Paulys real-encyclopädie der classischen altertumswissenschaft. By August Pauly et al. 2nd series. Vol. IIIA, No. 1. Stuttgart: J. B. Metzlersche, 1927. Columns 103-14.

Strabo. The Geography of Strabo. Trans. by Horace L. Jones. 8 vols. London: William Heinemann; Cambridge, Mass.: Harvard University Press, 1949.

Stratos, Andreas N. Byzantium in the Seventh Century. Trans. by Marc Ogilvie-Grant. Amsterdam: Adolf M. Hakkert, 1968.

Stucchi, Sandro. "Prime tracce tardo-minoiche a Cirene: i rapporti della Libya con il mondo egeo." QAL, V (1967), 19-45.

_____. "First Outline for a History of Cyrenaican Architecture during the Roman Period." Paper presented at the Libya in History conference. Banghāzī: University of Libya, 1968.

Sweet, Louise B. "Camel Raiding among the Bedouins of North Arabia: A Mechanism of Ecological Adaption." American Anthropologist, LXVII (1965), 1132-50.

_____. "Camel Pastoralism in North Arabia and the Minimal Camping Unit." Man, Culture, and Animals: Animals in Human Ecological Adjustments. Ed. by Anthony Leeds and Andrew P. Vayda. Washington, D.C.: American Association for the Advancement of Science, 1965. Pp. 129-52.

Syme, Ronald. "Flavian Wars and Frontiers." Cambridge Ancient History. New York: Macmillan; Cambridge: University Press, 1936. Vol. XI, pp. 131-87.

Synesius. The Essays and Hymns of Synesius of Cyrene: Including the Address to the Emperor Arcadius and the Political Speeches. Trans. by Augustine FitzGerald. 2 vols. Oxford: University Press, 1930.

_____. The Letters of Synesius of Cyrene. Trans. by Augustine FitzGerald. Oxford: University Press, 1926.

Tacitus. The Annals. Trans. by John Jackson. 4 vols. Cambridge, Mass.: Harvard University Press; London: William Heinemann, 1961.

Tarn, W. W. "Greece: 335 to 321 B.C." Cambridge Ancient History. New York: Macmillan; Cambridge: University Press, 1927. Vol. VI, pp. 438-60.

Thomas, Frederic C., Jr. "The Libyan Oil Worker." Middle East Journal, XV (1961), 264-76.

Thompson, L. A. "Settler and Native in the Urban Centres of Roman Africa." Africa in Classical Antiquity: Nine Studies. Ed. by L. A. Thompson and J. Ferguson. Ibadan: University Press, 1969. Pp. 132-81.

Thucydides. History of the Peloponnesian War. Trans. by Charles F. Smith. 4 vols. London: William Heinemann; Cambridge, Mass.: Harvard University Press, 1923.

Tillson, David S. Community Development Studies in Cyrenaica. Banghāzī [?]: Area Development Office, USOM, 1959. (Mimeographed.)

Tomlinson, R. A. "False-Facade Tombs at Cyrene." ABSA, LXII (1967), 241-56.

Toni, Y. T. "The Population of Cyrenaica." TESG, XLIX (1958), 1-11.

_____. "Social Mobility and Relative Stability among the Bedouins of Cyrenaica." BSGE, XXXVI (1963), 113-36.

_____. "Tribal Distribution and Racial Relationships of the Ancient and Modern Peoples of Cyrenaica." Annals of the Faculty of Arts, Ain-Shams University, VIII (1963), 153-91.

Torrey, C. C. "Ibn 'Abd al-Hakam." Encyclopedia of Islam. Leyden: E. J. Brill, 1927. Vol. II, p. 353.

Troin, J. F. "Observations sur les Souks de la région d'Azrou et de Khénifra." Revue de Géographie du Maroc, No. 3-4 (1963), 109-20.

Ṭurayyaḥ-Sharaf, 'Abd al-'Azīz. Jughrāfīyyah Libyā. Alexandria: Matbi'ah al-Maṣrā, n.d.

UNESCO-FAO. Carte bioclimatique de la zone méditerranéenne: notice explicative. Recherches sur la zone aride, No. 21. Paris: UNESCO-FAO, 1963.

UNESCO-FAO. Vegetation Map of the Mediterranean Zone: Explanatory Notes. Recherches sur la zone aride, No. 30. Paris: UNESCO-FAO, 1969.

United States. Army Map Service. North Africa. 1:250,000. Series P 502. Edition 1-3-AMS. Washington, D.C., 1961-1966.

_____. Beda Littoria. 1:250,000. Sheet NI 34-15. Washington, D.C., 1962.

_____. Derna. 1:250,000. Sheet NI 34-16. Washington, D.C., 1955.

_____. Libya. 1:50,000. Series P 761. Edition 2-AMS, First Printing. Washington, D.C., 1964.

_____. Marsá al Hilāl. 1:50,000. Sheet 3790 IV. Washington, D.C., 1964.

_____. Maţār Darnah. 1:50,000. Sheet 3890 III. Washington, D.C., 1964.

_____. Minţaqat al Qayqab. 1:50,000. Sheet 3790 III. Washington, D.C., 1964.

_____. at-Taḩīmī. 1:50,000. Sheet 3989 IV. Washington, D.C., 1964.

United States. Board on Geographic Names. Libya. Gazetteer No. 41. Washington, D.C.: Office of Geography, Department of the Interior, 1958.

United States. Geological Survey. Topographic Map of United Kingdom of Libya. Miscellaneous Geologic Investigations, Map I-350 B. 1:2,000,000. Washington, D.C.: Department of the Interior, 1962.

_____. Geologic Map of the Kingdom of Libya. Compiled by Louis C. Conant and Gus Goudarzi. Miscellaneous Geologic Investigations, Map I-350 A. Washington, D.C.: U.S. Geological Survey, 1964.

Vinogradov, Amal. "The 1920 Revolt in Iraq Reconsidered: The Role of Tribes in National Politics." International Journal of Middle East Studies, III (1972), 123-39.

Waddington, W. H. "Edit de l'empereur Anastase sur l'administration militaire en Libye." Revue Archéologique, XVIII (1868), 417-30.

Walser, Gerold. "The Crisis of the Third Century A.D.: A Re-interpretation." Bucknell Review, XIII (1965), 1-10.

Walser, Gerold, and Pekáry, Thomas. Die Krise des Römischen Reiches: Bericht über die Forschungen zur Geschichte des 3. Jahrhunderts (193-284 N. Chr.) von 1939 bis 1959. Berlin: Walter de Gruyter, 1962.

Ward, Philip. "Place-Names of Cyrenaica." Geology and Archaeology of Northern Cyrenaica, Libya. Ed. by F. T. Barr. Tripoli: Petroleum Exploration Society of Libya, 1968. Pp. 3-12.

Ward-Perkins, J. B. "Gasr es-Suq el-Oti: A Desert Settlement in Central Tripolitania." Archaeology, III (1950), 25-30.

_____. "A New Group of Sixth-Century Mosaics from Cyrenaica." Rivista di archeologia cristiana, XXXIV (1958), 183-92.

240

Ward-Perkins, J. B., and Ballance, M. H. "The Caesareum at Cyrene and the
Basilica at Cremna." PBSR, XXVI (1958), 137-94.

Warmington, B. H. The North African Provinces from Diocletian to the Vandal
Conquest. Cambridge: University Press, 1954.

Wheatley, O. J. Draft Report on Agriculture in Libya. [New York: United
Nations Mission to Libya, 1952].

White, Donald. "Excavations at Apollonia, Cyrenaica: Preliminary Report."
AJA, LXX (1966), 259-65.

White, K. D. Agricultural Implements of the Roman World. Cambridge: University Press, 1967.

Widrig, Walter M., and Goodchild, Richard G. "The West Church at Apollonia
in Cyrenaica." PBSR, XXVIII (1960), 70-90.

Winter, E. H. "Livestock Markets among the Iraqw of Northern Tanganyika."
Markets in Africa. Ed. by Paul Bohannan and George Dalton. Evanston:
Northwestern University Press, 1962. Pp. 457-68.

al-Ya'qūbī. Kitāb al-Buldān. 2nd ed. Bibliotheca Geographorum Arabicorum,
Vol. VII. Leiden: E. J. Brill, 1967.

Zohary, Michael. Plant Life of Palestine: Israel and Jordan. New York:
Ronald Press, 1962.

Zoli, Corrado. Espansione coloniale italiana (1922-1937). Rome: L'Arnia,
1949.

# THE UNIVERSITY OF CHICAGO
## DEPARTMENT OF GEOGRAPHY
### RESEARCH PAPERS (Lithographed, 6×9 Inches)

*(Available from Department of Geography, The University of Chicago, 5828 S. University Ave., Chicago, Illinois 60637. Price: $5.00 each; by series subscription, $4.00 each.)*

48. BOXER, BARUCH. *Israeli Shipping and Foreign Trade*  1957. 176 pp.

53. ACKERMAN, EDWARD A. *Geography as a Fundamental Research Discipline*  1958. 40 pp. $1.00

56. MURPHY, FRANCIS C. *Regulating Flood-Plain Development*  1958. 216 pp.

62. GINSBURG, NORTON, editor. *Essays on Geography and Economic Development*  1960. 196 pp.

71. GILBERT, E. W. *The University Town in England and West Germany*
1961. 79 pp. 4 plates. 30 maps and diagrams. (Free to new subscribers)

72. BOXER, BARUCH. *Ocean Shipping in the Evolution of Hong Kong* 1961. 108 pp.

84. KANSKY, K. J. *Structure of Transportation Networks: Relationships between Network Geometry and Regional Characteristics*  1963. 155 pp.

91. HILL, A. DAVID. *The Changing Landscape of a Mexican Municipio, Villa Las Rosas, Chiapas*
NAS-NRC Foreign Field Research Program Report No. 26. 1964. 121 pp.

94. MC MANIS, DOUGLAS R. *The Initial Evaluation and Utilization of the Illinois Prairies, 1815–1840*
1964. 109 pp.

97. BOWDEN, LEONARD W. *Diffusion of the Decision To Irrigate: Simulation of the Spread of a New Resource Management Practice in the Colorado Northern High Plains*  1965. 146 pp.

98. KATES, ROBERT W. *Industrial Flood Losses: Damage Estimation in the Lehigh Valley*
1965. 76 pp.

102. AHMAD, QAZI. *Indian Cities: Characteristics and Correlates*  1965. 184 pp.

103. BARNUM, H. GARDINER. *Market Centers and Hinterlands in Baden-Württemberg*  1966. 172 pp.

105. SEWELL, W. R. DERRICK, *et al. Human Dimensions of Weather Modification*  1966. 423 pp.

106. SAARINEN, THOMAS F. *Perception of the Drought Hazard on the Great Plains*  1966. 183 pp.

107. SOLZMAN, DAVID M. *Waterway Industrial Sites: A Chicago Case Study*  1967. 138 pp.

108. KASPERSON, ROGER E. *The Dodecanese: Diversity and Unity in Island Politics*  1967. 184 pp.

110. REED, WALLACE E. *Areal Interaction in India: Commodity Flows of the Bengal-Bihar Industrial Area*  1967. 210 pp.

112. BOURNE, LARRY S. *Private Redevelopment of the Central City: Spatial Processes of Structural Change in the City of Toronto*  1967. 199 pp.

113. BRUSH, JOHN E., and GAUTHIER, HOWARD L., JR. *Service Centers and Consumer Trips: Studies on the Philadelphia Metropolitan Fringe*  1968. 182 pp.

114. CLARKSON, JAMES D. *The Cultural Ecology of a Chinese Village, Cameron Highlands, Malaysia*
1968. 174 pp.

115. BURTON, IAN, KATES, ROBERT W., and SNEAD, RODMAN E. *The Human Ecology of Coastal Flood Hazard in Megalopolis*  1968. 196 pp.

117. WONG, SHUE TUCK. *Perception of Choice and Factors Affecting Industrial Water Supply Decisions in Northeastern Illinois*  1968. 96 pp.

119. DIENES, LESLIE. *Locational Factors and Locational Developments in the Soviet Chemical Industry*
1969. 285 pp.

120. MIHELIC, DUSAN. *The Political Element in the Port Geography of Trieste*  1969. 104 pp.

121. BAUMANN, DUANE. *The Recreational Use of Domestic Water Supply Reservoir: Perception and Choice*  1969. 125 pp.

122. LIND, AULIS O. *Coastal Landforms of Cat Island, Bahamas: A Study of Holocene Accretionary Topography and Sea-Level Change*  1969. 156 pp.

123. WHITNEY, JOSEPH. *China: Area, Administration and Nation Building*  1970. 198 pp.

124. EARICKSON, ROBERT. *The Spatial Behavior of Hospital Patients: A Behavioral Approach to Spatial Interaction in Metropolitan Chicago*  1970. 198 pp.

125. DAY, JOHN C. *Managing the Lower Rio Grande: An Experience in International River Development*  1970. 277 pp.

126. MAC IVER, IAN. *Urban Water Supply Alternatives: Perception and Choice in the Grand Basin Ontario*  1970. 178 pp.

127. GOHEEN, PETER G. *Victorian Toronto, 1850 to 1900: Pattern and Process of Growth* 1970. 278 pp.

128. GOOD, CHARLES M. *Rural Markets and Trade in East Africa* 1970. 252 pp.

129. MEYER, DAVID R. *Spatial Variation of Black Urban Households* 1970. 127 pp.

130. GLADFELTER, BRUCE. *Meseta and Campiña Landforms in Central Spain: A Geomorphology of the Alto Henares Basin.* 1971. 204 pp.

131. NEILS, ELAINE M. *Reservation to City: Indian Urbanization and Federal Relocation* 1971. 200 pp.

132. MOLINE, NORMAN T. *Mobility and the Small Town, 1900–1930* 1971. 169 pp.

133. SCHWIND, PAUL J. *Migration and Regional Development in the United States* 1971. 170 pp.

134. PYLE, GERALD F. *Heart Disease, Cancer and Stroke in Chicago: A Geographical Analysis with Facilities Plans for 1980.* 1971. 292 pp.

135. JOHNSON, JAMES F. *Renovated Waste Water: An Alternative Source of Municipal Water Supply in the U.S.* 1971. 155 pp.

136. BUTZER, KARL W. *Recent History of an Ethiopian Delta: The Omo River and the Level of Lake Rudolf.* 1971. 184 pp.

137. HARRIS, CHAUNCY D. *Annotated World List of Selected Current Geographical Serials in English, French, and German* 3rd edition 1971. 77 pp.

138. HARRIS, CHAUNCY D., and FELLMANN, JEROME D. *International List of Geographical Serials* 2nd edition 1971. 267 pp.

139. MC MANIS, DOUGLAS R. *European Impressions of the New England Coast, 1497–1620* 1972. 147 pp.

140. COHEN, YEHOSHUA S. *Diffusion of an Innovation in an Urban System: The Spread of Planned Regional Shopping Centers in the United States, 1949–1968* 1972. 136 pp.

141. MITCHELL, NORA. *The Indian Hill-Station: Kodaikanal* 1972. 199 pp.

142. PLATT, RUTHERFORD H. *The Open Space Decision Process: Spatial Allocation of Costs and Benefits* 1972. 189 pp.

143. GOLANT, STEPHEN M. *The Residential Location and Spatial Behavior of the Elderly: A Canadian Example* 1972. 226 pp.

144. PANNELL, CLIFTON W., *T'ai-chung, T'ai-wan: Structure and Function* 1973. 200 pp.

145. LANKFORD, PHILIP M. *Regional Incomes in the United States, 1929–1967: Level, Distribution, Stability, and Growth* 1972. 137 pp.

146. FREEMAN, DONALD B., *International Trade, Migration, and Capital Flows: A Quantitative Analysis of Spatial Economic Interaction.* 1973. 202 pp.

147. MYERS, SARAH K., *Language Shift Among Migrants to Lima, Peru* 1973. 204 pp.

148. JOHNSON, DOUGLAS L. *Jabal al-Akhdar, Cyrenaica: An Historical Geography of Settlement and Livelihood.* 1973

149. YEUNG, YUE-MAN. *National Development Policy and Urban Transformation in Singapore: A Study of Public Housing and the Marketing System.* 1973